Chapter One

Sam Sunday was behind a hedg
trousers were round his ankles   ...king a crap.
He wasn't sure how long the chicken had been in the
back of the fridge, but long enough, it seemed, to bear a
grudge. It had made a very hasty exit. He was lost and
late but, he told himself, he had to prioritise. Taking a
crap wasn't so much a priority, as an inevitability.

He was somewhere in the countryside. He never
drifted far from London, or any major city and, when
he did, it all looked the same. It hadn't been his idea to
hold the sales conference in the middle of nowhere, but
then no one had asked him.

"Damn," he muttered.

He had tissues in the car. Sam wasn't great at
forward planning. He was late because there was a girl,
and he could resist many things except a girl who
appeared to have even the slimmest interest in sleeping
with him. She was the first since Suzy, and he wasn't
going to squander the opportunity. It was priorities
again, and the possibility of any woman having sex
with him always went straight to the top of the list. He
thought he'd impress her with his prowess as a cook
and had knocked together something which, at the
time, seemed quite respectably tasty. He'd taken a
fairly blasé attitude to sell-by dates which is why, when
his bowels twitched, he knew not to ignore them. He
should have looked closer at the chicken, or even

smelled it, but there were other senses at play, and they were mostly in his trousers. He just wished he'd brought the tissues with him.

"Bugger," he said to himself.

He wasn't looking forward to the conference. They were always slow, grubby, humourless affairs, not made any less so by his boss, Derek. He wondered if his job might be in jeopardy. Not that he'd intended to become a photocopier salesman. As far as he was aware no one actually *intended* to sell photocopiers for a living. It just happened. In order to distract himself from the unpleasant position he found himself in, he imagined a small child who, with absolute certainty, did not want to be an astronaut, or a train driver, or a surgeon, but wailed, just after he'd taken his first steps, 'I want to be a photocopier salesman!'

"Shit," Sam said.

He brought himself back to the present and looked around the ditch. It was grassy and a bit thorny. He'd nearly sustained a serious injury stabbing the last thing he'd want stabbed. The ditch ran down to a small stream. There weren't any conveniently sized leaves with which, in the absence of the tissues he'd left in the car, he could wipe his arse. He certainly couldn't just pull his trousers up.

"Hold on," he muttered.

He'd spotted a blue bag further up the ditch. It was just behind him, but out of reach. That was becoming the story of his life. It would have been too convenient to have been within reach. He grabbed his underpants and moved crab-like in the direction of the bag. He didn't want to sully his trousers, and thought about taking them off, but the ground around was very damp, and he'd have to take his shoes off too. It wasn't going to be easy. He looked down. It was a bit of a mess. He'd been generous with the spices, which had disguised the sorry state of the chicken, but hadn't helped his stomach. The evening hadn't ended in tumultuous quantities of athletic sex either. The worse thing was that he didn't mind. That wasn't quite true. He did mind, but he wasn't quite sure whether there was still something between him and Suzy. He'd been with her longer than any other girl, which had prompted the grownup word 'relationship'. He crabbed his way closer to the blue bag.

"Nearly there," he muttered encouragingly to himself.

He knew the precise moment when it had all gone wrong with Suzy. They were both, as she'd frequently pointed out, over thirty, and ready for a more mature life. Sam didn't quite know what she'd meant by that and wisely didn't ask. But they were about to have sex and, while his penis was ready, Suzy evidently wasn't. She'd popped into the bathroom. He wasn't sure what she was doing, but she took a long time doing it, and eventually Sam had got bored. He'd waved his penis around to keep it interested. More time passed and he began to wave it in the style of a Star Wars light sabre.

It was only natural, he thought at the time, to add light sabre sound effects and, as he'd got that far, he'd added some dialogue. Suzy appeared and did not respond well to his declaration that she 'must feel the force'. Apparently it wasn't the kind of mature relationship she was looking for.

"Bingo," he said.

He'd reached the bag. He plunged his hand in and, as luck would have it, found a handful of paper. That would do the job. He grabbed it and began the repair work. It wasn't *that* absorbent, but it was better than nothing, and he could finish off with the tissues he'd left in the car. He threw the paper down the ditch. If he got back on the motorway, he reasoned, he could make up some time. He'd have to come up with something to keep his job. It was then that he looked down the ditch.

"Bloody hell," he said.

Something had distracted him from a rare moment of thinking about his job. It wasn't the ditch or the stream, but the paper he'd used to wipe his arse. It wasn't paper, or rather it *was* paper, but it was a special kind of paper, which was now covered in his excrement. He scrambled down the ditch.

"Bloody hell," he said again.

They were bank notes. £50 bank notes. He stood up. It was a little careless and his trousers were damp from the ground and possibly something else he didn't want to think about. He walked awkwardly to the blue bag. He recognised the bag, or the style of bag. It was one of those large Ikea bags. The handles were tied together, but part of the bag was gaping open. He thrust his hands in and pulled it open.

"Fucking hell," he said.

The road was remote and there was no passing traffic. It was oddly silent. It was just him and nature, yet his voice echoed as if he were in a library, or the back of a church. He knew he should be whispering. He knew he had to do something and do it pretty quickly. It wasn't just him and nature, there was him, nature and a very large blue bag which was crammed with banknotes. He had to get the hell out of there.

Chapter Two

"You're getting to an age," Suzy's sister had said.

Suzy's lunch with her sister had been less than satisfactory in which she was reminded of her apparently advancing years, and all the things her sister had and she didn't. She couldn't quite bring herself to tell her that it was all over with Sam. Not that her sister saw Sam as a great catch. Suzy was grateful when she got back to work and was confronted by her upbeat assistant.

"Why do you think, Bradley," she asked, "that they call it a 'catch' when a girl gets a man?"

"You had fun with your sister?" Bradley asked languidly.

"I mean, why a catch? Is it like they're falling from the sky?" Suzy continued without really paying Bradley much attention.

"Did she mention the age thing again?" He asked.

"Or is the catch that, in exchange for a house with a nice white picket fence, wifey has to become a servant and slave?" Suzy fretted.

"Does she think you should be married?" Bradley asked, certain he wouldn't get an answer.

"And sex slave into the bargain," Suzy ranted. "Who is catching who?"

Bradley knew that Suzy had both sides of this conversation covered and his best bet was to let her finish, or divert her.

"And wifey has to dutifully pump out babies, incubating hubby's genes, keeping the family line going and doing the washing and ironing," Suzy said.

She worried for a second that she had a less than positive perspective on the concept of family, but then decided she didn't care.

"You know the three witches are coming in this week?" Bradley asked, trying to divert her.

Suzy was an account handler in a small advertising firm and this was a new and major cosmetics client.

"Of course I do," Suzy said without really listening.

It was fortunate that there were no accounts that needed handling that afternoon, as she spent most of her time brooding about Sam. She had to remind herself that she had finished with him, although she was loath to mention this to Bradley. It just didn't seem quite finished. It wasn't official. For some people it required a post on Facebook to make it official. For her it was telling her sister, who would then tell her mother. And then her mother would call.

"You alright, babe?" Bradley asked, a little later.

Her mother would adopt her death-in-the-family tone and Suzy would be invited to an excruciating dinner after which she'd leave with the distinct impression that there was something wrong with her. The prospect of which wasn't quite a reason to give it a further go with Sam, but she wasn't going to ignore it either. There *were* some positive aspects to Sam. She thought she'd use Bradley as a sounding board.

"Sam's good looking isn't he?"

Bradley sighed, which she took as affirmation.

"I mean, I know his hair is a bit wild, but it's all there isn't it?"

Bradley nodded.

"And he's not that far out of shape, is he?"

Bradley frowned.

Suzy struggled to think of Sam's other qualities and decided not to share that strange Star Wars thing he'd done with his penis.

"Babes?" Bradley said hoping to redirect her to work related issues.

Bradley claimed heterosexuality, but acted as camp as a drag queen and addressed everyone as 'babe,' even the men. Suzy had found it spectacularly irritating to begin with, but had given up protesting, and now almost found it charming. It helped that he was good at his job, so good he frequently did hers, and he was good at covering for her when she was at lunch or, should a hangover arise, at home in bed.

"Oh, whatever," Suzy finally said.

As the full metrosexual, Bradley recognised this as the signal for 'relationship trouble,' which also smelled of gossip, which was one of Bradley's essential nutrients. And the work day had ground to an end.

"Fancy a quick drink?" he asked.

She knew the correct and only answer to this was 'no, absolutely not,' but it was Friday and Suzy had nothing else to do. And an evening with Bradley was like posting naked pictures of herself on Facebook. He was many things, but discreet was not one of them.

"A few of us are going down to the Crazy, Crazy Bar, babe," Bradley said.

The Crazy, Crazy Bar was the happiest drinking establishment she'd ever been in, with palm trees and coconuts, as if it were on a Caribbean beach. It was ran by a charismatic bloke called Kevin who everyone seemed to like. It was hard for her to resist. An hour later Bradley fetched a second round of drinks.

"So," he said casually, "how's it going with Sam?"

If Suzy told him it wasn't going, then Bradley would fly into action like a human Tinder, and round up as many single men of approximately appropriate age as time would allow. She wasn't sure she was ready to face that. If she said it was going through a rough patch, then he would want details and she wasn't giving him that either. That left the third option and, the longer she brooded, the more attractive her memory of Sam was becoming. It might have been the white wine.

"Shots," Bradley announced, before she could reply.

He launched himself at the bar and, with admirable efficiency, returned with a considerable bank of small glasses set in a wooden holder and containing alcoholic liquid, the nature of which appeared irrelevant.

"Go for it," Bradley said and passed one to Suzy.

Bradley had some talent for extracting information from an unwilling source, and knew how best to go about it. Two shots later Suzy had made a decision. It was a rose-tinted decision, fuelled by the alcohol and her sister's smugness.

"It's going fine with Sam," she said.

She said it with a flourish and walked out of the bar before she could change her mind, and in the direction of Sam's flat. She'd ingested enough alcohol to imagine a Richard Curtis scenario in which they had both missed each other and Sam delivers a long impassioned speech, but they both know he had her at 'hello.' That was how she hoped it would go. She approached his front door and pressed the buzzer.

Chapter Three

"I'm going to tear his fucking head off," Gary Beagle screamed.

He had no idea whose head he wished to tear off, but he was certain that he needed to remove *someone's*. He couldn't believe it. He'd chosen the most random point, located at the most arbitrary point, in the middle of nowhere, halfway to nowhere. In the land of nowhere. There was no reason for anyone to ever find themselves down this particular ditch, but some bastard had, and that bastard had taken the money. His money.

"I'm going to tear your fucking testicles off," he screamed.

He'd already decided on the gender of the thief, as it made the image of removing body parts much more palatable. For all his faults, and there really were a great many, Gary had never condoned violence against women. But he'd never felt quite as violent as he did at that moment. He'd checked and cross-checked the location, and he was certain this was it. There was no question of it. He'd counted and recounted the trees that led from a sign which pointed to a village, which was more of a hamlet, which nobody ever took. This was it.

"I'm going to rip your fucking kidneys out," he screamed, but he screamed it a little less loudly.

He didn't know why he'd elected to rip out kidneys. It was unlikely he'd be able to locate them, but he wasn't a man with a huge imagination and was struggling to think of how best he could administer pain. It was his bloody money.

"Fucking bastard," he said.

It was a 'fucking bastard' that was directed at who ever had stolen his money, and as a comment on his luck and, because he still had vestiges of catholicism in him, at God for being such a fucking bastard. Then a thought occurred to him.

"I'm going to pull your fingernails out," he said.

He found the image of exacting his revenge so painfully to be very comforting, particularly if it coincided with him being reunited with the money. His money.

"My fucking money," he whimpered.

By most definitions of ownership he would be pushing his luck to describe the money as his, as he'd stolen it. But, in his defence, he'd stolen it from someone who'd stolen it who, he was fairly certain, had stolen it from someone else. Or, if it hadn't been stolen, it had been acquired through very illegal means. In his eyes that gave his ownership some moral purity.

"Mine, mine, mine," he cried.

He sat down on the damp grass at the top of the damp ditch. There was no one for miles and, if there was ever a time for tears, this was it. He'd not cried since his father had hit him with his toy aeroplane. The plane had been beyond repair, but this situation, Gary told himself, was not beyond repair. He'd spotted something.

"What the fuck," he said.

Gary had an aggressive, intolerant nature. It was not unknown for him to be misogynistic and racist, and he possessed a minimal grasp of grammar. As a consequence he'd found a natural home in the police force. But for whatever reason, he liked to think it was his 'bastard luck,' he'd been sidelined, as many times as the cash, that was momentarily his, had changed ownership. If he was a train he'd be quietly corroding in a yard that hadn't seen a railway line in years. He was in a career cul de sac. It was more like a graveyard. It was so lonely that he'd begun to harbour dreams of escape. First he'd thought of escaping to Southend, but then he'd seen the blue Ikea bag and he'd upgraded his dream, and now it included the Caribbean, or at least it had. Gary was a detective constable in a rural part of the country which was more noted for incest than major crime. It was not a great grounding for sleuthing. Despite this, Gary knew a clue when he saw one. He picked it up.

"Shit," he muttered.

As a piece of deductive reasoning it wouldn't have troubled even Dr. Watson. But Gary's Inspector had said that Gary couldn't recognise the 'fucking obvious even if it was fucking obvious', and in this case he was wrong. Gary was holding a bank note, which on its own was clearly a clue. He wouldn't have recognised the faces of either Mathew Boulton or James Watt, even if he'd lined them up with the Harlem Globetrotters, but their faces were obscured with a further clue, and he'd correctly identified that.

"Shit," he said again.

It was excrement. Faeces. Stools. Crap. It was shit, and it was human shit, and Gary was pretty sure DNA could be extracted from that. That would make it a pretty good clue.

Chapter Four

The flat seemed warmer and cosier sharing the sofa, as Sam was, with a large bag of cash. The conference had been much more tolerable than he'd expected. But he'd been distracted. The presence of banknotes in the boot of his car was very distracting. But he'd got through the conference and made it home. The television was on and he'd bought a bottle of wine. The wine was the first foray into the cash. He feared that the cash might be 'marked,' although he wasn't entirely sure what 'marking,' consisted of, or whether the numbers were recorded. But the notes weren't new and consecutive, they were very grubby indeed. The problem was that Sam was not good at keeping secrets. He was a man who liked to share his thoughts and insecurities. It was very modern, but at the moment it was very inconvenient. He'd have to change.

"What," he said, pouring another glass of wine, "am I going to do?"

He needed someone to confide in. Two weeks earlier he might have confided in Suzy. She had been his girlfriend on and off for a couple of years. But they were on an 'off' period and, judging by her last remarks, it was more final than usual. She'd complained about a number of things. He looked at the cash and tried to think of what they were.

"I want to live with a grownup," Suzy had said.

It appeared that, in her eyes, he lacked maturity. He also lacked, and she was very clear about this, ambition, direction, consideration and he was thoroughly undomesticated. It had been very final, although he remembered thinking at the time that she was describing a dog, and not a boyfriend. But it was worse than that. They were getting, she'd told him, to an age. She'd left that sentiment hanging, thinking he was far more intuitive than he was, and unaware of its meaning. He wisely didn't point it out, and add it to his extensive list of deficiencies.

"An age," he muttered to himself, wishing he had some idea what that meant.

He drank a little more wine and took out a wad of notes. They were all twenties. He counted quickly and found there were fifty of them. One thousand pounds. It didn't look like much. He arranged it on the carpet. It was a rather ragged carpet, which he liked, but for which Suzy seemed to have a disproportionate loathing. He wondered why women did that. He placed two more thousands next to the first one.

"Thirty-three," he said.

He got up and looked at the mirror above the fireplace. Someone had left it in the street and he'd claimed it. It fitted quite well, and looked almost grownup. Thirty-three didn't seem like *that* much of an age. His black, curly – or as she'd put it unruly – hair was neither greying or receding. His face and his stomach were distinctly more filled out than they had been although, now he thought about it, Suzy had said chubby. He didn't remember her saying it with much affection.

He'd finished the bottle. Half an hour later he wished he'd bought more wine.

"Five hundred and seventy thousand," he said.

That was quite a lot of money. It filled most of the floor of his sitting room, but the amazing thing was that the big blue bag didn't look any emptier. There was well over a million quid. It was a lot to cope with, but he didn't want to leave it on the floor and go to the shop at the end of the road. It seemed too risky.

Then he remembered something. Suzy had cooked something with brandy and there was a bottle somewhere at the back of a kitchen cupboard. It took a while to find, as he took a rather unstructured approach to organising his kitchen which, now he thought about it, was a further criticism, and cupboards were randomly filled.

"Victory," he said as he found the bottle and grabbed a glass and went back to the sofa.

Looking at the notes was like surveying a kingdom. He arranged some more notes. It took some time and he lost count of the amount. Eventually it covered most of his sitting room floor. It was why he needed the brandy. He didn't much like brandy, and the liquid burned a hot path down his throat. It was very exciting, but it was also very dangerous. It was the sort of cash for which people were prepared to kill. And it wasn't like he could pay off his mortgage with it, or buy a new apartment, or maybe even buy a new car. How do people launder money like this and what did laundering money even mean? And someone might kill to get it back. This was something he had to keep secret. It was at this point, surveying the new kingdom and balancing the fear and danger, that the intercom blapped.

"Shit," Sam shouted.

It was a blap so loud and so unexpected, at a point at which Sam was poised on the knife-edge of paranoia, that he very nearly, and very literally, crapped himself. He went to the front window and pulled the curtain back an inch. He couldn't see anyone in the street, although it now occurred to him that if there had been someone in the street, he would have made his presence obvious. He would have to get better at this. He crossed the room and pressed the intercom.

"Hello?"

"It's me."

It was said in a flat, irritated voice. A female voice. It was Suzy.

What the hell was he going to do? There wasn't enough time to gather it together and how could he explain it? He could say it wasn't real. But, after their last meeting, in which there was talk of a lack of maturity, she wouldn't believe him. She might not even believe him if he told her he'd found it. He should tell her, but not like this. He'd have to bluff.

"Oh," Sam said sleepily, which wasn't the invitation she'd been expecting.

There was a pause in which Suzy's irritation was almost palpable.

"Can I come up?" Suzy asked, finally.

"I'm sorry, I'm really, really tired," Sam said, yawning ostentatiously.

Suzy's irritation hardened. She knew, that he knew, that if she stayed sex was more than likely and, in the considerable period she'd known him, he had never, and she was certain about this, declined an offer of sex. That left only one possibility.

"Have you got someone there?" she shouted.

She'd shouted it so loudly he hadn't needed the intercom to hear it. Sam stuttered in response and attempted to find the words that would save the situation, but Suzy added a final word, "Bastard!" She marched off leaving Sam with the feeling that it really was over, and that he would have to hide the cash, and not touch it. Spending it ostentatiously would be crazy. He had no idea whose money it was or what kind of a person they might be. It would be completely mad.

Chapter Five

"I kill them," Vlad said.

Vlad was cleaning his nails with a twelve inch hunting knife. He'd never been hunting in his life and his nails were actually quite clean, but he'd found that nothing sharpened prevarication more than addressing a man while holding a big knife. And this man was prevaricating.

"Yes, indeed. Be that as it may," the Lobster said.

The Lobster was his accountant. He lived in a permanent state of anxiety, with blood pressure which would have frightened a doctor were he ever to visit one. He coped with his anxieties by self medicating with a quite spectacular range of uppers, downers and alcohol. None of this had made him any less anxious and had resulted in a complexion so florid, everyone knew him as the Lobster.

"Be what as maybe?" Vlad said.

Vlad would have found the linguistic eccentricities of English confusing were it not for the fact that his real name was Lionel and he was from Leytonstone. But as Lionel from Leytonstone he got beaten up often and, when he'd left school, he discovered he was qualified for nothing, and he had an epiphany. It was as close to religion as anything was likely to take him and it was the simple realisation, while smoking a joint, that there was a pretty serious mark up on this shit. But he was tall and gangly and he was called Lionel.

"You find fucking money or I..." Vlad made an action with the knife.

The Lobster wished he worked for one of those big accounting firms with a tall, glass-fronted office in the city. But he hadn't exactly sailed through his exams. Or, if sailing was the correct analogy, he'd been in a boat that had taken in a lot of water. This had limited his job opportunities, which is why he found himself working for Vlad. His temperament would have been much better suited to auditing a set of accounts for a small publishing company than working, as he did, for a drug dealer. He went a little redder.

"I want fucking money," Vlad said.

Lionel had turned his tall and gangly body into a tall and intimidatingly muscular one and his hair had receded like a sunset. Then he'd become Vlad from a small town just outside Leningrad called Volkhow. He was very specific about it, and quite capable of talking about it with teary-eyed nostalgia and great detail. He'd spent time on Google Maps. He had a natural affinity for the Russian accent and had found a teacher located far from his manor and where no one knew him.

"Sosi moi hui sooka!" Vlad yelled.

Vlad didn't know that his teacher wasn't Russian either, just someone trying to make a living between acting gigs. His teacher's command of the language was, at best, approximate and mostly confined to swear words and neither Vlad, nor the Lobster, would have been keen to 'suck my cock bitch' as Vlad had commanded.

"No," the Lobster said, cowering.

It was at moments like this that Vlad found his true Russian spirit, not of the reflective Chekov-kind, but more the straight to DVD Steven Seagal stereotypical villain. The words exploded in his head like fireworks.

"Gandon! Gandon! Gandon!" He swore.

Vlad didn't know that the literal translation of this was a condom, or rather a very specific kind of condom. A used one. It didn't make any difference to the Lobster who thought he was going to die.

"I don't know anything," the Lobster pleaded.

There was a pause. A strange quietness fell over them. The Lobster found it hard to interpret this as a good sign but, as Vlad was cleaning his fingernails with a hunting knife, good signs were in short supply.

"Tee karova," Vlad whispered.

The words sent a chill down the Lobster's back. This was it. The final moment. He knew it would happen eventually. He shouldn't have taken the job, but he needed the money. It wasn't fair. The Lobster would have been less scared if he'd known that 'tee karova' translated to 'you cow.' Vlad had thought it was something rather more brutal, as brutal was how he was feeling. It was a lot of money and he wanted it back.

"Or I fucking, kill, kill, kill," Vlad said.

He stabbed the desk hard to punctuate each 'kill'. He was so in character that no one knew he was Lionel from Leytonstone and, on the rare occasions he had bumped into people from his past, they hadn't recognised him. Such was his immersion that middle Europeans thought he was a genuine Russian. This time he found the correct Russian words.

"Ubiystvo, ubiystvo, ubiystvo!" Vlad spat.

If ever there was a language for killing, or uttering threats it was, Vlad always thought, Russian. And he was very, very angry. He couldn't say for certain who it was who'd stolen his money and, even if he only had a vague idea, that would be enough for him to sharpen his knife on their intestines. He didn't think it was the Lobster as he had neither the courage, nor the imagination. And if he had stolen the money, he wouldn't be sitting in front of him sweating like he'd just got out of a sauna. Not knowing was prompting a significant amount of frustration and anger in Vlad. He brought the blade down again.

"Kill! Kill! Kill!" he screamed.

It would have been cathartic but, when he'd first acquired the IKEA bag in which he'd placed a considerable fortune in cash, he'd been shopping with Brandy. Brandy was his girlfriend and she had very clear ideas about interior design, and she'd filled so many trolleys he had to buy several large blue bags. It had taken hours and he'd felt like some of his life was passing him by. She'd even suggested he buy a desk for the office by which time he'd decided that it was easier, and quicker, to give in than protest. It was the IKEA desk which he now stabbed with the hunting knife and while it *looked* like it was sturdily constructed, it appeared to be no match for a hunting knife brought down with anger and strength. The knife sliced both the desk and his thigh.

"You go now," he said to the Lobster through gritted teeth.

Vlad was going to have to get himself to hospital.

Chapter Six

Sam knew it would be crazy, and dangerous, touching the money. Total madness. Only a complete fool would start spending the cash. Despite that, he was in a casino. He *had* intended to keep quiet about the cash. But there were two problems. The first was that he was now single, very single in light of his near encounter with Suzy, and the weekend beckoned. He was pathologically incapable of staying in on a weekend. It wasn't right. It conflicted with the natural order of things. And he had a huge pile of cash. He hadn't initially intended to take some, or get on the bus, or go to the West End or, and he had no idea how this had happened, enter a casino. But he had. He threw the dice.

"Sam! Sam!" the girls cheered.

The evening had escalated and Sam had picked up not one, but two Russian prostitutes, in so much as a prostitute could be picked up, and not that he was aware that they were prostitutes. He just thought he was doing great. It was certainly a rollercoaster ride in which the highlight so far was a short trip to a toilet in which he snorted a very long, and very expensive, line of cocaine off Ola's naked breasts, although it could have been Alina. But it had led him to conclude that he wished to make some fairly drastic changes in his life. For a start he'd like to press his face into more naked breasts. A lot more. They'd steered him skilfully back to the tables.

"Blow on it," he asked Ola.

This was an instruction that Ola was no stranger to and, as a precursor to future events, she blew on his hands, to endow the dice with the necessary good luck, although Ola already knew *she'd* thrown a double six with Sam. Ola was a pole dancer when she wasn't being a prostitute. Her breasts were more substantial than the rest of her would suggest, and they lacked movement, which was ideal for pole dancing. Anyone else might have concluded that a surgeon had packed in quite a lot of something that wasn't human, but Sam was having such a good time it didn't occur to him. He'd just assumed he'd not experienced enough breasts and that was something he'd like to change.

"Roll again," Alina said, stroking his inner thigh in a way which was distracting, but not distracting enough for him to stop spending money.

The girls operated with spectacular skill, as if spinning plates, and knowing precisely when another tug was required. Alina and Ola's work in the casino was very much win win, paid as they were, by both the management and, although he didn't know it yet, Sam. There was a third win in that they took a small markup on the cocaine, which had been on Ola's solid breasts, and was now in Sam's bloodstream. They were so skilled at this that they could run courses on fleecing men. They'd elevated it from a skill to a science, and then to an art form. This wasn't just degree level fleecing, these girls had a doctorate in the subject. Sam rolled again.

"Yes," they cheered.

Anyone else would have wondered why they'd cheered as he'd lost, but Sam was having too good a time to worry about that. He'd blown it with Suzy and he hadn't quite decided how he felt about it. An observer might say he'd got over it pretty quickly and, if there was mourning going on, it wasn't obvious to Ola or Alina. But when Suzy had slammed the door on their life together he'd almost felt lonely, except for the army of soldiers on his sitting room floor, the money he'd vowed he wouldn't touch, and the bottle of brandy.

"Again?" he asked.

Ola and Alina were a little surprised at his astonishing willingness to lose money, but they'd seen his wallet. Like a hawk hovering ten metres above an unsuspecting mouse, they could spot a significant wad of cash across a crowded, poorly lit room. And like the hawk, they'd gone in for the kill. They'd joined him not long after his arrival.

"You're a winner, Sam," Alina said.

Sam could have still been sitting in his flat with a lonesome bottle of brandy and a tempting pile of cash. Too tempting as it turned out, as he'd decided to refresh his wardrobe. He'd left the house with a grand to buy some clothes and then returned five minutes later to grab another grand. He'd dithered outside the door of his apartment, and entered and exited several more times until he'd finally hit the West End armed with ten grand. Oh, the joy of cash. And he had no idea where the evening would end.

"On the black," Ola suggested.

The girls, on the other hand, were working to a clear and defined objective and knew precisely where the evening would end. They nodded discreetly to each other, so discreetly that even the establishment's security cameras missed it, and they dragged him off to a hotel room. As sex was clearly on the agenda, and Sam had not had any for a while, it wasn't exactly a dragging. Ola had decided that he'd lost enough money at the tables, and therefore had fulfilled that part of their contract with the casino. The fear was that if he lost too much, there wouldn't be any left for them. Their work on their backs, and in the lap dancing bars of Europe, hadn't precluded an education and, as they understood the English liked to say, they knew exactly on which side of a slice of bread their butter should be applied.

"Where are we going?" Sam asked.

He had bought rather more than his fair share of what the house referred to as champagne. It was a pale, insipid fizzy liquid, which probably contained some alcohol, and into which Ola had inserted a decent slug or two of vodka. Sobriety would not be the route to the remains of Sam's wallet. They made a further gesture to each other, which was more like insurance, and decided to apply more butter.

"This way," Alina said.

There was a cab ride and an oddly ornate restaurant, and more champagne, and further dents to his wallet. Then there was a hotel. The hotel, and the room, looked a little rough, but things were quite hazy.

"How much?" he muttered as he paid.

It wasn't a question, more a shocked response at the figure quoted. It was enough, it occurred to him for a second, to buy a very sophisticated office photocopier. He was just about sober enough to recognise that it was a lot of money being asked, but he had other things on his mind. He was a little surprised to discover that he only had two grand left. It took him a while to take two away from ten and arrive at the conclusion that he'd blown eight. A few seconds later that wasn't the only thing that was blown. He was naked. It was as if a pair of lionesses had ripped his clothing off and were attempting to asphyxiate him with their sexual organs. He *did* remember thinking that if he had to go, this is the way he'd choose. The two grand didn't last long and nor did he.

Chapter Seven

Gary was at his desk. It was a tidy desk, as not a vast amount of work tended to move across it. Some police stations were a high tech fusion of the traditional and the modern, with clean walls and sharp angles. Gary's nick wasn't one of them, although it did have a really lovely garden. It was built in the thirties with small lead-lighted windows and wood panelling, and even the brightest fluorescent tubes were incapable of lighting the place up. It was a gloominess which matched Gary's mood. Gary didn't notice his Inspector approach him.

"What are you up to, Gary?"

Gary shrugged, as he thought it best not to mention to his Inspector that he was trying to retrieve at least a million quid that he'd stolen. That was another galling aspect. He'd not had the time to count it. But he'd been in a marked police car and he knew he had to stash it. He'd only had a moment to act.

"Oh, this and that," Gary replied.

The Inspector frowned. He would have hated lazy water-treading cops content to do the bare minimum while waiting for retirement to arrive, but he had only thirteen months, three weeks and four days to go and, if he spent his time trying to get rid of Gary, it would upset his golf handicap. He wasn't going to let that happen, and was content to let Gary shuffle as many papers from one tray to another as he liked. Now that the Inspector thought about it, there were three hours remaining on that day and he had not the slightest interest in wasting them on either Gary or police work. He walked away as Gary's phone rang.

"DS Beagle," Gary answered.

It was the lab. In the past week there had been one burglary, two graffitied signs, a stolen bicycle and two domestic disputes. Upper Norton was not a hotbed of crime, although there was some suggestion that the locals weren't averse to incest, and that was a crime.

"What's this?" the forensic scientist asked.

Both of them knew what it was. Gary had held onto the shit for a few days, as there had been no opportunity to pass it off on one of his trivial cases. He'd worried that, as it was no longer fresh, if that was the correct term for newly defecated excrement, it might be harder to determine the author's DNA. Oddly, it hadn't smelt any less shitty. Gary tried to remember the word he'd seen when he'd visited hospital. What was it? Then he remembered.

"It's faecal matter," Gary confirmed.

Gary was determined to discuss it like an adult and not like sniggering children talking about sex, which was not a view shared by the forensic scientist.

"Looks like shit to me," the forensic scientist said, adding, "like faecal money."

There was a pause. The laboratory was a pristine white establishment in a modern building rich in glazing and equipped with the latest technology and wallpapered with large flat screens. It looked pretty cool. But government cutbacks had been harsh and morale wasn't always high. This task seemed to be rubbing it in.

"Yes," Gary said.

Despite the cutbacks, the lab had performed a few forensic miracles and had some talent for extracting bits of this from bits of that, and obtaining a guilty verdict. They were clever people. They liked to categorise, they couldn't help themselves, and they'd worked out what they thought of as a 'Plod Scale'. They were frequently rather disparaging about the cognitive abilities of their police counterparts, and this scale placed the policemen they dealt with in an order much like the ascent of man. They saw Gary as hunched over, with a prominent forehead, and dragging a club.

"Whose shit?" the forensic scientist asked.

"That's what I want you to find out," Gary replied with uncharacteristic speed.

"Has there been a murder?" the forensic scientist replied.

Gary fumbled for a reply. He wished there had been a murder but, if there had been a murder, it wouldn't be him investigating it. The best he could manage was a dispute between two neighbours. Although one neighbour hadn't actually crapped on the property of another, it didn't seem impossible that he might have.

"A domestic dispute," Gary said finally.

"Do you know how much this will cost?" the forensic scientist asked.

Gary didn't. He didn't have the faintest idea. He had no idea how it was ratified and he didn't care. But he did care about the bastard that had stolen his money and he had every intention of finding him. The word 'detective' was, after all, in his job title. But he had chosen the grassy bank of a ditch in the middle of nowhere to stash the money precisely because of its anonymity, and because it was free of cameras. He had nothing else to go on, but a smear of shit. It was quite a substantial smear, there was no shortage of the stuff – he daren't speculate what the owner had been eating – but it was his best bet. He'd have to lie.

"No, but the guv says I've got to sort it. It's a bit close to home, this one."

There was a pause. Gary wished he'd joined the masons. It was at times like this that he imagined he could get stuff done with just a nod and a wink, or however masons communicated. But he wasn't a mason because no one had ever asked him.

"Okay," the forensic scientist said, and hung up.

Chapter Eight

"Who stole my fucking money?"

Vlad pronounced every word with a disproportionate amount of spittle. The Hump had his legs raised and was lying on a piece of gym equipment. This was unusual as he'd never entered a gym, or taken a moment's physical exercise, in his life. He'd been overweight for decades and, if it weren't for all the disastrous financial decisions he'd made, he wouldn't be far away from retirement. He only had one shoe on.

"I want my fucking money,' Vlad said.

Vlad had tried the Lobster, now it was the Hump's turn. He was Vlad's only official employee. His unofficial employees now ran to fifty, and he operated a terrorist cell type management structure in which most employees weren't aware of each other, and very few were aware of him. There was a chain in which the cash was passed ever upwards until it arrived at its final resting place, him. The individual sums weren't that great, reducing potential losses, but cumulatively it was pretty significant. And it had taken nearly a year to fill that blue IKEA bag.

"I don't know anything about any money," the Hump pleaded.

A bag no one knew about, and very few people could even have guessed, and no one in his employ, he reckoned, who would have the balls. Of course, if Vlad did find the culprit, he'd use the hunting knife and, who ever had taken his cash, would get to see his own balls from a much greater distance than before. It would be quite a defining moment for someone.

"Which thieving bastard, would you say, stole my bloody money?" Vlad demanded.

It often struck the Hump as strange that Vlad's grammar could vary so much. There were occasions when he could appear almost English. But this wasn't striking the Hump as that particular moment, as it was Vlad who had removed his shoe and had his big toe in one hand, and a hunting knife in the other. He didn't look like he was about to file his nails.

"I don't know," the Hump whimpered.

Vlad was an aggressive and violent man, but the state of the Hump's toenails disgusted him. Surely cutting your toenails was just basic grooming? It made the business of torturing seem rather unsavoury. It was as much because of the appalling state of the Hump's toenails, than the possibility he might have stolen a fortune from him, that prompted Vlad to stab the knife into his foot.

"Arrrgh!" the Hump screamed.

Vlad had spent the morning in hospital. His thigh was bandaged because of the injury he'd sustained when he'd plunged the hunting knife through the desk. The doctor said he very nearly hit a major artery. He'd remember that for the future. He'd limped out of the hospital still wondering into whose thigh he was going to plunge his hunting knife. And that thought had taken him to the Hump. The Hump ran the skip hire business, which was Vlad's legal front. He was called the Hump not because he was quick to anger, or was prone to taking offence, but because he had a large camel-like hump on his shoulder. He'd spent some years in denial about it and used to look around in surprise should someone mention it. Consequently, with the advent of political correctness, and the success of the Paralympics, it was as if it had vanished. Then he came to work for Vlad.

"Who, you humpy bastard, took my fucking money?" Vlad said.

The purpose of the business was to launder the proceeds of his more lucrative illegal work. Cash was the problem. He'd been trying to figure out a way of laundering it and taking it back to his native Russia, when he reminded himself he didn't come from Russia. Leytonstone wasn't that far away.

"It wasn't me," the Hump said.

Vlad didn't think the Hump had actually stolen the money, but he thought he might have some idea about who had, and could be a little more proactive in the matter. During Vlad's transition from Lionel he'd read lots of self help books, and was a big fan of the proactive. Sitting on his arse, and wondering who had stolen his cash, was much more frustrating than torturing someone he was pretty certain hadn't. There was a word for it, what was it?

"Cathartic," Vlad suddenly said, and dropped the Hump's foot.

It was a less than cathartic experience for the Hump, who assumed that 'cathartic' was a Russian word and, from his longstanding association with Vlad, would guess that it translated into something like disembowel. As far as he could gather it was a language which only had words for stabbing, punching, hitting, kicking, disembowelling and impaling. He wondered if they had a word for daffodil.

"Let's start again," Vlad said.

He untied the Hump's feet and pushed him off the bench. He was irritated to find that the bastard had got blood all over his bench. He found some tissues, while the Hump lay in a moaning heap on the floor.

"K picked up the money as usual?" Vlad shouted.

Vlad liked to use letters for all of his operatives. He liked to call them operatives too, he'd got that from one of his books. The letters tended to confuse the Hump, who wasn't that great at letters. He wasn't that brilliant at numbers either, which had been one of the limiting factors in his career.

"Yes," the Hump managed to say.

"Bloody hell," Vlad said.

The Hump closed his eyes, assuming that he was about to have another body part stabbed. Perhaps his 'cathartic'. But Vlad was just annoyed he'd run out of tissues and, despite the so called wipe-clean vinyl used in the construction of the gym bench, some of the blood was stubbornly refusing to come off. It was possible it was blood from the last person, but Vlad doubted it. He was very meticulous about his gym equipment. They were in the basement of one of his lockups. It had started life as an inspection pit, until Vlad saw the potential, and discreetly dug it out until it was quite a substantial hidden space. He went upstairs.

The Hump had a large enough stomach for his feet to be rarely visible, which was why he took an out of sight, out of mind view on cutting his toenails. He also hadn't attempted to touch his toes since flared trousers were in fashion. He looked a little like a turtle who'd had been put on his back, or a dog chasing his tail. He reached down to grab his foot, but each time it seemed to run away. It was most exhausting. Eventually he grabbed it. He wasn't sure what to do next, as he feared his back was going to give out, until he saw a roll of gaffer tape. Vlad always had lots of gaffer tape. Vlad really liked gaffer tape.

"What you doing?" Vlad said, back in full Russian character.

Vlad didn't listen to his reply and continued to try and remove the bloodstains from his bench. He needed something a little more abrasive, but all he'd found was an old rag and a local paper. He dumped the bloodied tissues into the paper. It was then that something caught his eye.

"Hold on," he said.

The Hump thought he was referring to his use of the gaffer tape. He knew that Vlad could be proprietorial about the stuff, but it didn't seem unreasonable to use just a little bit to stem the bleeding. But it wasn't that. Vlad had found something in the paper.

"Have you seen this?" Vlad asked.

The Hump lay in a defeated and bloody pile and thought it odd that Vlad should ask him about local events, not least as he was rarely *au fait* with the latest gymkhana.

"No," the Hump said cautiously.

With one hand, and with astonishing ease, Vlad grabbed the Hump by the shoulder and pulled him to his feet.

"This," Vlad said, pointing.

The Hump read the article.

"The police have been investigating a series of burglaries in Aston Road," Vlad read out.

"Is that where the money was?" the Hump asked.

"The police have searched surrounding properties," Vlad said.

"The police," the Hump and Vlad said.

Chapter Nine

Suzy had planned to stay in and watch the latest Poldark. She'd recorded them and saw her Saturday evening as an endless orgy of Cornish skullduggery, with gratuitous shirt removal and, in her case, white wine. She had not intended to go to the pub, but Bradley had insisted. He'd decided to adopt her like an orphan, or a stray cat.

"I'm fine," Suzy said for the fifth time.

He was like a dog with a bone who wouldn't let it go. She hadn't intended to leave the pub and head for a club either. But once they'd got in a cab, and she'd already consumed a few drinks, it seemed like nothing could hold them back. The capital flashed past them as the cab driver swung them through back streets like, she thought, a Star Wars fighter pilot. She wished she hadn't thought that, as she knew it was precisely the sort of thing that Sam would have said, and she was trying to forget him. But the world was passing her by at great speed. It felt like a metaphor for her life, which was passing her by at an alarming rate. She decided, and only because she'd had too much to drink, to enlist Bradley's help.

"They say you know who the one is," she said.

The cab had a very unofficial look to it, and it thumped and crashed over potholes with the music set at a sufficient volume to remind the driver of the soundtrack of his Algerian life. The windows were open, mostly to air the car a little from the fried chicken the cab driver had just consumed. It was a little chilly. And Suzy had posed her question without any frame of reference. It was apropos nothing. Despite that, Bradley knew where she was coming from.

"The one?" Bradley asked casually.

Suzy had no idea why she'd said it. She'd never for a moment thought that Sam was the one. That was until she'd kicked him out. He seemed a lot more appealing now.

"Was Sam the one?" Bradley asked.

"No," she said firmly, and then "I don't know."

"Which is it, babes?" Bradley asked.

"If only it was that bloody simple," Suzy said.

Bradley shrugged. The driver looked in his rear view mirror, which was a remarkable achievement as he was turning into an alleyway populated with pedestrians and cyclists. They were both waiting for more explanation.

"Okay," Suzy explained. "I didn't know, at first. There was no lightning flash realisation that he was going to be my life partner until, until, what do they say in the vows?"

"Until death us do part," Bradley and the cab driver said.

"Yeah, that. But then after a while, when he'd been around a while, after some time, you know," Suzy said painfully petering out.

"You knew?" the cab driver asked.

"No," Bradley said, "I think she just meant 'you know' as a figure of speech."

"So, she didn't know?" the cab driver asked attempting to clarify her position.

"I don't know, did you know?" Bradley asked Suzy.

Suzy shrugged and Bradley tried to help her along.

"Where did you meet Sam?"

It was the first time Sam's name had been mentioned, although the cab driver had already assumed it would be a Dave, or a Steve, or a Sam. They weren't very creative when it came to names in this country, he often thought.

"It was in a pub," she said.

Now that she thought about it, it was entirely typical that they'd met in a pub. The signs were there.

"Didn't you meet at Andrea's birthday party?" Bradley asked.

"That's right," she said.

"That wasn't in a pub."

"Wasn't it?" Suzy asked, confused.

For a second, and it might have been grasping at straws, she wondered if her failure to remember the location of their first meeting was an indication that he *was* the right one. It was possible that nothing else mattered.

"It was at a flat in Peckham," Bradley said.

"Peckham?" Suzy said.

She had no memory of ever being in Peckham, although she could be in Peckham now for all she knew. Then she remembered the flat. It was pretty grotty, with wood-chip paper on the walls, which was a lazy decorating solution that hadn't been fashionable in at least two decades. And everyone was smoking. They were smoking an assortment of things, which gave the place an unpleasant, fetid air. Sam had made a beeline for her.

"You're right," she said finally. "I remember."

Now that she thought about it she couldn't be sure that it wasn't her that had made a beeline for him. What was a beeline anyway? Do bees travel in a direct line? She didn't think so, she thought they meandered, sticking their noses, or proboscises, or whatever they're called in flowers along the way. Had Sam done the same thing and pollinated other women on his path towards her?

"What happened next?" Bradley asked.

It was clear to Suzy that it wasn't remotely clear what had happened next. She decided to skip over the path that brought them together, and whether it was, or wasn't, in the manner of a bee. She was certain they'd met as soon as she'd arrived at the party.

"It was full of smoke," Bradley said.

"I remember that," Suzy said.

"Weren't you smoking that stuff that Stanley had brought?"

Suzy had no recollection of that, but then if she been smoking it, it would explain why she had no memory of it. It was a very effective eraser.

"I don't think so. Anyway we left together and went to a pub," she said.

It was an old pub with worn and sticky floorboards and there weren't many people and there was no background music. It was oddly silent.

"Wasn't that the wine bar on the corner with all the mirrors?" Bradley asked.

Now that Suzy thought about it, it might have been. Why had she thought it was a grotty old pub? One thing that was for certain was that this wasn't the story she'd tell her grandchildren. She'd have to make a better one up.

"I don't know," Suzy finally admitted.

"Never mind," Bradley said in an attempt to be consoling.

"I don't think anyone knows who the one is. Life is not that simple," Suzy said.

"I knew," the cab driver said.

"You knew your wife was the one?" Bradley asked him.

"Since I first saw her," the cab driver confirmed and added, "married twenty-eight years."

Suzy didn't think it likely that an Algerian unlicensed cab driver could make her feel inadequate, but he had succeeded. Twenty-eight years seemed like an unobtainable goal, a massive ambition, and a life sentence, all rolled into one.

"Very happy marriage," the cab driver confirmed.

Suzy was beginning to hope that they'd nearly arrived at their destination, wherever that might be, but she decided she'd pined enough and was ready to have some fun.

"Does she live in England?" Bradley asked the cab driver.

"No, she's in Algeria," the cab driver said, adding, "very happy marriage."

Bradley and Suzy looked at each other concluding that the key to a happy marriage was to have at least two countries between spouses. The cab came to a halt.

"Where are we?" Suzy asked.

She'd lived in London all her life, but frequently found herself completely lost. If she didn't have a mobile phone she'd spend most of her time walking around lost. She wondered if she could get an app on her phone which would navigate her through life.

"Camden Town," Bradley said.

Suzy was surprised. She'd been to Camden Town loads of times and it still looked alien to her. At least Sam knew where to go. That, she suddenly realised, was why she was lost. She was used to following Sam.

"Are you hungry?" Bradley asked.

Suzy shrugged. Was she so used to someone else organising her life that she was incapable of doing it on her own? Did she not know when to eat? She had to take a stand against this uselessness that was enveloping her.

"Yes. I am hungry."

Bradley steered her through Camden market and it all began to look familiar. They arrived at a stairway leading to a first floor restaurant. The walls were oddly ornate, with an Indian or Moroccan influence.

"I know this place," Suzy suddenly said. "I've been here before."

The ornate carved feel continued into the restaurant. It was large with an odd glamour with women dressed in elegant, and sexy, evening wear. There was a touch of the tacky about it too.

"The girls from Essex like this place," Bradley said, giving them a good eye.

The fine dividing line between elegant and sluttish was frequently broached with naked cleavage, legs and backs in abundance. She followed Bradley's gaze. It appeared that there was some truth in his protestations of heterosexuality. Suzy felt distinctly under-dressed, although she only ever wore clothing like that in bed, and not with any intention of sleeping.

"I really like girls from Essex," Bradley said.

"Is that so?" Suzy said.

Although Suzy had no interest in Bradley she had to wonder, now that his sexuality was established, along with her status as a single woman, why he had precisely no interest in her. What was wrong with her?

"Do you pick up a lot of Essex girls?" Suzy asked.

"My fair share, babes," Bradley said.

"And you like them slutty and obvious?" she asked Bradley with more than a hint of derision in her voice.

"*Everyone* likes them slutty and obvious," Bradley said unaware of any tone, derisory or otherwise, and taking in the sights that the restaurant offered.

"Hold on," Bradley suddenly said, "is that..."

Then he stopped himself. There was a table in the corner at which there was one man and two women. The women had that Essex thing going, which is why he'd noticed them. Or, put another way, if they'd displayed any more cleavage it would include a nipple, and any more leg, a buttock. They looked a little like hookers although, ironically, if they were, they were giving away a lot for free. But it wasn't the three girls that drew his attention.

"What's that?" Suzy asked.

"Oh, nothing," Bradley said.

Suzy knew when an 'oh nothing' meant something significant and looked around. As she scanned the room she made a decision. She was going to buy a knock-out dress as part of her new life as a singleton. But she hadn't spotted the thing that had aroused Bradley's attention. It had taken Bradley a moment too. Bradley was a man who liked his clothes, and had in his possession an impressive array of suits, all of which could be defined by their manufacturer. And the man he'd noticed was wearing Armani. It wasn't a place in which Armani was a surprise, what was a surprise was that it was Sam. That was a surprise.

"Okay," Bradley said, redirecting her, "what shall we eat?"

She looked down at the menu, her mind elsewhere and then, in an unfortunate coalition of events, she looked up and she saw him. He'd gone to the bar and returned with a bottle of champagne. He was dressed in a way she didn't recognise. He was at a table of two laughing women and worse than that, much worse, he looked a million dollars.

Chapter Ten

Sam woke with a surprisingly clear head. It was clear in the sense that there was no pain, an indication that perhaps the brandy, champagne and cocaine had been of a good quality. It was just the previous evening that was a little hazy. He was alone in the bed, but he did have a slight recollection that there had been sparks flying the previous evening, but that might have been because the sheets looked like they were made of nylon. No one troubled him when he left the hotel and, although his pockets were entirely empty of cash, he hadn't lost his travel card. He grabbed a collection of newspapers and jumped on the bus.

Sam scanned and turned the pages like a man possessed. He started with the trashy breast-revealing papers and found nothing. He progressed to the ones that took themselves seriously and featured piety and hypocrisy in equal measure, and found nothing. He removed the irrelevant sections of the serious papers, the ones that thought they ran the country, and found nothing.

"Nothing," he muttered.

Surely if someone had mislaid what looked like more than a million quid they'd mention something? There was no mention of money lost or stolen. This suggested that the money had to be dirty, even before he'd wiped his arse with it. It would, most likely, be drugs money. And therefore very dangerous. Any uncharacteristic displays of wealth would betray him immediately. They would expose him and he'd be in very severe danger. He looked out of the window of the bus and was surprised to see a car showroom. It was even open on a Sunday. There was, he reasoned, no harm in taking a look. He got off the bus.

He'd noticed the place before, but he'd never realised that their selection of cars was so extensive. And so pornographic. He wandered through the maze of cars in a slight daze. He'd looked at cars before, but they'd never seemed quite so affordable. That wasn't to say they weren't expensive, some were hideously so, but he had more than enough cash in his apartment to buy any of them. That hadn't happened before. He hovered a little longer next to one car.

"Would you like to sit in her?" a salesman said.

Sam hadn't seen the salesman appear. The salesman had slid up to him as if he were lubricated. He had much in common with the Russian prostitutes, and would have danced round a pole if it would have secured him a sale.

"Isn't she beautiful?"

Sam cringed a little at the genderising of the car. Suzy would have given him short shrift but, Sam thought, she *was* beautiful. He slid into the car, as if he'd been doing so all his life. As if they were made for each other.

"A test drive perhaps?" the salesman asked.

Sam would have left, he really would, but there was something magnetic about the car. It was black, but not just any kind of black. Nothing was just black or white anymore, they were all a kind of black. And this one had one of those demonic names. It might have been Raven's black, he couldn't remember. But there was something prophetic about it. He knew he had to resist, and he knew there was a limit to the amount of cash they'd accept. And cash was all he had. Then the salesman lent over him and pressed a button.

"Oh," Sam muttered, as if trapped in a sexual experience.

The roof whirred open. Sam admired the leather upholstery around him, but it was not like any leather a cow had ever worn. It was red, but not Hotspur red, or St James red, or Ruby red. It was blood red. The roof and the red leather acted like a tractor beam pulling Sam into a mothership. He had to resist.

"I can't help it," he muttered.

"I beg your pardon?" the salesman asked.

He'd like to say he was the kind of salesman who enjoyed arranging the perfect marriage between customer and car. He'd like to say he apprised them of all the appropriate information, such as the costs, and potential depreciation. He'd like to say he pared the price down to offer the finest value. He'd like to say he thrived on trust and repeat business. But he was a salesman on commission with an occasional cocaine habit. He didn't give a shit.

"Sorry, did I say something?" Sam said.

Sam gripped the steering wheel. He couldn't stop himself. The salesman could see there was something strange going on, but he knew the consequences of not taking lunatics seriously. Lunatics had rights too and, more specifically, they had money. And this car was lots of money.

"It's so beautiful," Sam muttered.

There was the red and the chrome and a bit of wood, which didn't look like a distant cousin to a tree, but something that had been hand-chosen, carefully-felled, lovingly-sliced and fanatically-polished. It was beautiful and Sam wanted it.

"How much?" Sam managed to ask.

It was hard for the salesman to hear as it came out as a throaty rasp. But he was the kind of salesman who could detect interest in a blind man. And right now he could sniff out a sale and a hefty commission.

"Forty-nine thousand, nine hundred and ninety-nine pounds," the salesman said.

What was near as damn it fifty grand still managed to sound like forty something to Sam, and it never ceased to astonish the salesman how many of his punters, when wrapped in desire, could only ever round a large figure down. There had been moments when he'd revealed the price and it was as if he'd strapped the punter into a bullet proof vest and fired a round straight at them. Not this punter. He seemed to smile. It was a little moronic, but it was a smile nonetheless, and it looked a little triumphant.

"Do you take cash?" Sam asked.

"Cash?" the salesman asked.

"Cash," Sam confirmed.

The salesman drew in his breath. He had concerns. There were issues to do with money laundering and tax evasion, but the salesman didn't care about either. He could see the sale drifting away from him, like Kate and Leonardo on the Titanic.

"All of it in cash?" the salesman asked.

"Yes," Sam confirmed.

"I'll ask," the salesman said.

It was with a heavy heart that the salesman extracted himself from the beautifully crafted interior and went to seek the owner. He didn't know much about the owner, it wasn't the kind of environment in which the staff were taken out to encourage camaraderie, and there were no fruit bowls regularly restocked. The owner didn't care about the health or welfare of his employees. He was not a man who worked tirelessly for the community, or for the underprivileged. He did it for the money. But there were limits.

Sam watched the salesman and the owner through the window. They were in the back office, next to a safe which didn't have as much money in it as the owner would like. Sam ran his hand over the seats, as if he was caressing a naked woman. He admired the redness. And he thought about the drug dealers who very probably owned the money and he looked again at the blood red upholstery. And Sam wondered whether his blood would stand out. He left the showroom before the salesman returned.

Chapter Eleven

Vlad had threatened everyone that could be threatened and then, for good measure, he'd abused a traffic warden and kicked a basket of fruit that sat outside a fruit and veg shop. None of it had helped. He'd read the papers to get a lead on which police force had searched one of his properties, and it came down to a small remote station in a place called Upper Norton.

"What did he look like?" he asked his neighbour.

The many properties Vlad owned were held in a variety of offshore companies, which ensured that he was kept a handy distance should things go wrong. And something had gone wrong, although no one had instigated an investigation. It was worse than. They'd just taken the money.

"He was kind of tall, like you, with dark greasy hair and a belly," the neighbour said.

The neighbour had no idea that Vlad was a drug dealer. Her greatest concern was house prices and, while a drug dealer would have been very bad, Russians were good. Russians only invested in the finest areas, she'd told her friends at the book club. They'd looked at her doubtfully, but she'd not noticed.

"Was he in uniform?" Vlad asked.

The neighbour admired Vlad's wide shoulders and muscular arms. She'd mentioned those too at the book club. She'd described him as a Russian Darcy, which was an indication both of how little she knew him, and that she'd never actually read *Pride and Prejudice*.

"Oh no," she said, "he had this horrible saggy black leather jacket on."

"Thank you," Vlad said, smiling charmingly at her.

A small plan was emerging in his head. He smiled again and left. He'd parked his car far enough away for it not to draw attention. When he got there there was a small boy sitting on the bonnet.

"Money for looking after your motor," the boy said with his arm outstretched.

"Fuck off," Vlad said and the boy, who came from a very rough family, did.

Vlad's car was big, black and shiny, and cost a huge amount. It was fast and Germanic and four wheel drive. It was tall and commanding and stood out a bit, particularly the way he'd specified it, with enormous wheels and windows so dark a tint wouldn't describe them. It would have made the manufacturer cringe and was *precisely* as a stereotypical drug dealer might want it. It wasn't a good car for undercover surveillance. He stopped at the skip yard and found the Hump.

"Give me your car keys," Vlad demanded.

The Hump dithered a bit, as his walking had become impaired as a result of his previous meeting with Vlad. He didn't dither for long.

"Can I take your car?" the Hump asked.

Vlad looked at him. It was a multi-nuanced look, which didn't prompt the Hump to pursue the matter.

Vlad eased himself into the Hump's battered Ford Fiesta. It was more of a shit-box than he'd thought. It was the price of doing some surveillance, which would reveal the copper who had thieved his cash. He hoped it was worth it, as it was pretty uncomfortable.

Vlad headed for Upper Norton station. It took him a while to recognise it was a police station, as it was nothing like the grey concrete affairs in Russia – not that he'd been to Russia – and nor was it much like the nick in Leytonstone. It had a very well tended garden.

Vlad's mobile chirped. He checked the screen. It was Brandy.

"I need looking after," Brandy said, without waiting for pleasantries.

'Looking after' was Brandy's term for sex, and she was a girl who needed a lot of looking after. They'd met at the gym and most of their time was spent exercising in one way or another. They'd didn't relax much.

"I can't," Vlad said. "I've got some business to take care of."

That week Brandy had finally moved into his loft apartment. She didn't ask what 'business' meant and he didn't tell her but, as the apartment was large with a good balcony and a fine view, she didn't quibble.

"When will you be back?" Brandy pouted.

It had quickly emerged that, while she was quite spectacular in the bedroom, she was far less accomplished in the kitchen. Vlad had to do the cooking once he'd done her. It was an arrangement that was still working well for them, although it was occasionally tiring.

"It will be late," Vlad said.

He'd been a little hesitant about her moving in, as things had moved too fast for him to tell her that he wasn't actually Russian.

"Okay," Brandy said in a squeaky how-am-I-going-to-manage voice.

Vlad suspected she'd manage okay, as her greatest talent, aside from sex, was getting people to do things for her. He hoped she wouldn't, but also hoped that she didn't burn the building down trying to toast bread.

"See you later," Vlad said, but she'd already hung up.

Vlad sat and watched the police station. After an hour it felt like time had stood still. The station looked like a watercolour and no one, and nothing, had moved. He was worried he'd fallen into a coma. Vlad was many things, but he wasn't a patient man, and this surveillance malarkey required stacks of it. An hour later his mind wandered. It arrived at Brandy. Brandy moving in was a big thing. She was a big thing. She wasn't fat, or anything, but she was a big presence. Eyes followed her. She was a very good looking girl with her clothes on, but with them removed she was eye-wateringly spectacular. She'd taken Vlad's breath away, and that was before she'd thrown herself on top of him and removed any remaining breath.

"Hello," Vlad said.

Someone was leaving the station. But it was no one who remotely filled the description. Then that was it for another hour. He was astounded that the police did so little. It left him alone with his thoughts and they moved onto deeper territory. While he really enjoyed sex with Brandy, and he admired her body – maybe worshipped was a closer word – he feared that there wasn't much depth to their relationship. Vlad was a drug dealer and hadn't exactly immersed himself in emotional and intellectual intercourse, but he knew there must be more. He liked being with her, and they did talk, although at the end of a conversation he was hard pushed to remember the content, or if there had been any. But he wondered if there should be more. At the same time, and it was really irritating, he thought about her constantly.

"Hold on," Vlad said.

A shabby looking man with greasy, almost-black hair and a pot belly had appeared. It was his stretched, shapeless black leather jacket that clinched it for Vlad. He followed him. It was a short drive and it finished at a pub. It wouldn't have taken long to walk to the pub, but it seemed that the man he was following was better at drinking than walking.

Chapter Twelve

Gary had a pint in one hand and a cigarette in the other. It was a rural pub, but it had its own website in which it spoke warmly about its cosy, friendly and authentic quality. A more accurate description would have been old and grubby. In that sense it was as authentic as Gary was, but much less friendly. He scowled.

"You okay, Gary?" the landlord asked.

It was really a request for Gary to stop smoking, but Gary wasn't the kind of person to pick up on signals delivered with subtlety. His career had assiduously resisted promotion for many reasons. Prime amongst them was that Gary was a quite hopeless detective, without insight, or imagination. But, as he didn't do anything of much use, he was rarely in a position to be reprimanded, and that seemed to suit everyone fine. The other problem was that he was lazy and had never much cared why someone might have done something to someone.

"Do you mind, Gary," the landlord tried again.

That was until he'd found himself in temporary possession of a fortune. It focused the mind. Gary was sat by a small inglenook fireplace, which was burning, and smoking merrily. It was hot, and he was sweating, as he hadn't got round to removing his leather jacket. It was a black, shapeless garment which he'd worn longer than the cow before him, and which had been cut in a manner that had never been fashionable in all the decades he'd worn it. Unless there was a fashion holocaust it was likely to remain so, although Gary didn't care. He wore it all the time. He was thinking.

"If it's not too much trouble, Gary," the landlord ventured.

Gary didn't often think. Clearly *some* thinking must go on as he got up, ate, defecated and went to work, but in all other areas his brain was very rarely pressed into action. Like an old dog that wasn't often taken out, it wasn't responding well. He tried to remember his basic training, but it had been a long time ago and, in his case, it had been very basic.

"Will you stop fucking smoking," the landlord suddenly shouted out.

The landlord had begun to boil and Gary hadn't noticed. Why would he? Gary had other things on his mind. Despite that, he stubbed out his cigarette.

"Give us another pint, mate," Gary said.

He approached the bar with his empty glass and, when the landlord had refilled it, he passed over a grubby looking note. The landlord took it and looked at it suspiciously.

"Shit, where's this fifty been?" the landlord asked.

Gary thought it best he didn't tell him, as the landlord had hit the nail on the head. It was one of the shit-stained notes that Gary had sent to forensics for DNA. The good news was that it had come back, no one had noticed or drawn attention to it, and it was definitely human. The problem was that there were no matches on the police computer.

"Dunno," Gary said, took his pint and change, and sat down.

He had a map with him. He'd marked the spot where he'd left the money and he was looking at the roads and the villages that surrounded it. Why would anyone drive down that road? It led to a hamlet of three houses. That was three possible suspects, he thought. It wasn't far from the pub. Gary got up and approached the bar. He lay the map down in front of the landlord.

"Do you know who lives there?" he asked.

"Yeah, that's the vicarage," the landlord said.

It felt a little like a door had closed in Gary's face. If he was of a more sensitive disposition he would have found this familiar, but he was more focused than usual.

"Why do you want to know?" the landlord asked.

Gary couldn't see much harm in telling the truth.

"I want to know who drives down this road."

The landlord nodded and turned to serve someone else. A small crowd peered over his shoulder with mild interest. Gary looked gloomily at the map, as if the answer was about to jump out. Luckily for him, it did.

"The conference centre," a man next to him said.

"What conference centre?" Gary asked.

The man lent over and pointed at the map. Gary followed his finger.

"Hope Spring View," the man added.

"Why would you go down here to get there?" Gary asked.

The man next to him paused, took a huge mouthful of frothy beer and told him, "You wouldn't."

He was a man who had not met Gary before, and was not aware that Gary was gifted with a very short temper, and no sense of humour. Gary was about to reach for his badge, hurl it in the man's face, and explain precisely what line of work he was in, and why he shouldn't take the piss, when the man said, "Sat-navs keep taking people down there."

It took Gary, whose thinking process was less refined than most, a moment to grasp the significance of this. It was like pulling a one-armed bandit and watching all the lemons line up. Then he got it. Gary left his pint on the bar and raced to the car. There had been nothing to motivate him to move at anything more than walking pace all his life, but this was a genuine and exciting lead. Half an hour later he was at the conference centre.

Chapter Thirteen

The following Monday Suzy rearranged her desk and tried not to think about Sam. If she were to be honest with herself and, at that moment she was being anything but, she was more than a little surprised to see an Armani-clad Sam with two beautiful, if rather slutty, women. She couldn't figure out whether that was better than if she'd seen him with just the one girl. He couldn't be having sex with both of them, could he? She made the mistake of asking Bradley.

"Sam?" he said throwing in a dramatic pause. "It looked like it to me."

Bradley had only met Sam once, but he'd heard plenty about him through Suzy. The problem was that Bradley wasn't quite the sympathetic shoulder he appeared to be. Bradley had a vested interest.

"You know you've got a meeting with *Justepourmoi*?" Bradley said.

"Of course I do," Suzy said, without really listening to him.

"They're in the boardroom now," Bradley said, pointing to the boardroom.

"Who are?" Suzy asked.

"*Justepourmoi*," Bradley said.

"Now?"

Bradley nodded.

"Fuck it," Suzy said.

Justepourmoi were the new cosmetic client. They were the three witches. They were French and chic and always obscenely buffed. They were an all female team, and they were buried deep in immaculately applied makeup in which every line was banished, and they wore dresses of sublime chicness, and shoes of steaming sexiness. She hated them.

"Fuck, fuck, fuck," Suzy said.

She'd completely forgotten, and consequently she was wearing jeans, the line and form of which had not been cast by a highly qualified designer of great imagination or taste. They'd been thrown together in a sweat shop in India with the sole purpose of speed of construction from material whose cheapness held more than a hint of child labour about it. They were cheap, and not in an art student ironic way. She was wearing a sweat shirt. She hadn't intended to, but her mind had been elsewhere. It was as if the Sam that she'd knocked about with had become Brad Pitt. It was the lure of the now unobtainable.

"What the fucking hell am I going to do?" she asked Bradley.

The three witches Delphine, Sandrine and Elodie would flail her alive. They'd throw her on the boiling pot of stylish, sexy chicness and she'd be roasted alive. She'd won the account *because* she'd spent three hours knee deep in makeup, and had harvested *every* designer accessory and clothing she, and the office, possessed. They were notorious for dumping agencies and she was dressed in a style which they could only interpret as homeless crack addict.

"Be calm," Bradley advised, although he appeared to be enjoying the experience a little too much, "you've just come from the gym."

"Gym? I don't go to the gym!" Suzy said, sweating like someone who just had.

"I know that, but they don't," Bradley said.

"Of course," Suzy said and, with a slightly manic look she searched for more bullshit, "I was exercising with a client. Maybe Nike? What do you think?"

"I think you shouldn't say the name of the client, but you could imply it," Bradley advised.

"Brilliant! I'll drop a hint about a tick, how does that sound?"

The pressure was making her anxious, and it looked like the only tic she'd acquired was facial.

"Excellent," Bradley advised.

Suzy got up, grabbed a fresh pad of paper, for the creative inspiration that would surely flow, put up her hair and jogged to the boardroom. As she hadn't jogged in some time it was fortunate that the boardroom wasn't far away. Just before she got there she thought she'd mention the marathon she was running for charity. It needed to be a charity that the three witches would approve of, which ruled out the political or anything controversial like child labour or vivisection, as they probably did both in the manufacture of their cosmetics. Suzy jogged on the spot while she tried to think of an appropriate cause. She had to decide soon as she'd be unable to communicate while she collected her breath. How about those little chic dogs that women in Paris use as accessories? It seemed good enough. Suzy entered the boardroom. It was empty.

"Bradley!" she shouted.

He was standing behind her grinning. He was holding what looked like shopping.

"They will be here in three hours," he said.

Before Suzy could shout at him he added, "And look what I've got for you."

He held out a dress.

"Nicole Farhi," he said.

Suzy admired the dress. It looked like it was her size, too. Only a gay man would know that, and know what true in-your-face chicness looked like. It would knock the witches down and prevent her from being burnt at the stake, or lowered into the ducking pool. (Author's note: that is the only time in what must be a million words in which I've actually meant to write ducking.) Bradley had something else hidden behind his back and he produced them like a magic trick. They were shoes. But not mere shoes, they were more a statement of sexual intent.

"Manolo Blahnik," he said.

She looked at them in awe. They were the holy grail of sexy shoes, and Bradley had sourced a pair for her. They were her size, too. How did he know?

"I have more," he said, and Bradley turned and walked back to the office.

It seemed to Suzy to be a slightly camp walk but she wasn't complaining, as this wasn't just saving her bacon. It was serving it up like a Michelin starred chef. When he arrived at her office, there was more.

"Victoria's Secret," Bradley said.

He passed her a bra which looked like a work of art and a month's salary all rolled into one.

"I'll let you try it on," Bradley said and left her office, closing the door behind him.

Five minutes later Suzy looked like she could join the coven and burn the fashionless at the stake of style.

"And I've got you a makeup appointment in thirty minutes," he said.

Suzy was spectacularly grateful, and she'd completely forgotten about Sam. It was incredible how well everything fitted. Even the bra. How did he know? What was it about gay men?

"Thank you, thank you, thank you," she said making worshiping bows.

"What would you do without me, babes?" Bradley smiled.

He was many things, but gay wasn't one of them. The bra size wasn't a lucky guess. He'd been studying her breasts forlornly for years.

Chapter Fourteen

"Oh well," Sam muttered to himself. "It was only ten grand."

They weren't the kind of words he thought he'd ever say but, in the end, it *was* only ten grand. And there was plenty more where that came from. It was on the bus that he began to formulate a philosophy. It was the ten grand philosophy, which he was guessing was the largest sum of cash that most people would be prepared to accept without raising too many money-laundering, tax-dodging questions. When he got back to his flat he checked the money.

"Hello my little beauties," he greeted what had previously been soldiers, and had been elevated to beauties.

His admiration of the stack of notes was interrupted by the vibration of his phone. He looked at it with irritation. It was Derek. He answered it with the greatest reluctance, as photocopiers couldn't be further from his mind.

"Where are you?" Derek asked.

"Derek," Sam said with undisguised irritation, "it's Sunday."

There was a pause as Derek reddened with his own irritation.

"It's Monday," Derek said.

"It is?" Sam said, "are you sure?"

Derek was very sure it was Monday. He'd waited all weekend for Monday as his wife had given him an endless list of tasks, which he'd been forced to do, as she'd developed an unstated passive-aggressive withdrawal of conjugal favours should they not be completed. Derek had ticked every box and fallen asleep on the sofa. The good thing about Monday was he was in charge of the day. He set the tasks.

"I am very bloody sure it's Monday," Derek said.

"Shit," Sam said.

Derek had an impulsive thought. It's worth noting that Derek had never had an impulsive thought in his life. His life was a list of tasks, which he worked through in a methodical fashion. He was not a man with a great deal of imagination and had no idea that his wife wasn't passive-aggressive but she was waiting, once the fence was fixed and the children were at choir, for him to throw her on the bed and ravish her. It was proving, on her part, to be too big a hope.

"You've got some holiday to take," Derek said. "It's a light week. Take the week off. Go and do an 18-30 or something. Get some action."

"Okay," Sam said. "I will."

Sam often wondered about his boss's obsession with 'getting some action' but, as he surveilled the piles of money, now was a good time to do just that. His flat was located on the first floor, which was the top floor of a Victorian house with a communal entrance. It had a closer on the front door which rarely remained open, but offered no great security. The ground floor flat was empty as his hippy neighbour was finding herself again. Something, he noted, she was never able to achieve at home. She travelled a lot. There was a further basement flat which wasn't visible from the road and was accessed from the rear of the building. An elderly couple lived there and he rarely saw them. His own front door was flimsy and, because he occasionally lost his keys, often left unlocked. That afternoon he bought three new locks, a series of steel reinforcing strips and a keyhole viewer. He'd had to buy some tools. He was no great master of the art of DIY and would have called someone in, but didn't want to draw attention to the flat. His work was not elegant, but he made sure it was solid. It wouldn't be an easy door to break down.

After that he set about looking for more cunning hiding places for the cash. He'd seen films in which apartments were ransacked, either by the villains or the police, and he understood common hiding places were in sofas, under the floorboards and in wall cavities. It would be wise, he told himself, to look for the uncommon. It needed to go in something that would ordinarily be considered solid. At the moment it was still in the blue IKEA bag in his airing cupboard. Not that he used the airing cupboard to air anything, and would have shoved his sheets in there were it not for the fact that he only possessed one set. This had prompted Suzy to bring her own, which he still had. He wondered if she'd come and collect them, or if they would be his last memory of her. He shook his head and returned his thoughts to hiding cash. He looked around the flat.

He had one bedroom, a sitting room with a kitchen at one end and a bathroom. It was a limited space to hide quite a large object. That left the floors, ceilings or walls. He closed his eyes for a moment and imagined people with machetes and sledge hammers ripping through his flat. He couldn't be certain that, if he cut a hole in the wall or ceiling, he'd be able to re-plaster it without a big mark saying 'cash hidden here'. He needed to hide it somewhere else. It was while he was thinking about the somewhere else, that he had a eureka moment. It was an inspired solution.

"Of course," he said.

A year earlier the boiler had broken down and it had been replaced with a new one. It was the kind that provided constant hot water, which had made the copper hot water cylinder in the airing cupboard redundant. The plan, or it might have been Suzy's plan, was to make it into a small wardrobe. It was a job that was on Sam's to-do list, which was the kind of list that never received ticks. But the cylinder was still in place and looked like it was plumbed in and functioning. He had to buy some more tools. Then a little later he had to buy a few more.

It took him all day to remove the cylinder, cut out a large hole in the bottom, fill it with most, but not all of the cash, and put it back in place with all the plumbing apparently intact. By eight o'clock he was back in London's west end. This time he had twelve grand on him.

Chapter Fifteen

"I don't care," Brandy said.

It was day three of Vlad's surveillance operation and Brandy was feeling distinctly underappreciated. There were many things that Brandy could handle, but that wasn't one of them. Vlad had also realised, because neither of them had conventional jobs, just how much time they were spending together with this new living arrangement. It was quite demanding. She was quite demanding.

"I've just got to sort this bit of business. It shouldn't take long," Vlad said.

He was less than impressed by the detecting powers of Gary the copper, but he was certain he was on the right track.

"You need to attend to this business first," Brandy said.

She said it with a flourish and she was, in an instant, entirely naked. Vlad hadn't noticed that she was only wearing one item of clothing. The only area in which Brandy was economical was the quantity, although not necessarily the price, of the clothing she wore. She liked to taunt men with considerable hints of flesh. If he hadn't noticed her clothing before he did notice, because it was hard not to, her spectacular body. If he hadn't explored every inch of her he'd swear that she was a surgeon's construction. She was almost cartoon-like in her pneumatic qualities.

Half an hour later Vlad was back in the battered Ford Fiesta. The car was giving him unnatural longings for the power and comfort of his big, chunky fuck-off motor. He got to the station just in time and waited for Gary.

Gary was a creature of habit. He left the station at the very dot of five o'clock almost every evening and went directly to the pub. This evening he didn't stay long in the pub and came flying out as if on a mission. Vlad followed him. Vlad had no idea where Gary was going, and whether he'd drop by wherever he'd stashed the cash. That was the one thing that was disturbing Vlad: he would have expected Gary to be splashing cash around, which meant he was either very clever, or he didn't have the money. He'd taken a good look at Gary. He didn't look clever.

But Vlad was pretty certain that Gary was the only copper who could have taken the cash. As he spent most of his life in a Russian accent he occasionally missed English idioms, and he hoped he wasn't barking up the wrong tree, or on a wild goose chase.

Gary drove for quite a long time, and it began to occur to Vlad that he might run out of petrol. That would be very annoying. Vlad had nearly abandoned the mission when Gary pulled into the Hope Spring View Conference Centre. He left the car idling and wondered what to do. He'd never talked to Gary and knew nothing about his life but, as he'd watched him pitch from station to pub, he thought it unlikely that this would be a sexual liaison. He couldn't decide whether to get out of the car or not. The car decided for him and rumbled a little and then came to a very silent halt. He turned the key, but knew it was hopeless. The needle on the fuel gauge had stopped hovering and had made a desperate lunge. The tank was empty.

"Bollocks," he said.

He got out of the car and entered the conference centre. Gary was at the reception desk.

"Just part of our enquiries," Gary said slapping his badge on the desk.

The conference centre was located in an area which had no natural beauty. The owners had been told, via a focus group, that the word 'view' would increase their booking rate. It had presented problems as they did not have a handily located mountain, or a canal, or a river, or the sea. There was a municipal dump, but they didn't have to ask a focus group about the potential that posed. There was also a profusion of pylons, but no one thought Pylon View would be a good idea. There wasn't a spring either but, between the months of March and May, it *was* spring and that was very nearly enough. The word 'hope' seemed to complete it.

"Enquiries," the receptionist repeated.

Hope Spring View was not close to motorway links, or an airport, although it was on a flight path, and there were no thriving cities located nearby. There was precisely no reason for anyone to visit Spring View, and it was built with the blandest architecture of absolutely no merit. As a poorly conceived venture it stood head and shoulders above all other enterprises, and would have fallen into disrepair were it not for two things. The first was that it was a number one location for extramarital assignations, much favoured by executives and their secretaries on the basis there was absolutely no possibility that their wives would find them. The other was it was ideal for cheap conferences for companies who were borderline solvent. There seemed to be no shortage of those.

"So that weekend," Gary said, "there was DW photocopy supplies, Jaxit Pest Control, Botox International, and the University of Newham."

"Yes, that's right," the manager said, adding, "do you mind if I ask what this is about?"

"Yes," Gary said with some aggression.

The receptionist didn't say anything. She assumed, from his generally shabby appearance, that Gary was a private detective, and although he had slapped his warrant card on the desk, she hadn't really looked at it. She *had* seen things at Hope Spring View. She'd seen old men with young women, and old women with young men, and a few old men with old women, and old men with young men, and couples with additional men or women. And that didn't include the transgenders, or those of indefinable gender. She was very fastidious about checking the bedding the following day. There wasn't much that would surprise her. She was very discreet.

"Have you got all the names of everyone who stayed?"

The receptionist nodded and turned the book in defeat for Gary to look at. Gary looked at the huge list of names. This was going to be a lot of work. He took out his phone and photographed them. It wasn't until he was driving home that he realised that they'd also listed their addresses, which meant he could eliminate quite a few names. He hadn't noticed the car tailing him as he'd arrived at the conference centre, and he hadn't noticed its absence as he left. Nor did he notice a tall, muscular, and very angry man, who'd found himself stranded in the middle of nowhere.

Chapter Sixteen

"Zis is very nice," Delphine said.

Suzy had produced flip charts and mock-ups and a huge range of competitors' products. At least she was getting the credit for it, even though Bradley had done most of the producing.

"Very beautiful," Elodie said.

There was no question that Suzy had this meeting, and the three witches, in the palm of her hand, and she looked a million dollars. She rarely hit a mark anywhere near that, particularly when left to her own devices. She liked to look good, but she wasn't really invested in it like the witches. But Bradley had dressed her like a doll.

"This," Suzy said, "is how we see the seven ages of women, and how the marketplace sees it."

Suzy was a more gifted actress than she thought, as much of the stuff that Bradley had put together she'd hardly read. She sounded like an expert on the subject.

"It is good for a woman of a certain age," Sandrine murmured.

It was hard to see her lips move. She might have had an alternative career as a ventriloquist, as Sandrine rarely said much, smiled or frowned. She hadn't frowned since 1981, although 1981 was a moment to frown as it was her fortieth birthday. Since then she'd worn a mask of makeup which precluded smiling as well and, to look truly super all the time, actual conversation. Her main concern, her only concern, was how anything affected 'women of a certain age', which Suzy had picked up on a long time ago. Specifically when 'a certain age' arrives Suzy had not determined but, she thought, it was after the sixth, or seventh, flush of youth had been thoroughly flushed.

"Oh that *is* gorgeous," Bradley said.

The witches smiled at each other. They loved the presence of a gay man, it was so chic. Bradley wiggled his hips for good measure. He had quite a talent for performance too.

"And that," he said fingering a colour chart, "is simply divine."

When the meeting was concluded, Elodie lent over to Suzy and asked, conspiratorially, "I love that dress. Is it Versace?"

Suzy smiled. There was such a confusion as to why women wore clothes. It was usually suggested that, as part of the mating process, it was to attract men. There was some truth in this, but nothing quite beat the approval of a very chic person of the same gender. But Suzy couldn't for the life of her remember who Bradley said had designed the dress. She didn't want to admit that it didn't really interest her, and she was more likely to be able tell a Porsche from a Maserati. The dress looked great and that was all that mattered and, if Elodie said it was an Versace, it probably was.

"Yes it is," Suzy said.

But Sandrine had overheard her and was sufficiently motivated to break her habit of barely speaking.

"I think zat is a Nicole Farhi," she whispered with a slight unavoidable ripple of her lips.

There was a brief pause when it seemed likely that Suzy would be exposed as someone who couldn't tell her Manolos from her Louboutins, or in this case her Versace from her Farhi, and Bradley wasn't sure if he should intervene.

"Of course it is," Suzy said quickly, and the moment passed.

"And let me guess," Elodie said, "the shoes. They are very beautiful shoes," she paused again, as the beauty of the shoes overwhelmed her, "they are Valentinos?"

Elodie looked at Suzy. Elodie had been married a number of times, but had been divorced rather more and had got to an age where her perfect and longest lasting union was *with* a pair of shoes. She had a shrine to them in her spectacularly chic apartment in Paris and spent more time there than with her children.

"Er," Suzy said, trying to recall what Bradley had said.

Bradley had positioned himself behind the witches and was shaking his head.

"No, they're not Valentines," Suzy said.

"Valentinos," Elodie corrected her.

"Yes, I mean no," Suzy said.

Elodie leant in further to find out who had designed the shoes, but Suzy's mind remained blank. Bradley was pointing to himself, and then holding his hand up indicating an 'O' and then pointing down. Suzy was not a great fan of charades, but she could sense the importance of getting this one. Bradley was pointing at himself. That could only mean one thing.

"Gay," Suzy said slowly.

She tried to think of a designer called Gay. She couldn't think of any. Fortunately it sounded like she was revealing the name with a dramatic delivery rather than fumbling, and the women smiled. She wondered what the 'O' meant. It seemed as if Bradley had mined it with a pained expression on his face. Was the 'O' meant to be a sphincter? Then a name came to her.

"Burn," she said, "Gay Burn."

"I've not heard of her," Elodie muttered.

"Oh, she's very good," Suzy said breezily.

Elodie studied the shoes carefully and said, "They look like Manolo Blahnik's."

There was a pause, as Suzy thought that perhaps he had said Manolo Blahnik, although she couldn't understand why he'd mimed Gay Burn. It occurred to her that Gay Burn may not be a fashion designer. She needed to recover before her mighty fashion faux pas became evident.

"Gay," Suzy said, "is an emerging talent and, if I were to lay a criticism at her door, I'd say she's taken a little too much from the house of Manolo."

There was a further pause as Suzy tried to recall Manolo's surname.

"Blahnik," Bradley said.

"Indeed," Elodie said.

"That was close," Bradley said, after the witches had left.

He pointed at himself and said, "man," then he produced an 'O' with his fingers and said, "O," and followed it with pointing at the ground, "low."

"Manolo," he said.

"I thought you meant Gay Burn," Suzy said.

"She's not a designer," Bradley pointed out.

"Is she not?"

"No."

"Oh," Suzy said.

"And she's not a she either," Bradley said.

"There's a bloke called Gay?" Suzy asked adding, "There's a name that's tempting fate."

"He's Irish. It's from Gabriel," Bradley said.

"Oh."

"And I'm not gay," Bradley added.

Suzy looked at him doubtfully. She suspected he was going through his Kiki Dee phase, in which Elton John declared that she shouldn't go breaking his heart, when everyone knew there was no chance of that happening. They worked in a modern, tolerant, liberal environment. No one cared which way Bradley chose to butter his bread. But it was up to Bradley how he dealt with it.

"Of course," she said.

Bradley would have said something, but she'd lost interest in his sexuality and needed to attend to other matters.

"Right," Suzy said flatly. "This costume is coming off."

"No, you can't," Bradley protested.

Bradley hadn't done all that work for nothing. It was part of a plan.

"We must go out and celebrate," he said.

Suzy could see the sense in that. It had been a blinding meeting and they had, or rather Bradley had, saved what could have been a disaster and turned it into a storming victory. She could do with a drink too. It didn't take long for Bradley to steer her out of the office and into the nearest pub. He would have chosen somewhere that was cutting edge and trendy, but he wanted to get some alcohol into her before she changed her mind.

"I can't walk far in these bloody heels," Suzy complained.

There were practical issues too, and Suzy was grateful she didn't have to walk any great distance with the witches, who glided in their heels. She imagined that their feet were so accustomed to near vertical high heels that they were no longer human shaped. They probably looked like a pair of inverted Cornettos.

"White wine, please," Suzy said when they got to the pub.

Bradley didn't say anything, but returned with two mojitos. This part of his campaign may have lacked subtlety, which is not to say that Suzy had the remotest idea he was interested in her, but he knew from which front it was best to attack. Alcohol was not an option. Besides which, Suzy just saw it as two colleagues celebrating. Two friends, nothing more.

"Cheers," she said.

Chapter Seventeen

It was past midday and Sam was sleeping. Or he would have been if it weren't for his phone, which was vibrating noisily on the table next to him. He had a smile on his face. It had barely left his face since he'd found the money. He suspected he knew who was calling, and he knew he really should answer it. It had been a hell of an evening. He was on fire. He'd become a babe magnet with a gravitational pull so strong they couldn't stop themselves. At least that's how it felt. He wasn't entirely deluded. He knew that the money, the cash, the moulah, the dosh, was a factor. But, whatever it was, it had been a hell of an evening.

The thing was that he'd not heard anything. There hadn't been any news reports about the money, and no one had knocked on his door. Every day the money was in his possession he felt a little more secure. And that prompted a little more of the reckless in him. He was just self aware enough to realise this. But what could he do? The power of temptation was too much. He wondered how he was going to entertain himself today. He was very tempted to take a trip away, Ibiza or somewhere, although he was enjoying holidaying at home. It was at home, but with a huge stash of cash for company. Then there was his job.

Sam was just a gnat's genitals away from ditching his job. The temptation to launch into a life of rampant rampantness was very tempting. For a fleeting second he wondered if he could lead a life of unending shallowness. Then he thought about the previous evening. Bloody right, he could. But it wasn't just play. He had things to attend to. The Armani suit looked great, but they'd insisted that the trousers need some re-tailoring, and there were a couple of shirts too. Was it a couple? Now he thought about it, it was half a dozen he'd ordered, if only because it gave him the pleasure of saying 'I'll have a half a dozen of those'. The phone was still vibrating.

Sam picked up his phone and looked at it. It was Derek. He'd wondered if Suzy was going to call him. He wanted to call her, but he wasn't quite ready. He had a little more rampant behaviour to get out of his system. It would probably only take a few days, he assured himself. Sam decided that at the end of the week he'd go back to work, and call Suzy. There was a possibility that Sam wasn't being honest with himself, as he was held in the addictive grip of a large pile of cash and what he could with it. He knew he should think about laundering it and turning it into useful assets, but why do that when there was so much fun to be had?

"Derek," he said, looking at his phone.

He had no idea why his employer was calling him when he was on holiday and he let the phone vibrate and squirm. It rang for a long time, which suggested Derek had changed his mind and really needed him, but Sam had other things on his mind. Thinking it might be Suzy made him feel a little guilty. But it was her who had kicked him out. It might have been the light sabre thing that had been the turning point. She simply hadn't felt the force like he had. Or he wanted to have fun more than she did. Not that they hadn't had fun, but they'd been together long enough to want, she'd said, the normal next step of things. Sam hadn't asked exactly what that entailed, but guessed it was marriage and kids. It didn't involve waving your dick around like a light sabre.

Now that Sam was fully awake he decided to make it into town. He'd never been into central London quite so much as he had now that he had cash in his pocket. He got up and realised he needed to go to the bank, and the cash machine. He found his new, and barely used, adjustable spanner and undid the nuts holding the copper cylinder in place. He leaned it back and a few bundles of cash tumbled out. He was growing very fond of this cash machine. He left the house and waited for the bus. It hadn't arrived two minutes later, so he hailed a black cab. He hadn't sat in one of those for ages. He even managed not to look at the meter, which was turning like a frenzied arcade machine. His stomach rumbled and he decided that the shopping would have to wait.

"Know any nice restaurants?" he asked the cabbie.

Sam had spent a lifetime assessing the merits of eating establishments by the price of their house wine. This was lunch without restriction.

"What's your budget?" the cabbie asked.

"No budget," Sam said, as casually as he could.

The cabbie frowned, as the new influx of cheap Uber cabs had curtailed his eating out habits, and he wasn't a man who appreciated the good fortune of others. He dropped Sam off at the most savagely expensive restaurant in town. It was run by an embittered chef who had not won, or been nominated, for a Michelin star and who hated his clientele. He had been close to flambéing himself in what he thought would be a classy gastronomic suicide. He'd covered himself in brandy and held the blow torch, but he decided he hated his clientele too much to carry it out, and the torch had run out of gas. The next day he raised the prices. He knew he was ripping people off, but he didn't care. He took pleasure in it.

"Have you booked?" the chef shouted at him.

"No," Sam said.

"Why the bloody hell not?" the chef said.

Sam was surprised to find that this level of brutal rudeness was a component of expensive restaurants and struggled to find the right answer.

"Sit there," the chef instructed.

The more the chef hated his clientele the more he'd raised the prices, but rather than put people off, the restaurant had begun to flourish. The food hadn't improved, and was still as mediocre as one food critic had described it, but that hadn't stopped people coming. He hated them for their wealth and stupidity, but he no longer wanted to create a chef brûlée, and instead he'd shown his loathing in abruptness, which had made way for outright rudeness. And people liked that too. Sam was lucky to get a table, and it was there that he met the Contessa.

Chapter Eighteen

"Bloody hell and damn," Derek shouted.

His wife didn't like it when he swore and there were a lot of words with hard 'c's and 'f's he was desperate to get out of his body, but the picture of his young wife and children perched on his desk was holding him back. But it felt like the words were backing up in him like a blocked drain. Derek was furious. There were nine Canon AD79s coming in, there was an ink order from Palm pharmaceuticals and they were out of coffee. And he'd sent Sam on holiday. It was a mistake and Derek needed him. But Sam wasn't answering his mobile. Derek had sent him three texts telling him he had to come back to the office, but he'd heard nothing. Worse, he suspected Sam might be on one of those Ibiza holidays where everyone has sex. Derek had spent most of his adult life wishing he'd gone on one of those when he was younger.

"Damn again," he muttered.

He wasn't sure how he was going to manage to get everything done and pick the kids up from school. His wife was playing in a tennis tournament. There were times when he thought he'd made a big mistake with his wife. For a start she was, as she often said, a 'good ten years younger' than him. That 'good' translated into the more accurate number of fifteen. Worse, although it should have been better, she was quite presentable looking. That wasn't to say she was gorgeous, or that men admired her in the street, but by the standards that Derek's life had set she wasn't too bad. She was easily the best looking woman he'd ever done it with, not that Derek had done it with that many women, and she was, as someone had pointed out, 'way out of his league'.

"Derek?"

It was his secretary. His wife had very little input into the running of his business, but she was very specific about his secretary, who had neither brains nor beauty. His wife knew a bit about secretaries, as she had been one herself, and she understood their power. She liked control and didn't need competition.

"Yes?" he replied.

The problem, Derek often thought, with marrying a younger woman who was so conspicuously out of his league, was that he had to work hard at servicing her demands. And she was a very demanding woman.

"There's someone to see you," his secretary said.

His secretary had her own views about things, although she knew that she'd be the last person to be consulted and, when it came to Derek's wife, they weren't very charitable views.

"Derek Withers?" a man asked.

Derek looked at him suspiciously. He had near Terminator qualities when it came to evaluating a client's potential photocopier needs just from their appearance. This man was heavily built and overweight which, with a slight slouch, disguised his height, not that he wished to disguise it. It was more as if gravity resented him. He wore a leather jacket which sagged almost everywhere. Derek preferred men in suits and, if not suits, then fashionable designer wear was acceptable, and what he'd expect from media types and occasionally architects. Derek's instinct was that this was not a man who required a photocopier.

"Yes, can I help?" Derek said uncertainly.

Derek was shitting himself. He'd made a few further conclusions. If the leather-jacketed, slightly thuggish man didn't require a photocopier, then he was very probably from the Inland Revenue, and if not them, then worse than them. The VAT. They were bastards and absolutely the very last thing he needed now was a VAT inspection. They were the Gestapo.

"Detective Constable Gary Beagle," Gary said, introducing himself.

Derek had claimed back the VAT on the new kitchen his wife had insisted on. And the sofas in the new conservatory. Worse than that, the conservatory. It was worse than an inspection. They'd come to arrest him. Derek's shoulders slumped. This was it. They were going to take him away. He felt defeat rush over him and, with it, came a feeling of relief. He couldn't keep it up. He needed a wife who inhabited a league several notches below, perhaps his secretary, who was gifted with neither brains nor beauty. He wondered if his secretary would visit him in prison.

"Your company attended a conference centre Friday the eleventh," Gary said.

Derek nodded, while he could still nod. For a second he'd imagined that they'd brought back hanging and this was it. The big man in the saggy leather jacket sat down. Derek realised they'd both been hovering by the desk. This felt like a good sign. He sat down too.

"Would you like a coffee?" Derek suggested.

"Please," Gary said.

It was then that Derek realised that they'd run out of coffee. He made signs to his secretary, who pretended not to notice, while Gary continued.

"Did all your employees attend?" Gary asked.

Derek was getting an inkling that he might not be facing hanging or prison. This sounded like someone else's misdemeanour and, in this regard, Derek was more than happy to lend his fullest assistance.

"Yes, how can I help?" Derek said.

"That's five people," Gary confirmed.

"Yes," Derek said proudly.

He'd built this bloody business from nowhere to the kind of business that turned over enough money to be able to disguise both a kitchen and a conservatory in its accounts. All the other employees were out on the road guarding their territories and bringing in work that he and Sam would process. Aside from today, when he was forced to handle it on his own.

"Are all your employees still working for you?" Gary asked.

Gary had worked harder that day than any other in his career in the police force. He'd talked to people and made connections and then it had all come down to one question. If you'd just found more than a million quid, would you carrying on working for a pest control company or, in this case, a photocopier company?

"Yes, of course," Derek said, still a little suspicious.

Now that Derek had concluded that he was not being inspected he wanted to tell Gary that he had a four bedroom detached house and a very beautiful wife and a BMW. Actually, he had two BMWs. The company paid for his wife's convertible. Derek had a salesman's mentality, and he really liked the metal and the props. It would have stayed that way but, as Gary had given up on getting a coffee, and realised that this was a dead end and had hauled himself up to leave, something occurred to him.

"Has anyone taken a holiday?"

Gary sighed. He'd checked everyone in a relentless three days of actual detective work and no one had deviated from their lives. He was sure it was someone buried in that list.

"Holiday?" Derek said.

Derek could have pointed out that it was his idea for Sam to take a holiday, although Sam had mistaken a Monday for a Sunday. He could have said that, but he was angry with Sam for leaving him in the shit, even though he hadn't.

"Yeah," Derek said angrily, checking to see if he'd received a text and adding, "Sam Sunday."

Gary looked at the list and found Sam's home address. He was getting an excited stirring. This sounded promising.

"Is that his home address?" Gary said.

Derek peered at it through his multi focusing glasses.

"Yes," he said.

Gary didn't say anything, but Derek had one more thing to say.

"He's not answering his phone either."

Chapter Nineteen

Sam had seen the texts from Derek and ignored them. The Contessa, on the other hand, was much harder to ignore.

"I want you fuck me again," the Contessa said.

Sam tried to concentrate. The Contessa was a very demanding woman who didn't let many things stand in her way. It had started when she'd seen Sam at the ludicrously overpriced restaurant. It was a good hunting ground for her. They'd linked arms, or she might have linked his with hers, and there had been a casino along the way. Sam had hardly entered a casino in his life yet he'd fallen into two within a handful of days. She'd steered him to the other side of the table. And Sam, who was not remotely skilled at gambling, lost ten grand. It didn't seem to matter to him as she let her fulsome breasts rest on the table. They were breasts that worked hard for her and probably deserved the rest. They focused Sam's attention more than the roulette wheel, after which they went to her apartment.

"Do this way," the Contessa demanded.

She was quite capable of speaking clear English with perfect grammar, but knew there was nothing quite so sexy as her Hispanic accent in which she did not believe in pronouns. They were the enemy of her sex life and the Contessa's whole existence revolved around getting laid. She had a tremendous gift for inheritance and had acquired four substantial fortunes without having to resort to scheming or, God forbid, work. This left a lifetime of entertainment, and few things entertained her more than a young buck giving her one.

"Righto," Sam said dutifully.

There was a fleeting thought that he might have got himself into something deep, although, if he thought about it, this was a metaphor that also applied to having sex with the Contessa, who was way beyond more than the mere first flush of youth. He didn't know, as she hid it well and expensively, but even middle age would be a youthful description.

"Is very nice," the Contessa said, her eyes closed.

Sam did as she directed and, because she knew what was what, it prompted the desired response. He watched her writhe in obvious delight and he took a minute to look at the rest of her. Although all the crucial parts of her were bared, she wasn't entirely without clothing or, more accurately, she wore very highly crafted lingerie.

"Faster," the Contessa demanded.

They were entirely natural – the breasts, that is – and untouched by a surgeon or a personal trainer's regime, although the lingerie was lending them a gentle and subtle directional hand. It was more questionable as to whether it was natural for Sam to be having sex with a woman who was older than his mother but, right at that moment it wasn't a situation that required much thought. Twenty minutes later it was brought to a happy conclusion.

"Very good," the Contessa said.

The evening had passed by at such speed that Sam hadn't taken a moment to look around him. They were in her apartment, but it wasn't like any apartment he'd ever seen before. It didn't bear even a passing resemblance to his flat, although both served as accommodation. It was set in a very grand building just a stone's throw from the casino. It was good luck, rather than planning, although the Contessa always said, 'if you want to go fishing live near a river'. It was a phrase that worked better in Spanish, but it was one of her own expressions, which was drifting into the language.

"This is an amazing apartment," Sam said.

It was very impressive, with high ceilings, deep windows and ornate plasterwork much like the ballroom in a renaissance palace. And this was the bedroom. It would one day be the subject of a television documentary in which several experts, over six episodes, deconstruct each piece. Sam found it hard to look past the vast bed on which they were sprawled. It was a vastness which came in handy when the Contessa enjoyed a particularly big haul from one of her fishing expeditions.

"It used to be the king's," the Contessa said casually.

"Oh," Sam said.

"It took eighteen months to make," the Contessa explained.

"Nice," Sam observed.

"It took ten men to lift it because the King said it mustn't creak, as he occasionally entertained his mistress when his wife was in the next bedroom."

The Contessa shook it to demonstrate that some hundred or so years later it still didn't creak, not that these things remotely concerned her.

"You want a Cointreau?" the Contessa asked.

"Sure," Sam said, although he couldn't remember if he'd had one before.

A uniformed man suddenly appeared, which Sam found a little shocking given their sprawling nakedness, but the servant didn't seem to notice. Instead, wearing an expression which could not be any more sombre, he delivered one glass of Cointreau to either side of the huge bed. It was quite a long walk and Sam was astonished at the speed of his entry although, as the servant had been in the Contessa's employ for twenty years, he knew precisely when the Cointreau was required. It was more a function of the speed of Sam's exit.

"Thank you, Peralta," the Contessa said.

Peralta bowed as if attending a formal occasion, and not the coital union of a naked young man and a late middle aged woman with her ample naked breasts fully on display.

"I don't know what I'd do without Peralta," she confided in Sam.

The Contessa was delighted with her new plaything, and it prompted her to make a spur of the moment decision.

"You come with me?"

Sam smiled. Most of the time he didn't have the slightest idea what she was saying and this was no exception, although most of her instructions had been of a sexual nature, and he wasn't sure if he could come again with her, not without a lengthy rest. Despite that, he responded in the affirmative.

"Sure," he said.

"Good, we pack," the Contessa said.

Peralta appeared, although Sam could see no evidence that he had been beckoned.

"We pack," she told Peralta.

Sam began to sense that 'come with me,' in this one particular instance was not a sexual instruction and required a little elaboration.

"Where to?" Sam asked innocently.

The Contessa hadn't heard him as she was issuing extensive instructions to Peralta in Spanish, which is always much louder than English, and frequently appears to have no breaks or pauses. It didn't matter, as Peralta knew what to do. When she finished speaking, Sam realised he'd have to ask again.

"Where to?"

At that moment Sam had every intention of at least responding to Derek's texts, and maybe even going to work. He had a few visits to make and was reasonably certain he could close some deals and earn a healthy commission. Not that it was on his mind at that moment, but it wasn't *that* far from his mind either. Although he didn't know that the Contessa owned a Gulfstream. He didn't really know what a Gulfstream was. He wasn't sure if he wanted to find out.

"Monte Carlo," the Contessa said with an enticing smile.

Chapter Twenty

Vlad had given up on the Ford Fiesta and created an awkward journey for the Hump. It didn't concern Vlad, who was back in his black four wheel drive beast. It was a very conspicuous vehicle, but he'd concluded that Gary wouldn't have noticed if he'd driven into him.

Brandy had been putting pressure on him to get a move on, and he had. He was sitting outside Gary's flat. He didn't care that Gary was a copper. He'd lost patience with him. He had a crowbar and his hunting knife. The flat was round the back of a plain-looking block built in the fifties. It looked rather nasty to Vlad. He drove round the block and slipped out of the car, flipping his hoody up, and walking briskly with his head down. He was walking on the tips of his toes with purpose.

There were a few different versions of Vlad. There was the one his mother very occasionally saw in which he was still Lionel, there was the one when he was with Brandy, which had quietly evolved until she subtlety held more power, and then there was this one. This was the Vlad who'd set up a small empire dealing light narcotics and occasionally using intimidation and violence. He'd arrived at Gary's front door. He heaved it open with the crowbar and his shoulder, and he thought about all his cash that had been stolen. And then he went a little crazy with the hunting knife.

"Bloody hell," Vlad muttered.

It was amazing just how much mess a proper search can make. First there were the obvious places, like the bookshelves and clothes drawers. Then, once everything had been hurled on the floor to reveal nothing behind, there were the sofas and the mattress. Only a knife will do for that. A flurried knife attack on both, left foam and padding everywhere. Failing that, there were the floor boards. That involved the removal of carpets and underlay. That made quite a mess too. The crowbar was useful and, with it, most of the floor boards had been ripped up. Nothing. That left the walls.

"Shit and fuck," Vlad shouted.

While Vlad as not a man with a sweet and gentle nature, he didn't always feel the need for violence. He had to gee himself up a little to keep his aggression at a point between simmering and boiling. It was a strange reversal of fate that he'd been following a copper. He was certain that this copper had taken the money and yet he'd not found a bean. He'd been a little shocked to find that coppers lived in such shabby flats, but he'd not been apprised of Gary's divorce history.

"Shit," Vlad said and punched a hole in the wall.

There was nothing behind it, so he punched a few more. Ten minutes later Gary's flat looked like a building site in which there had been a heated dispute with contractors who had not been paid, and Vlad had to reluctantly admit that the money wasn't there. He shoved his hands in his pockets, covered his head with his hoody, and strolled back to the car. Ten minutes later Gary came home.

"Oh my god," Gary said, looking at the devastation.

He found a kitchen chair, which was wood and was one of the few things that hadn't been butchered in some way, and sat down. He pulled out a bottle of scotch. He poured himself one. It wasn't big enough. He poured some more. Then he wondered what the hell he was going to do. He drank the scotch. It helped, but it didn't tell him want he needed to do, so he poured some more scotch.

"Bugger, bugger, bugger," Gary muttered.

That didn't help either. The obvious thing was to call it in. Or, as other people would say, phone the police. But if he called his colleagues, they would ask questions. It was obvious someone was looking for something. Even the dumbest detective, which was an accolade Gary might enjoy, would be able to figure that out. And it would invite further questions.

Gary poured some more scotch. He couldn't call it in. So he began to tidy up. He had some gaffer tape and bin bags under the sink and attempted, with reasonable success, to stuff the stuffing back into the cushions of the sofa, tape them up, and turn them round. He tried the same with the mattress, but it felt like he was fighting a losing battle, as every time he stuffed some stuffing in one hole, it would bulge out of another. It was after this battle, and at a point half way down the bottle of scotch, that he tripped. It was hard to say if it was the alcohol, or the fact that the flat was strewn with trip hazards, but he landed on a floorboard which was not secured. His foot went through the floor and through the ceiling of the flat below.

"Shit," Gary screamed.

For some reason he couldn't figure out, the structure of the ceiling, which was old timber laths and plaster, had decided to grip his leg, which was dangling above Mr and Mrs Singh's dinner table. Fortunately Mrs Singh had yet to serve their supper. There had been bashing noises coming from upstairs all day and they had assumed that there was renovation work going on but, as they were a little afraid of Gary, they decided not to say anything.

"Mr Beagle?" Mrs Singh shouted.

There was something about the shabbiness of the shoe and jeans above it that suggested to Mrs Singh that this was most surely Mr Beagle from upstairs. The leg kicked about, although she couldn't be certain if this was in response to her question. Gary swore a bit more and eventually managed to extract his leg. He looked through the hole.

"Hello, Mrs Singh," Gary said, more cheerfully than the circumstances would normally dictate.

"Good evening, Mr Beagle," Mrs Singh said.

She looked at him in silent wonderment.

"I'll get it fixed," Gary said and put the floorboard back and threw the carpet over it.

He went back to the kitchen chair and poured some more scotch.

Chapter Twenty-One

Sam was discovering that, as well as butler, Peralta was also chauffeur and, he was soon to learn, pilot. Peralta was waiting outside Sam's flat while Sam packed, found his passport and decided how much money to take with him. How much cash did a trip to Monaco require? Did he want to go to Monaco with the Contessa? It had never occurred to him before that he could actually be shagged to death. He plugged his phone in. The battery had died and he'd been grateful for it.

He got his plumbing gear out. In the last week he'd carried out more plumbing than the rest of his life and he was getting quite adept at it. It was just like a cash machine, and like his local ATM, he was making rather more withdrawals than he'd planned. He leaned the cylinder over and pushed his hand in. It was then that his mobile began to make a series of bleeps and noises suggesting that someone was keen to communicate with him. It made him jump and he cut his hand on the jagged edge of the hole he'd made on the underside of the cylinder. It bled a bit. Sam wrapped it in a fresh-looking fifty and grabbed a few bundles. The note wasn't the most absorbent, and he absentmindedly replaced it with another. He guessed he'd taken about twenty grand. That seemed enough.

Sam took one last look at the flat and left, making sure that the door was securely locked. Although he didn't live in the worst part of London, the Contessa's black Rolls looked slightly out of place. Much like the Contessa, the car was elderly, but beautifully preserved and, just like the Contessa, it had only appreciated in value. It hummed along effortlessly with a chink from the cut-glasses and the tick-tock of the clock.

"You cut your hand," the Contessa said dramatically.

Sam had forgotten about the cut and the fifty pound note he'd wrapped it in. He grabbed a tissue and covered the fifty, but it wasn't the sort of thing that the Contessa would have missed. She felt a little like a spider who'd weaved a web and caught a fly. It wasn't an analogy she much liked as, in her younger days, she was quite the queen bee, but she had to be realistic. Although she couldn't help wondering what kind of a fly she'd caught. It was strange, even by her standards, to use a fifty pound note as a plaster. It didn't matter for the time being, and she put her hand on his knee, and moved it up his thigh to make it clear what should happen next.

Sam hadn't noticed that the blackness of the Rolls extended to the windows, and the divide between them, and Peralta. A few minutes later he discovered that the lambs wool carpet was thick and cushioned his knees comfortably, and that the Contessa never wore knickers. It was while his face was buried between her legs, and she was issuing very specific instructions, that a few things occurred to him. Despite being a man who had always been motivated by sex, he had to question whether he was up to the task. This was very tiring and he had no idea what was going to happen once they arrived at Monaco.

The second thought was to do with photocopiers and Derek. It was more a feeling of guilt. The Contessa was making too much noise for a third thought, which suggested that, at the very least, he was a man who took instruction well. Half an hour later they were both light headed, although in Sam's case it was through exhaustion, and they arrived at the airport.

Chapter Twenty-Two

"It's why they make you queue to get in a nightclub," Bradley said.

It irritated Suzy, although almost everything Bradley said irritated her, but he left it hanging annoyingly in the air, and begging for her to ask exactly *how* her situation was in any way related to a queue at a nightclub. She tried to resist, but couldn't stop herself.

"How?" she said with obvious pain.

"It's why you're more likely to go into a busy restaurant with hardly any tables available, than an empty one with a nice seat by the window," Bradley said.

If there was an explanation buried somewhere in there, Suzy couldn't see it and, as far as she could tell, he was inviting her to ask the same question.

"How?" she said with undisguised irritation.

"It's like..." Bradley began.

"Don't tell me what it's like," Suzy shouted.

Bradley pouted. He hadn't quite exhausted his bank of similes. He could see his audience had lost its patience.

"The more desirable your Armani-clad Sam is to other women, the more you want him. The more others want him, the more attractive he becomes."

"I don't think so," Suzy lied.

She knew he was right. If Sam had been lying in a shallow pool of his own vomit dressed in polyester, she would know she'd done the right thing when she'd ended the relationship. Now that she'd conjured the image in her mind she couldn't help elaborating on it a little. She would be on the way to somewhere glamorous with a Brad Pitt-type companion. They might have been hobnobbing with the stars. Now that she thought about it, and because it was an image that she was able to manipulate, she was with someone younger than Brad. She tried to think of younger good looking actors, but as she didn't go to the cinema, or watch enough television. She couldn't think of any.

"Very nice suit, though," Bradley said.

Bradley's natural calling would have been a suit salesman, as his interest in cut and cloth bordered on the obsessive.

"It looked made to measure, too," Bradley added.

How, Suzy had to wonder, did Sam manage to find the time, let alone the money, to order a made to measure Armani suit in the brief time they'd stopped going out together? It didn't make sense.

"It was probably off the peg," Bradley said, giving the suit conundrum further thought, "but adjusted to fit. It looked very good across the shoulders."

Suzy didn't know what a suit that looked good across the shoulders looked like. But she did know that Sam had looked good. And he was neither in a pool of his own vomit, or worse still, dressed in polyester. He was with two attractive, if a little tarty, women.

"Great looking women," Bradley said.

It wasn't, in her moment of crisis, a very helpful comment. Suzy felt the need to deflect it a little.

"Do you think they were prostitutes?"

Bradley had experienced many things including, but not restricted to, a wide range of narcotics. He'd even, via the modern medium of Tinder, experienced a very significant number of sexual partners. But he'd never paid for it, nor met someone who had. And in Bradley's world, if he hadn't experienced it, it didn't exist.

"No," he said with certainty.

This didn't help and, for a moment, Suzy couldn't stop herself wondering whether Sam had sex with both of them. It was that thought that made her realise that she missed the sex. After work that evening she went home via Sam's flat. It was in the opposite direction of her own flat, but she couldn't help herself. When she got to his road she began to wonder what she was doing there. She walked past the flat a couple of times. Each time she looked up at the last minute. She wasn't sure what to do, or what she expected to see. She didn't really want to see the shadow of sexual activity projected onto his blinds. Worse, it would be the kind of sexual activity which would involve more than a pair of people.

"Shape up," Suzy said to herself.

She turned round, crossed the road and walked past his place and in the direction of her home. She would have gone straight home, but she saw a car appear. She couldn't stop herself. She had to find out. She looked around and saw a narrow alleyway filled with bins. It was across the road from Sam's fiat and gave her a good view. She slid into the shadows and watched. A large, overweight man got out of the car. He appeared short of breath. He wore quite the most hideous black leather jacket she'd ever seen. It seemed to sag in every direction, although she suspected that the man underneath also sagged in every direction. The man approached Sam's front door. She could see him raise his foot as if he were going to break it down. His foot didn't get too far and he gave up and used his shoulder instead. On the third thump the door flew open.

"Oh my god," Suzy said.

This was unreal. Her thoughts were disrupted by a burbling noise. A large black car had drawn up. It was directly in front of her and she slunk further into the shadows. A large bald-headed and absurdly muscular man stepped out of the throbbing car. He was looking at Sam's flat.

Chapter Twenty-Three

Gary was sitting on the toilet. To an onlooker he was doing nothing, just staring into space, but he was thinking. It wasn't his most exercised organ and it would have probably taken someone else a couple of minutes. But it had led him to a decision. It was an actual plan of action and it was why he was in Sam's bathroom. He'd done a quick, discreet search of the flat and had found nothing.

He'd identified, or forensic had, from the shit-stained notes, the DNA of whoever had taken his money. It therefore made sense to take a sample so he could confirm, or eliminate, Sam Sunday. The annoying thing was that there seemed to be very little in the bathroom from which he could take a sample. There wasn't a toothbrush or, more conveniently, a hairbrush with a mass of hairs. There was very little of anything. They were pretty big clues and further evidence that Gary was no Sherlock, and it took him a while to conclude that Sam had gone away. Once he'd made that leap he felt certain he was on the right track. Sam Sunday was the man.

Gary had a further problem. Who had ransacked his flat? He didn't know, but he did know it was likely to be whoever he had acquired the cash from in the first place. He'd have to be careful from now on, he decided. He also decided that he had to locate the cash first. It was his only opportunity to live the way he'd dreamed of ever since the money had first passed through his hands. His dream involved leaving England on the first flight and buying a villa in the sun, and very probably not far from a bar. He hadn't noticed that his dream life was the same as his real life, but with added sun. It didn't matter, as it had galvanised him into action. Gary had broken into Sam Sunday's flat. It hadn't been difficult. But he needed to be certain it was him.

There wasn't much evidence in the kitchen either. There were no unwashed forks, or half eaten sandwiches wrapped in his saliva. He would have given up, but something caught his eye. It was a crumpled piece of paper by the airing cupboard door. He picked it up.

"Interesting," he said to himself.

It was a fifty pound note. Fifty pound notes were rare enough, crumpled up and apparently discarded was rarer still. This one was covered in blood. Gary left as quickly as he could and, that afternoon, he did two things. He sent the note to the lab and he studied some CCTV camera images. They came from a camera at the end of Sam's road. It took ages and reminded him just how dull detective work can be. There was almost nothing of interest until a large black Rolls Royce of the sort built in the fifties, or early sixties, appeared. It was while he was studying these images that his phone rang.

"The blood and the shit," the forensics man said. "They belong to the same person."

Gary was excited. He had no notion that he could have derived so much satisfaction from doing his job. At five he went home and tried to fix up his flat a little and then, just after midnight, he broke into Sam's flat again. This time he attacked it with the same fervour that someone had attacked his flat and with the knowledge, as the shit and blood samples had verified, that he was in the right place. He bought a Stanley knife with him and he tore the mattress apart and ripped the sofa to pieces. He was like a crazed animal.

"Not a bloody thing," Gary said.

He hadn't found a thing. The money was stashed somewhere else. He left with an angry and brooding spirit and, despite his intention to be careful, he didn't notice a large black four wheel drive vehicle tailing him, nor did he notice a slightly pissed girl watching him from across the road. He was going to have to do some more detective work. He was even beginning to think he might have a talent for it. He was going to track down Sam Sunday.

Chapter Twenty-Four

"Ernest is here," Lady Jane said.

The Contessa was having a dilemma. It was the kind of dilemma she liked, positively cherished even. Ernest was a whirlwind, like one of those big planets with loads of moons constantly orbiting it. Wherever Ernest was, so was fun. And sex. She wasn't sure if her new muse was flagging already, she'd have to pace him.

"Wonderful," the Contessa said and, as if he'd been cued, Ernest appeared.

"My dear Contessa, how are you?"

"I'm wonderful," the Contessa said.

"Do you have some entertainment with you?" Ernest asked.

"I do," the Contessa said and Sam appeared, as if he'd been cued.

"Oh lovely, darling," Ernest said.

Ernest liked boys, which was not that unusual, but he also liked girls. That was quite unusual, particularly as he liked them in equal measure. He looked at Sam appraisingly, with enough evident lust to make Sam perspire.

"Well, if you wear him out I have a little..." Ernest paused as he thought of the correct word, "... entourage."

Again, as if they had been cued, a small crowd of young beautiful things, who were more than a little high, appeared. Sam looked at them in amazement.

After the flight in the Contessa's jet, in which there was a substantial bed, and his arrival at her Monaco apartment, which had an even larger bed, he was beginning to think he was living in an alternate universe. And he shouldn't be there.

"Will you be eating at the Palais?" Ernest asked.

"Of course," the Contessa replied.

"We shall see you then," Ernest said and he disappeared with a flourish and his planets followed, orbiting him joyously.

Sam's phone rang. He looked at it, unsure what to do. Ernest's departure had left a vacuum and, as his relationship with the Contessa hadn't featured much conversation, an awkward silence. More surprisingly, he could see Suzy's face flashing on his phone. He hadn't expected that. He'd not seen her since the money had appeared and he wouldn't let her in. He'd wondered what to do about that and had chosen to do nothing, but then his life had been travelling at some speed since then.

"I'll tell you what, darlings," Ernest had reappeared.

Ernest had stretched his long neck and elegant head round a huge gilt-laden panelled door. It was hard to see if his satellites, or they might have been apostles, were rotating behind him. Sam thought a bit more and decided that they were acolytes.

"How about a little drinkies on the little boaty?" Ernest said.

"Marvellous, darling," the Contessa said.

Sam thought that she was parodying him for a minute, but realised that she actually talked like that. They all talked that way. A minute later, he too, was caught in the gravitational pull of Ernest and, he discovered ten minutes later, his immense wealth. The little boaty rose from the water like a block of flats. Unlike the gin palace power boats that surrounded it, it had three masts that were so high that his guests, who were also frequently very high, were in danger of falling over should their eyes follow them to the top.

"Beautiful isn't it," one of Ernest's acolytes said.

She was tall, as tall as Sam, and she wore a bikini top which made it a challenge to look her in the eye. He couldn't tell whether she was referring to the yacht, or the newly acquired, and equally beautiful, lumps that had been applied to her chest. Sam went for the boat.

"I like the wood," he said.

"Oh, we all like a bit of wood," she said, smiling.

It was a sexual innuendo that was so blatant that it passed Sam by, and he managed to look confused, and hideously out of his depth. She lay her hand on his waist.

"Oh I see," Sam spluttered.

The tall, elegant acolyte looked at Sam as if he were from another planet, a strange planet in which people toiled from Monday to Friday in order to provide food and lodging. It was a strange concept she'd heard about, but had never quite grasped. She smiled at him. Another acolyte appeared by his side.

"I think he means the teak," he said.

He was a slim, fine-boned man, barely out of boyhood, and effeminate enough for Sam to question his gender.

"Teak?" she said.

"It's a wood," the fine-boned man replied.

The tall, elegant acolyte looked around and finally noticed the swathes of wood on the deck. She'd spent the last six weeks on the boat and hadn't spent much of it compiling an inventory of materials. Instead she'd ingested quality narcotics and had rampant sex. The rest of the time she'd squandered in blameless sleep.

"Teak," the fine-boned man said, "Ernest has it revarnished every year. I hear it costs a hundred thousand dollars."

"Nice," Sam said.

"Champagne, darling?" Ernest said, appearing from nowhere.

Ernest pressed a champagne-filled flute into Sam's hand and smiled at him. Ernest's life was filled with pleasure and not a moment of regret and, along the way, he'd consumed more than his fair share of quality narcotics. The small side effect of which was that he was incapable of remembering a single name, including many of his ex wives and a few of his children. He called everyone darling apart from those with titles who, unaccountably, he could always remember.

"Isn't she beautiful, darling?" Ernest said.

Sam smiled and said, "Yes, the teak is beautiful."

Ernest chuckled a little lascivious chuckle and said, "I didn't mean my little boaty."

As Ernest was gazing at the solid orbs on the acolyte's chest, his meaning was very clear.

"Yes, she is," Sam said.

Sam had extended his vowels and expressed the three words in a lavish way that fitted the company he found himself in. He was being drawn in. He sensed he was capable of altering his speech patterns and convincingly deploying 'darling' at the end of a sentence. In addition to the teak, there was leather and chrome and a palpable, and comforting, feeling of well-established wealth. He was finding the gravitational pull strong and he was falling into Ernest's orbit. It didn't worry him that he might be acolyte material. It beat selling photocopiers.

"Shall we all hook up together?" Ernest said.

While this was obvious to the tall, elegant acolyte and the fine-boned man, the inference passed Sam by. If Ernest had drawn a picture, Sam would have struggled to connect the dots. In his previous and more normal life, it might have meant a beer or two together in a local pub. He watched as Ernest leaned over and lightly caressed the arm, and then the naked stomach of his tall, elegant acolyte.

"Not for me," the fine-boned man said.

"He's so straight," Ernest said, laughing.

"Him?" Sam asked.

"Oh yes," Ernest said.

This should have been a big enough clue for Sam, but he'd landed on a planet in which social conventions, and speech, were not the same. Ernest raised his arms, when Sam thought about it later it seemed like it was in the style of Dracula, and he and the tall, elegant acolyte were manoeuvred down a deck and into a lavish cabin.

"Wow," Sam said.

For a second he'd been preoccupied by his preconceptions and assumptions about the fine-boned man's sexuality, so preoccupied he hadn't grasped the significance of it. Now he was blown away by the breathtaking extravagance of the master bedroom. He'd never seem a room like it. It was at least double height and the ceiling had a star-like array of crystal chandeliers. He'd thought that the Contessa had a big bed because, up until now, he'd been saddled with beds created on the regal scale, in which not much sat above king size. This was the size of a small island, floating in a sea of the deepest pile carpet he'd ever encountered. He wondered what the hell Ernest did on a bed that size. He turned to ask him.

"Oh my god," Sam said.

It seemed as if Ernest was intent on showing him. He'd shed his clothes. He was tall, spindly and with a slight pot belly. There was a small string of black hairs which meandered along his chest, occasionally losing interest and fading out, and then continuing in a rush of enthusiasm until they terminated at his genitals.

They were baby smooth. Sam was taking in the horror of his nudity at the same time as being a little distracted by the assemblage around Ernest's genitals. It appeared as if he was a man who came with both bells and whistles. It was a little wilder than just a Prince Albert. And, despite the weight of the metalwork, and Ernest's evident middle age, a substantial erection. Sam turned to the tall, elegant acolyte.

"On my god," he said.

She too, was entirely naked. Sam ran through the conversation that had preceded their arrival at the bedroom and realised that there hadn't just been a hint at a possible assignation. They'd practically drawn him a picture. A picture he'd failed to grasp. But it was worse than that. He'd been wrapped up in his prejudices and overwhelmed by the grandeur and wealth. And the fine-boned man had declined the invitation to 'hook up'. The reason lay in front of him. The tall, elegant acolyte with the beautiful breasts also sported a substantial erection.

"Oh my god," Sam said again.

The tall, elegant acolyte with the significant erection moved towards him to his left, while Ernest approached from his right. There was something military about it. And Sam was unfamiliar with the correct social convention should one find oneself in such a position. The door opened and they all looked round. It was the Contessa.

"Do you need saving?" she asked Sam.

Chapter Twenty-Five

Gary was celebrating the end of a good day and the beginning of his holiday. The DNA sample had been tested and Gary's theory had been confirmed. Sam Sunday was the man who'd wiped his arse on his cash. Better still, he'd tracked down the Rolls Royce and the Contessa, he'd even found the flight log, and he'd located her Monaco villa. He never knew that detective work could be such fun. And now he was going on holiday. Or that's what he'd told his colleagues. He was going to a small principality in the south of France. He was going to Monaco. He'd packed and was ready to take the flight first thing the following morning.

"Fuck off," he said to a young couple.

The young couple glared at him.

"Move," he said, and they did.

That evening, in common with most evenings, he was in the pub. He didn't want a crowd of young people around him and he chose to ward them off in the only way he knew how. It made the landlord nervous. Gary had planned to restrict himself to three pints. Despite that, he was enjoying his fifth when a large shadow sat in front of him.

"Fuck off," Gary said.

Gary wasn't someone that people usually challenged as, although he looked dishevelled and overweight, he looked a little nasty too. It took a big man to confront him. He didn't have the widest vocabulary, but didn't think he required more than two words.

"You stole my fucking money," Vlad said.

He delivered it with the halting lilt of a very annoyed Russian. Gary looked up. Gary too was an angry man, with nothing to lose, and unlikely to make analytical assessments as to whether he could take this sizeable bloke. He would give it a go if he had to.

"Fuck off," Gary said.

Vlad knew he was taking risks confronting a policeman. The last thing he needed was someone looking into his affairs which, given he was a drug dealer, were best left unlooked at. But that money had been his retirement fund. Not so that he could give up work, but to make his work a little more legal or, who knows, entirely legal. He'd worked hard for that cash.

"You found it by accident. You didn't tell anyone and you didn't think you'd get caught."

"Fuck off," Gary replied.

The landlord looked at them nervously. He'd seen fights before and two big men could make a mess of his pub. He'd like to say he wasn't having that, but he could see that whatever happened was outside his control.

"And someone stole the money from you," Vlad continued.

This part was conjecture, but it was a theory that Vlad had been working on that seemed to fit everything.

"Fuck off," Gary said.

Gary was getting a little concerned. Although he thought of the huge stack of money in the blue IKEA bag as his, it wasn't. He had sort of stolen it and, as it was a considerable lump of cash, it would be reasonable to assume that it had been acquired illegally. The big Russian didn't look like a librarian. This could be trouble.

"And I want my money back," Vlad said.

Vlad knew that this line was best delivered with a prop of some sort. A flash of a gun handle would have been good, but he didn't have a gun. He'd thought about it often, but the acquisition of a gun could cause as much trouble as it solved. He removed the hunting knife from the inside of his jacket. It had come with a holster, but it was one that was designed to sit on a belt and on his hip. While that would look great, it was a bit too obvious. He'd modified the holster to hang from his shoulder and it was only half successful as he'd stabbed himself a couple of times while working it out. As luck would have it a little bit of stray, but useful, light glinted on the blade.

"Fuck off," Gary said a little uneasily.

Vlad wasn't sure how to handle this. Ordinarily, at this point, he would expect some whimpering and grovelling. He was going to have to issue a threat.

"You want I cut your balls off?"

Although Gary didn't use his testicles very frequently he didn't want them to be cut off, he really didn't. But he wanted the money too.

"Fuck off," Gary said, but with much less edge.

Vlad sighed. There were many things Vlad hated. He wasn't too bothered by injustice, he could live with climate change, and had no views on world starvation. Although packaging drove him crazy. His large hands made it difficult to open small boxes and cellophane wrapping was, in his view, the work of the devil. It was why he'd bought the knife in the first place, although his anger at packaging which deliberately, and wilfully, resisted opening had occasionally meant that he had ripped apart both the covering and the contents. The other thing that he really hated was dirty fingernails and he proceeded to ensure their thorough cleanliness by picking at them with the knife. Once his nails were immaculate he was going to have to do something.

"Fuck off," Gary said again, but something in his voice let him down and it came out with a slight squeak.

The landlord would have loved to have got rid of Gary, but he didn't want his pub wrecked either.

"Shall I make a call?" the landlord offered.

The words hung in the air. Who was going to call whose bluff? If Gary got help he might have to explain himself, although it was unlikely that the big Russian would admit to the theft of illegally acquired cash.

"I do you a deal," Vlad said, getting more Russian.

Vlad was pragmatic by nature. He had a choice. He could follow the detective, get his money back, and kill the detective. It wouldn't be easy and, from what he'd heard, the detective wasn't up to much, and probably wouldn't find his money without help. The other complication was that no one in their right mind goes around killing people, let alone cops. The penalty was too great. If he killed a cop, even Gary, they would throw everything at him. It would be mad. It wouldn't get him the money either. He could easily make Gary think he was mad and threaten to kill him, or he could do something more radical, and in many ways unthinkable. They could work together.

"Fuck off," Gary said, but put his hand up to the landlord to indicate that he had it under control.

"We both find him and I give you ten percent."

And Gary paused. They both knew what this meant. They were negotiating. And if they were negotiating, they were going to work together. Gary knew it was risky, but he also had a feeling that if he was too greedy the Russian wouldn't honour his cut. He also knew that if he told him to fuck off he wouldn't get rid of him. He'd either have his testicles removed, or the Russian would follow him everywhere. That would make things difficult.

"I know who's got it. Fifty percent," Gary said.

"Sam Sunday, fifteen percent," Vlad said.

Gary hadn't expected that. The Russian must have been following him. But he hadn't followed him into the station. He didn't know about the Countess and the jet.

"I know where he is now. Thirty percent," Gary said.

Vlad paused. He knew that whatever he agreed to he shouldn't agree too easily. Thirty percent was a huge amount of money. It was too much money. He looked down at Gary's drink.

"I get us some drinks," Vlad said and got up.

Despite the landlords shaking hands he poured the pints at top speed and Vlad returned to the table.

"Twenty-five percent and no trouble," Vlad said.

Gary knew how much money there was in the bag, or rather he didn't, but he knew there was a hell of a lot and twenty-five percent of a hell of a lot was still a hell of a lot.

"How do I know I can trust you?" Gary said.

"How do I know I can trust you?" Vlad said.

There was an uneasy silence, while they tried to work it out.

"He's not in the country," Gary said.

"Far?" Vlad asked, fishing for information.

Gary shrugged and said, "France."

It wasn't quite France, but France was a big country and Vlad would need more than just that to find him. More than that, Gary had photos of Sam, one from his driving license and the other from Facebook. He could identify him. It was Gary who found the solution.

"Passports. I'll hold yours and you'll hold mine," he said.

Chapter Twenty-Six

"What shall I do?" Suzy asked Bradley.

She didn't know at what point Bradley had become the sounding board for all her anxieties, but he was conveniently there, so she decided he might as well be.

"Call the police?" Bradley suggested.

It annoyed Suzy that she hadn't quite got it out of her head, and now she wished she had entered Sam's flat. But she had this feeling that Sam was in trouble. As far as she was aware he'd not been in trouble before. Perhaps it was something new like wearing Armani. He'd not done that before either. She was pretty certain you had to sell an awful lot of photocopiers to wear Armani.

"He might be in trouble," Suzy said slowly.

"Have you thought about calling him?" Bradley said.

That was the obvious thing to do. She hadn't even thought about it although, now that she had, she could see there were a few problems. Firstly she'd broken up with him and then, beyond that, he'd had someone at his flat, and then beyond that, he'd been in the restaurant with two girls. Come to think of it, *that* was the last time she'd seen him. It wouldn't be her best memory of him.

"I will, but it's difficult," Suzy admitted.

She imagined that Sam's memory of those events would be a pretty good one, but it wasn't quite the Sam she remembered. He was sociable and liked to have a good time, but he wasn't exactly wild. She tried to think what it was that had prompted her to break it off with Sam. Was it something about maturity? She feared the problem might have been with her.

"Are you going to the pub later?" Bradley asked.

Suzy had no pressing engagements, worse than that, if she actually owned a diary it would be frighteningly bereft of entries. There was very little going on. She might as well have a drink.

"Okay," she said.

An hour later, and at the very chime of five thirty, most of the staff on her floor reconvened to the pub. She was surprised there were so many people she didn't know. Their faces looked vaguely familiar, but names and conversation had never flowed, as she'd made a policy of avoiding work drinks. She took a better look at her colleagues.

"Who's she?" she asked Bradley

"Mandy from accounts," Bradley told her.

"Accounts?" Suzy said dismissively and adding uncharitably, "that is one enormous arse."

It might have been out of snobbery, or stereotyping, but Suzy had also decided, early in her work life, not to talk to the accounts staff. There was a reason why they were usually located in a lightless basement, or an airless loft room.

"What about him?" she pointed.

"That's Stan. Stan works in the post room."

Suzy didn't know they had a post room, although she guessed there was some system for getting the post to her desk. Then someone else appeared on her horizon. He was moving slowly, like a cruise ship.

"What about him?" Suzy asked.

She said it slowly, emphasising every syllable, in a way which was just a touch prurient and, at the same time, suggested an obvious interest. He was tall, slim and dark skinned. Now that she looked closer, and she was inclined to, she noticed he was dark skinned because he was black. She wondered where the point was that took someone from dark skinned to black. She'd had friends of varied ethnicity, but they'd all been female. She'd never been out with a black man.

"That's Pete," Bradley said.

She entertained herself by looking a little more at Pete and not making any effort to disguise it. Then it occurred to her that he might also be in accounts, or the post room or worse, he might collect the rubbish. Did they have a department that catered for that? They must do, she thought, as the rubbish disappeared as magically as the post appeared. She had to ask.

"What does he do?"

"Pete?" Bradley said with irritating nonchalance.

"Yes, Pete," Suzy said through gritted teeth.

"Pete works in legal."

Suzy hadn't uttered a single word to Pete, but she was getting quite excited. Legal was exciting. There weren't any television dramas about accounts departments, or post rooms, at least none that she was aware of, but there were plenty about glamorous lawyers. And they weren't always fighting worthwhile causes, many just made bucket loads of money and lived well. She liked the sound of that too.

"Can you introduce me?" Suzy asked.

"He's not your type," Bradley said and tried to turn her away.

"I think I'll be the judge of who is and who isn't my type," Suzy said, pulling herself back, and into the flight, of the wondrous Pete.

"You don't really want to be introduced, do you?" Bradley said.

"God, yes," Suzy said, as quick as a snap of knicker elastic.

Bradley sighed and weighed up whether it would be better for him to introduce her, or allow her to throw herself at him. He decided he might be able to control it if he introduced her.

"Pete," Bradley reluctantly called.

Pete glided over, giving Suzy a little more time to drink in the fluidity of his movements and what that might possibly suggest. Bradley watched with a sense of doom and defeat.

"Suzy," Bradley and Suzy said at the same time.

Pete smiled revealing about, although it was hard for Suzy to give a precise estimate at this juncture, a thousand glittering white teeth, and he extended his hand. Suzy shook it. It was enormous. It's also worth pointing out that at this point that she was referring to his hand, but it hadn't even been necessary for Pete to say 'hello'. He could have had her way before that.

"Pete," Pete said.

"I hear you work in the legal department," Suzy said, trying to compose herself.

"I do," Pete said. "What do you do?"

"Account handling," Suzy said.

For a second she wondered if 'account handling' sounded the same as 'accounts' or 'post room' to somebody who had a law degree. She was fairly certain there weren't any dramas about account handlers.

"Yes, of course. You were involved in the Florex campaign," Pete said.

He had a rather grand voice with a sort of depth that seemed to shake the floor. For a second she wondered if choosing a boyfriend was like choosing a dress. Some things suited some people, and not others, but everyone had to ask themselves whether they could see themselves 'in' a certain dress. Obviously 'in' was way to crude a way of thinking of things, except that was *exactly* how she was thinking. Although another word would be with. Could she see herself with Pete? Surely if he was good enough for 'in,' he must be good enough for 'with.'

"Really? How come?" Suzy said, drawing herself back.

"There were legal issues," Pete said mysteriously and then added, "Would you like a drink?"

"A white wine would be nice," Suzy said, and Pete turned to the bar.

"Go," she said to Bradley, but Bradley pretended not to notice.

"Leave," she hissed, but Bradley just looked aloof and remained standing next to her.

"Fuck off," she told Bradley, just as Pete turned back with the drinks.

"I beg your pardon," Pete said playfully.

Bradley grunted and disappeared in the direction of Mandy from accounts with the plentiful arse, thinking that she looked just like the mountain-climbing type of challenge, and new experience, he was ready for. He tried not to look over his head at Suzy and wished he hadn't, as she was gazing at Pete with evident lust. He needed to get over Mandy so he could get over Suzy. Suzy was driving him crazy with her indifference.

"Hey," Suzy said to Pete.

She didn't know much about this kind of pick up, but she was content just to gaze at Pete and conversation, although nice, wasn't mandatory. Bradley's departure might have left a silence were it not for Pete's near infinite skill at picking up women, which was so highly crafted that it appeared to Suzy that she was enjoying the kind of rapport on which longterm relationships were built, without even exchanging a word. As Pete smiled, she felt like she was caught under the bright glare of stage lights. That was, until Mandy hove into view. It was as if her huge arse had acted as a moon and eclipsed the sun. Pete liked a bit of booty and a generous backside and, as Mandy turned, it became quite obvious that God hadn't spared her chest in the construction of her buttocks. And Pete *really* liked big tits. The sun disappeared so quickly that Suzy feared for a vitamin deficiency. It turned out that Mandy was as interested in Bradley as he was in her.

It was a little while after, after Suzy had consumed a few more drinks, that she decided to call Sam.

Chapter Twenty-Seven

"Look Vlad, you give me your passport and I'll tell you where he is. That was the deal."

Vlad knew that was the deal, but he was reluctant to show his passport. He didn't show anyone his passport. He hadn't shown Brandy his passport. He had Gary's passport in his hand. He'd checked the picture and it was a reasonable likeness. It was Gary. He was even wearing the same leather jacket. That jacket hadn't missed much in his life.

"Okay, I give you passport," Vlad said in his customary Russian accent.

Gary took it, but didn't look at it. He didn't want to waste any time.

"Okay, he's in Monte Carlo, in Countess Camisuli's villa. I've got a flight booked to Monaco first thing."

Vlad thought about this. There were two issues. The first was that they had to travel together. They didn't trust each other enough, or even at all, to meet there. The second was that Vlad, built as he was like a well constructed outhouse, was terrified of flying. He'd only done it once and it had scared the hell out of him. He'd needed therapy.

"We take my car," Vlad said.

"It's quite a long way," Gary pointed out.

"We take my car," Vlad repeated, making it clear he had no intention of negotiating.

"Okay," Gary said, thinking it was unlikely that his own car would make it.

They drove to Gary's flat, picked up his suitcase, and went to Vlad's apartment. There was no question that one was a flat and the other an apartment. The tatty hall and the twenty-two stairs to Gary's place, the only exercise he ever took, was a rather different experience to the wood-panelled lift which swished to the top floor. There had been a few moments when Gary had wondered whether he'd made the right decision stealing the cash. When the doors slid open and he saw Vlad's loft-style, high-windowed home, he'd wished he'd turned to crime rather earlier. Not that Vlad's life was without problems of his own.

"Brandy, this is Gary," said Vlad, a little uncomfortably.

"Pleased to meet you," Brandy said with the tone of someone who wasn't remotely pleased.

Brandy liked to think she had standards, even though she had not introduced Vlad to any of her friends, and Gary looked a little lame to her. She'd also told Vlad that he couldn't carry out any business in the apartment. She looked warily at Gary. Gary tried not to look at Brandy. Brandy operated a clothing policy which left very little to an imagination even as limited as Gary's. Gary found it hard not to look, as he'd never seen such a vastness of cleavage on such a stick-thin body. Vlad didn't notice, as he had things to do and pack, and it was for that reason he said to Brandy, without giving it a moment's thought, "We're going to Monaco."

Vlad continued, unaware that he had a made a faux pas of such monumental proportions that it could prompt a war in most middle eastern counties, a few in Africa and destabilise Europe. The silence that descended was so stony that it could have built a wall between Mexico and America. Even Gary noticed it and he was widely regarded by colleagues, and former wives, as the world's least intuitive and sensitive man. And then Brandy exploded.

"There ain't no fucking way," Brandy squealed, "you're going to Monaco without me."

Gary was thankful he wasn't standing any closer to her, as she appeared to have all the qualities of a grenade. She'd said it with such force that her breasts, which would ordinarily be immune from movement in any earthquake registering under seven on the Richter scale, actually bristled. Vlad often felt they were expressive enough to have valid opinions of their own.

"It's bus..."

Vlad stopped. He'd almost said the word 'business,' and that was forbidden in the apartment. He tried to think of another way to express it and very nearly burst into Russian.

"The thing is," Vlad tried again.

Gary could see Vlad's muscles moving in his jaw, he could see a further ripple below his tee shirt and, because he'd experienced a little of this in the past, he could see inevitable defeat motoring his way.

"We have to leave now," Vlad said.

This was a tactic. In the three years they'd been together Brandy had never, without exception, done anything rapidly. Going out involved a makeup reconstruction and deconstruction, seven changes and then a combination of accessories that would challenge a statistician. Packing for a holiday took a week, much of it spent in department stores water-boarding Vlad's credit card. The concept of 'now' was alien to Brandy, but Brandy knew a bandwagon when she saw one, and disappeared into the bedroom. Five minutes later she lugged out the largest suitcase Gary had ever seen, which was of sufficient size to house all his life's possessions. Thankfully Vlad was as strong as a forklift, which would have been the only other way of getting it from the apartment to the car.

"Do you really need..." Vlad began.

But he didn't have enough air to deliver the thought and lift the case at the same time, and he was a man who could bench press more than a hundred kilos. Brandy gave him a look. It was similar to the scathing look she'd delivered to Gary, but it held the added threat of withholding sex. She'd been forced, due to the limited time, to be quite selective with her wardrobe.

"You want me to look beautiful, don't you?"

This was Brandy's response to many arguments, and she deployed it much like saying 'it is God's will'. It confounded Vlad every time. The worse thing was that he was fairly certain that this wasn't Brandy's entire wardrobe and the irony was that Brandy was a girl who liked to wear the flimsiest, and most minimal, clothing. Half an hour later they were on the road to Dover and, despite the size of Vlad's car, there was some cramming required to house both a passenger and Brandy's case in the rear of the car. And, as Brandy had insisted on taking the front seat, it was Gary being crammed.

Chapter Twenty-Eight

Sam had not answered Suzy's calls. It was just as well, as she had no idea what she was going to say to him, and couldn't say for certain how she felt. She'd decided to buck her ideas up, as her father might have said, and she was driving to his flat. She wondered why she rarely drove there, and then remembered that most evenings with Sam had involved alcohol. That didn't sound very healthy to her. There weren't many things she'd left in Sam's flat, but there were a few, and she didn't fancy lugging them back on the bus. Mostly they were sheets, as she hated the threadbare, worn sheets that hadn't bothered Sam. She was sitting outside his flat.

She'd been there for a while and the car had misted up a little, but she hoped it would give her an idea about how she truly felt. At least that's what she'd told herself. It wasn't giving her any blinding inspiration. It wasn't like she was expecting him to walk on water or, now she thought about the miracle he would most likely opt for, change water into wine. She just had a feeling that there was *something*. She just didn't know what.

"Damn it," Suzy muttered, and got out of the car.

The main door to the flat was still hanging open. She knew that Sam's neighbour, who lived on the ground floor was away. She was a bit of a hippy and had gone to Sri Lanka, or India, or it might have been California.

She'd gone to find herself. Suzy wondered if she needed to find herself. She shook her head and starting climbing the stairs to Sam's flat. She found his front door had been forced in the same way. She pushed it gently and looked in.

"Bloody hell," she said.

The place had been ransacked. Suzy panicked and ran back to the relative safety of the car. Then she wondered what she was going to do. What did she have to lose? They were nice sheets, but they weren't *that* nice. She phoned Sam. This time he answered.

"Suzy?" Sam answered.

She was surprised he'd answered, even though she'd called him and, once again, she had no idea what she was going to say to him.

"Where are you?" she asked.

"I'm in France," Sam said. "Well, Monaco actually. Montecarlo."

Suzy found this news very irritating, as the only place they'd gone away to together was Bruges, not including a trip to Southend. She couldn't include Southend, although it had been quite a nice trip. A good hotel. She refocused her thoughts.

"What are you doing there?"

Sam couldn't easily answer that, but it didn't matter as Suzy got to the point.

"Someone's wrecked your flat."

It focused Sam's attention. That was real and more than a little bit frightening.

"I saw two men," Suzy continued, "a tall muscular shaven-headed bloke and a shabby looking overweight bloke in an old black leather jacket."

"Oh shit," Sam said and added, "You were at my flat?"

"Yes," Suzy said trying not to get irritated, "I thought I'd get my sheets back."

There were lots of things going through Sam's mind and, by a coincidence, sheets weren't that far away.

"Did you get the sheets?" he asked.

"What? Didn't you hear me? Someone has ransacked your place. There's stuff everywhere."

"Yes, yes, but did you get your sheets?" Sam asked.

"I just saw the mess and ran out," Suzy admitted.

"Are you near?"

"I'm outside."

"Well, you don't want to leave without your sheets," Sam insisted.

Suzy couldn't believe he was taking the wrecking of his flat so well and seemed more concerned about her sheets. It was very weird.

"If you think so," Suzy said slowly, and got out of the car.

She walked up the broken concrete path, stepped through the two broken doors and back into Sam's flat.

"It's pretty bad in here. They've ripped the sofas up. And the mattress. There are holes in the wall. They've pulled the floor up."

"What about the sheets?" Sam asked.

Suzy opened the airing cupboard door. The sheets had been pulled out, they had little red flowers on them. There were the sort of sheets that looked a little naff in photographs, but actually looked quite nice in the flesh, or the cotton, Suzy thought. They were there.

"I've got them," Suzy said.

"What about the rest of the airing cupboard?"

"What do you mean?"

Suzy was realising something else. Men were clearly from a different planet, and she would never understand them. If her flat had been robbed and wrecked she'd be asking very different questions.

"Is the airing cupboard intact? You know, the tank and everything?" Sam said.

Suzy looked in, just a little bewildered.

"Yes, it's fine."

Chapter Twenty-Nine

By the time they'd arrived at Dover, Gary had found a position which wasn't actually painful and, as he'd had a few pints earlier, allowed him to fall asleep. It involved pressing his face against the window and the edge of the door, and had created a crease across his face which looked like he'd been on the wrong end of a gang fight. He would have remained asleep, but Brandy had fired a burst of what she thought of as refreshing perfume, which acted as smelling salts for Gary. In any greater density it would have asphyxiated him. They were queueing to get onto the ferry.

"Passports," Vlad said.

Gary passed Vlad's passport to him. Vlad opened the window and passed them over with his credit card. A few minutes later they were through the barriers and Vlad returned his passport to Gary. It was while they were waiting to load that Gary took a closer look at Vlad's passport. Vlad had meant to have a word with him about it but, since Brandy had got on board, he'd not had the opportunity.

"Lionel?" Gary said.

Brandy knew many things about Vlad. She knew when he was hungry and when he wanted to have sex, which was most of the time, and she knew when he was angry, and when he was anxious. She didn't know that his real name was Lionel and that he was born in Leytonstone. Vlad turned round to look at Gary. It was hard for him to see as Brandy's case was obscuring his view, but it was important to convey the message.

"Not now," he said firmly.

Gary understood. In that moment they'd forged a further alliance and strengthened the very small amount of trust that existed between them. It didn't matter, as Brandy hadn't noticed, and was studying her iPad.

"I want a swimming pool," Brandy demanded.

It took a moment for Vlad to realise that she was referring to hotels in Monte Carlo. She was flicking through a web page, and it was evident that budget was not one of Brandy's criteria. Since the loss of Vlad's cash, and the feeling that his business was being looked at, he'd postponed two deliveries and had done very little dealing. Consequently he had to rely on the vagaries of the skip hire business which, he'd discovered, was far less stable than the demand for narcotics. He wasn't feeling very flush.

"Bloody hell," he said, looking at the price.

"Hermy-tage," Brandy said with the linguistic skill of someone who'd barely mastered her own language.

"Shit," Vlad spluttered.

Vlad was in charge of most of his life. In business and in the gym people did what he told them, and that was how he liked it. But when Brandy was around he was relegated to a passenger, and Brandy drove as if she were always seconds away from a car crash. He needed to grab hold of the steering wheel.

"We are only here to pick up a package," Vlad said soothingly.

But Brandy did not take this news soothingly.

"Package? Who said anything about a package. Is it drugs? Are you picking up drugs?" Brandy yelled loud enough for border control, and customs, to hear and so loudly that Gary now had a profound ringing in his ears.

"No, it's not drugs!" Vlad hissed, aware that border control and customs weren't far away and, if that wasn't enough, he had a policeman crammed in the back seat.

"What is it?" Brandy demanded.

It often irritated Vlad that, while Brandy loved the trappings of drug dealing, she seemed to disapprove of every other aspect of the business. She did her best to put it as far away from herself as she could, and Vlad often wondered what would happen should he be caught and incarcerated. He couldn't picture her visiting him. He put it out of his mind, and decided to combat this latest onslaught with some banter with Gary.

"What are we picking up, Gary?" he said cheerfully.

It wasn't an immediate success as it didn't seem to illicit a response. He turned to Gary. Gary was looking out of the window. He wasn't being rude, or sullen, or difficult. He couldn't hear a bloody thing. Vlad's eardrums were more accustomed to Brandy's frequent explosive outbursts. He decided to come clean, or at least cleanish.

"We're picking up some money," he said.

Brandy took this in and decided, that as she very much liked money, this was okay.

"It's next to the casino," she said.

"What is?" Vlad asked.

"The Hermy-tage," Brandy said.

It was clear that the steering wheel was back in Brandy's hands and there wasn't much he could do. There were moments when he wondered why he put up with her, particularly as the moments when he didn't wonder were relatively brief in duration. The girl was a sexual phenomenon. Vlad had never known anything like it. It was just the other twenty-three and a half hours in a day he had to endure.

"Credit card," Brandy commanded.

Vlad handed it over. His credit cards and bills were all in his Russian name, and Brandy was no stranger to them.

"Book a double and a single," he said.

He said it loudly so that Gary could hear. They needed to stay close to each other. But Gary was looking out of the window experiencing a kind of sensory deprivation, as part of his body had become numbed by the weight of Brandy's suitcase, and his ears were ringing loudly enough to make his head rattle.

A couple of hours later they were in France and heading for Monaco.

Chapter Thirty

It was morning when they arrived at Monte Carlo, and Vlad was exhausted. Gary and Brandy had slept soundly and noisily with a cacophony of snores that even Vlad's mega-watted car hifi couldn't defeat. He was going to have to grab at least two hours sleep before they went looking for Sunday.

"The Hermy-tage," Brandy announced.

She'd been following the signs to the casino and Vlad, who'd driven for about fifteen hours, wasn't sure if he was awake or trapped in a bad dream. The Hermitage wasn't difficult to find, and he was too grateful to find that it was the kind of hotel that parked his car to worry about the cost. The car looked at home in the carpark even if Vlad, Brandy and Gary didn't.

"Isn't this beautiful?" Brandy said.

Gary looked nervously at the prices, while the concierge looked at him as if he'd slept in the doorway. Gary's head had sunk in the course of the journey, and his face looked like a car crash of imprints and, as very little blood was able to circulate while he was pressed up against Brandy's suitcase, he was having difficulty walking. Brandy was delighted, walking on air, as she admired the tall hall, the opulent decor and the staff uniforms. This was why she was with a Russian, to get away from her squalid east end upbringing. Not that it had actually been squalid, just that her mother had kept her on a bit of a leash and held what Brandy considered to be reactionary views on matters such as sun beds.

"This way," they were directed.

Brandy strutted in her four inch heels, giggling with pleasure. Vlad placed one foot in front of the other zombie-like, while Gary staggered like he was waiting for a double hip replacement. There were four men behind them grappling with Brandy's suitcase. One was carrying Brandy's coat. For Brandy less was very much more and she'd managed, like a Russian doll, to cast off a few layers leaving a vast expanse of leg, which almost ran out by the time it reached her skirt. Her pink running shirt managed to be both tight and baggy in equal measure.

"Dear god," Gary muttered.

He'd never seen anything like it. It was a stark reminder of the barrenness of his own life. The good news was that it was bringing back circulation to his body, including parts in which blood rarely circulated.

"Your room, sir."

Gary took a last look at Brandy's departing form and Vlad grabbed his arm. He thought, for a second, that he was going to be reprimanded for his lechery, but nothing could have been further from Vlad's mind.

"Give me a couple of hours," Vlad said.

Gary nodded and entered his room. Although it sat at the bottom end of the hotel's tariff, it was by far and away the nicest hotel room he'd ever stayed in. He dropped his case on the bed. By Brandy's standards his bag was as minimal as her clothing and wouldn't have accommodated her collection of bikinis, let alone her cosmetics. But it was sufficient for two pairs of socks and underpants, which Gary would only deploy should circumstances absolutely dictate it, and an un-ironed shirt, which he'd only worn once. Now that he looked at it he saw a rip under the armpit. Not that Gary cared. He wasn't a man who gave his appearance much thought. The cash was the reason for the journey and if Vlad, or Lionel, as he'd discovered, was true to his word then he'd be up a couple of hundred grand, and that would be enough to buy a nice place in Spain, and take not so early retirement. Perhaps then he'd think about stretching his sartorial standards.

Gary sat on the bed and played with the television in the hope that there might be some of that continental pornography he'd heard about, then he looked at the minibar, and then he decided it was too early for either. He lay on the bed and closed his eyes and, as there wasn't a coffin-like object crushing him, and no perfume asphyxiating him, he fell asleep. It was less peaceful in the neighbouring room.

"Vlad," Brandy shook him.

Vlad had landed face-first on the huge double bed and had collapsed into an instant, immediate deep sleep. That left Brandy and her bra-less perkiness on her own. And Brandy didn't like being left on her own. But it was more than that. There were few things that made her hornier than a lavish hotel room. As far as she was concerned, sex was the sole purpose of the hotel room. It was the ultimate aphrodisiac. She shook Vlad.

"Vlad," she said, soothingly.

At this point a surgeon could have removed Vlad's spleen and he wouldn't have noticed. But that was not the organ that Brandy was interested in.

"Vlad," she said a little louder, and a good deal less soothingly.

The surgeon could have hoiked his appendix out too.

"Vlad," Brandy screamed.

She screamed it so loudly it woke Gary in the neighbouring room, and caused a car accident in the street outside. It was like a screech, or the sound of car tyres skidding. It didn't wake Vlad. One of Brandy's many qualities was persistence. When Brandy really wanted something, she really had to have it. She normally got it.

She turned Vlad over. In her experience of men, which was far wider than she'd admitted to Vlad, the route to a man, although that could easily be root, was contained in the remote control located in his trousers. Despite Vlad's weight and size, Brandy managed to drag his trousers off. It was a testament to her determination. She yanked his underpants off and applied her world class fellating skills to an organ that looked distinctly disinterested.

"Mmm," Vlad seemed to say.

Brandy took this as a good sign and worked a little harder, although there was no evidence that that hardness was extending to Vlad, which was disappointing. She continued undeterred. There was still very little response. She tried a little light biting. If there were degrees of biting, a sort of scale, she would consider this to be playful. That would be more in the manner of a nip than a divot. She would have left it there, but the allure of the hotel room seemed to be acting on the lower half of her body, and she wasn't getting the response she'd hoped for. She stepped it up a little. The next level above playful, in the biting scale, was probably the bottom end of the sadomasochistic scale, and might involve a little bit of light redness. It wasn't quite playful either, as Brandy was getting pretty irritated by the situation. She really didn't feel that Vlad appreciated her. She knew everyone else did. She'd heard that Mona Lisa's eyes followed you around the room. She didn't know about that, but she *did* know that everyone else's eyes followed her. She caused quite a stir wherever she went,

"Vlad!' she shouted.

The drivers of the car crash outside heard it and raised their eyes. Gary did too and was now fully awake and, with the help of his mobile phone, he was tracking down the Contessa's villa. It was conveniently within walking distance. Vlad was still unconscious, and Brandy was making decisions, one of which involved a further step on the biting scale. A second later Gary heard the result of those decisions and Vlad's scream.

"You fucking mad bitch!" Vlad screamed, breaking from his normal protocol.

As Brandy had moved up the bite scale, Vlad felt that someone had ripped out both his spleen and his appendix. Strangely, it prompted the response Brandy was looking for and she didn't waste the moment and jumped straight on him. Ten minutes later Vlad was awake and Brandy was fast asleep. He staggered onto his feet, pulled his underpants and trousers on, and left the room. He knocked on Gary's door.

"Are you alright?" Gary asked.

Vlad struggled to muster a reply, although he was inclined to say 'not really.' Half an hour later they were in the Contessa's back garden.

Chapter Thirty-One

Sam walked naked onto the balcony. He had not been, in his previous life, prone to overtly flashing his nakedness but, after having had more vigorous sex than he'd ever had, it seemed perfectly normal. He let the warm sun tumble over him. He sniffed the air, and it smelled good. The house was set in a terrace of similar buildings, which were replete with architectural jewellery and detailing. The Contessa's bedroom was at the top of the house, and the balcony ran the full width. It had a stone balustrade on which Sam leaned nonchalantly. There was a surprisingly generous garden and the view was quite clear. It might be possible for someone to see him standing naked, but it was unlikely and, if they did, he didn't care.

"What are you thinking?" the Contessa asked.

Sam was thinking about the conversation he'd had with Suzy. It was the first time they'd spoken since they'd split up, and they hadn't really said much. He'd just asked her about the money and, as far as he could tell, it was still hidden in the old water cylinder. He still wasn't sure what he thought about Suzy.

"Thinking?" Sam said.

The Contessa had appeared behind him. She was also naked, or as naked as she ever allowed herself to be, with lingerie accoutrements guiding her flesh helpfully. She stood proudly and Sam couldn't resist looking at her breasts.

"You have fantastic breasts," Sam said.

It was the nearest thing to a compliment he'd managed.

"*Digo la condesa, poniendo sus enormes tetas sobre la mesa,*" the Countess said.

"I beg your pardon?" Sam said.

"You have an expression - as the actress said to the bishop," she explained.

"I suppose," Sam said slowly.

"That is the Spanish equivalent."

Sam didn't know what to say. He didn't know that it was a phrase that was rumoured to have originated from the Countess.

"What does it mean?"

The Countess laughed and looked at the view. Sam followed her gaze. He knew it couldn't, and wouldn't, last forever, and he felt a bit of fraud. He could never be an acolyte and fit in with the world of Ernest. But it was nice taking a holiday from reality, so he told the truth, or some of it.

"I could be in rainy Croydon trying to flog a photocopier to a skip hire company next to a dump."

It was a sentence which painted a picture so bleak, and at odds with the beauty of the Contessa's existence, that it was as if he'd farted. But the Contessa wasn't entirely fooled.

"How does a photocopier salesman lose ten thousand at the tables?" she asked.

The Contessa had fended off plenty of unfavourable suitors in the past and had a knack for seeing through them. It might have been her greatest skill.

"That's a bit of a story," Sam admitted.

"Not many people use a fifty pound note as a plaster either," the Contessa pointed out.

Sam wanted to tell her the truth, but the truth was boring, and he knew the Contessa didn't like boring. It was better to say he'd won it, or claim it as an inheritance, or even say he stole it. He found it didn't say much about him at all, other than he'd been lucky. And, right at the moment, looking at the beauty around him, he felt very lucky. It was a moment worth savouring.

Then he heard something. Sam hadn't noticed anyone looking at them and hadn't seen anything to disturb the peace. But he definitely heard someone say something, and it was in English. It jangled with the serenity and made him feel just a little apprehensive. He turned and took another look at the Contessa's magnificent breasts and felt instantly calmer. They were very therapeutic.

"Some people are looking at us," the Contessa said.

She wasn't concerned by a potential voyeur – she might even have welcomed it – but they looked a little unsavoury. She liked her men to be so savoury that they were good enough to eat. And Sam, who clearly harboured a secret which was very probably of a criminal nature, was quite delicious at the moment.

"That's him," one of the men said.

Sam saw two men whose appearance looked suspiciously like a description he'd heard recently. Then it clicked. This was trouble. Big trouble, of a kind he'd never been involved in before. One was tall, jowly, overweight, seedy and wearing a worn, shapeless and unfashionable black leather jacket. The other was taller still and wore a tee shirt which didn't disguise his muscularity. There was a brief flicker of a second as they froze and looked at each other.

Sam exuded guilt. The one in the leather jacket wore a fixed expression with his mouth open in wonderment. He was looking at the Contessa's breasts. The other stared at him with hatred, menace and a very clear undercurrent of violence. He was the one that moved first. He kicked a door down. The door was beautifully constructed of solid oak, of a density which would have made it a challenge to drive a nail in, and with elaborate mouldings which were finely crafted. It didn't stand a chance when confronted with an angry drug dealer with a propensity for lifting weights, inflicting damage and an acquired Russian accent.

"Shit," Sam spluttered.

He was trapped. He couldn't go downstairs, and there was no other exit. He had seconds to react.

Sam climbed onto the stone balustrade and onto the roof. It was an old roof made of Roman tiles, and it might have been slippery were Sam not barefooted. He was bare everything. Entirely naked, but there wasn't enough time to collect his clothes, and even less to put them on. He crawled up the roof, grateful that the pitch was fairly shallow, and up to the ridge. It gave him a very striking view of the city and he couldn't help taking a quick look. He could see a large American-style caravan with the words 'Jesus Saves' on the side. He hoped it wasn't a sign and picked his way along the ridge until he made it to the next building and, from there, he made it to the next. It was an escape made without much of a plan and he got lucky.

He was lucky because Gary could have tracked his progress, but he was too mesmerised by the Contessa's breasts. He was also lucky because Peralta had a gun. That trumped muscles. It was the gun and the scar across Peralta's face, along with the Contessa's insistence that Sunday had made his escape, that convinced Vlad. And Sam had one further piece of luck. It was the housekeeper of a neighbour seven or eight houses along who had, that morning, put out the washing of the master of the house.

Chapter Thirty-Two

Bradley wasn't ready to give up on Suzy. It hadn't been difficult to steer her towards a pub, as her social life post Sam was a little barren. But strange things were happening.

"Someone had cut up his mattress?" Bradley asked.

Suzy nodded. She knew she'd regret telling Bradley, but once she'd started it had gushed out, and she hadn't spared the details.

"And there were holes in the wall?" Bradley asked.

She'd already told him this so wondered why he felt the need to ask again, but then, as he'd established with Sam, men thought differently. They were a mystery. What was that book about Mars and Venus? They weren't far enough apart in her view.

"And the floor?"

"Yes," Suzy said.

Sam had ended the call abruptly, but he'd said 'thanks'. It didn't sound like much, but it sounded like he meant it. In all the time she'd known him he'd been an open, and very easily read book. Now he was a walking mystery, raising new questions every time she talked to him, or laid eyes on him.

"What were they looking for?" Bradley asked.

"Looking for? What do you mean?"

"A burglar might force open a door, he might pull clothing out of a drawer, he may even pull a sofa apart, but holes in the wall and raised floorboards. They were looking for something."

Suzy digested this. It made sense.

"I don't know," she admitted.

"The big question is whether they found it."

Suzy played the brief conversation she'd had with Sam through her head. It had been an odd sort of a conversation.

"He didn't seem that worried," she said.

They both knew what this meant and Bradley, who was a man who could win prizes for being inquisitive, knew which way he wanted it to go. He wanted to take a look at that flat.

"Shall I get more drinks?"

Bradley also knew that it would require a little courage to get into the flat, and the Dutch had a lot to say on the matter. He wondered what a Dutch army knife would look like and if it had fourteen different tools for opening wine and beer bottles.

"Good idea," Suzy said.

"We're going to have to go there," Bradley said when he'd got back.

Suzy didn't say anything, but looked at the little array of drinks he'd brought back with him.

"What's this?" she asked.

"Mojitos and chasers," Bradley said.

"Who the hell has chasers with mojitos?" Suzy asked.

"We do," Bradley said and knocked back a chaser.

Bradley really wanted to know what secret Sam was hiding. He'd met him a few times and didn't mind him. He'd wanted to hate him, so not minding him was pretty good. Of course, Bradley had a secret of his own. It wasn't exactly a secret, as everyone in the office knew and all his friends knew. Even the friends of his friends knew. The only person that didn't know was Suzy.

"Sod it, why not," Suzy said and threw back her chaser.

It burned an alcoholic path down her throat and it made her feel stronger and more confident. It was all an illusion, but that didn't bother her.

"Cheers," Bradley said, and raised his mojito.

Bradley was absolutely, uncontrollably, head-over-heels in love with Suzy, and she was the only person who was not remotely aware. Not even a hint of it. Nothing. He needed a little courage. He'd moved in nicely as her confidant, now he needed to move in as something more. Today would be the day. When they left the pub, and set off on their mission, it was obvious that they would have to do so by bus. Driving was out of the question. Suitably fortified, they left the pub.

"Are you alright?" Bradley asked, looking around, as it seemed as if Suzy had disappeared.

Suzy had fallen in a hedge.

"Oh fuck it," Suzy said.

The hedge had broken her fall, but there was quite an aggressive thorny bramble woven through it.

"Pricks," Suzy shouted.

Bradley couldn't tell if this was an insult.

"Brad! Can you get me out of here?"

Bradley carefully picked the thorns out of her clothing, which involved quite a bit of intimate poking about. He might have miscalculated the de-inhibiting powers of mojitos. And chasers.

"Thanks," Suzy said, and they staggered on.

It took a while for the bus to come, and a further time to walk to Sam's flat. When they got there they were much more accustomed to the alcohol in their system, which is to say that they weren't, were a breathalyser to be applied, any more sober. They just felt it. The communal front door was still hanging forlornly but, as it wasn't visible from the street, no one had noticed.

"Oh shit," Bradley said.

There was something about the hanging door, and the way it had been attacked, that reminded Bradley that there had been violence. He wasn't so sure about this now that he'd sobered up a little.

"I'm not sure this is a good idea," he said.

Suzy looked at him. She had just endured numerous rounds of mojitos and chasers. She'd spent ages waiting for a bus.

"We're here now," she said flatly.

Bradley realised that it looked like he was wimping out, which was precisely what he was doing and which, he knew, did not look good. He'd have to bluff.

"Damn right," he said.

She gave him a disbelieving look and walked though the open door without checking to see if he was following. He had no choice, although he left a couple of paces between them. Just in case. They entered the flat.

"Fucking hell," Bradley said.

It was worse than he'd thought, although the state of Sam's flat had not been uppermost in his mind. He looked around. His flat was bigger. Should he mention that? He decided to mention it later on the trip back on the bus. Since he was bluffing he upped his game and tried to play detective.

"What were they looking for, and why didn't they find it?"

Suzy decided she didn't much care anymore. She had other things on her mind. The chasers and mojitos were mounting a rebellion. She was going to throw up.

"Are you alright? Bradley asked.

He'd hoped that this evening they could share something together. It would be his moment.

"I think," Suzy said.

There were little flicks of something around her mouth and, if Bradley were to hazard a guess, he'd say it was vomit, which was rather killing the moment for him. He'd blown it again. He always seemed to say and do the wrong thing.

"He seemed really interested in the airing cupboard," Suzy suddenly said.

They looked at it. It looked like an airing cupboard. Although why any cupboard in which there was clearly no exchange of air could be called 'airing' was a mystery to Suzy. It was all a mystery. And then something unsavoury arrived in her mouth. She put her hand out to steady herself, closing her eyes.

"Are you okay?" Bradley asked.

Suzy was fighting a small battle in which her stomach, and the alcohol was leading a charge. Bradley, rather gallantly he thought, produced a hankerchief. It was quite a fine one, with his monogrammed initials. Suzy spat the vomit into it and gave it back to him.

"Fucking hell," Suzy said.

Here eyes had cleared and they had focused on something.

"What?" Bradley asked.

Suzy pointed. She had used the copper cylinder to steady herself and, strangely, it had leant back slightly. More strangely it had, like a Las Vegas one armed bandit, chucked out a bundle of bank notes.

"Fucking hell," Bradley confirmed as he picked it up.

Chapter Thirty-Three

Ashton Hoffman-Lendetta was having an artistic crisis. Those who knew him wouldn't be surprised by this, as he lived in a perpetual state of artistic crisis. But this was worse than most. In the past both the establishment, and buyers, had loved whatever surrealist mish-mash he came up with and, were it not for the fact that he actually regarded himself as a genius of some proportions, it would seem as if every reinvention was just a little bit cynical. He thought of himself as a Bowie kind of character, but increasingly there was a growing suspicion that he was like the landlord of a pub with a business plan who carried out a refurbishment every five years. He'd fallen out with most of the art critics at some time or other, and then launched a vendetta against them. Or, as the press had called it, a Lendetta vendetta. He was feeling a bit isolated.

"More paint!' he shouted.

There was no one else in the house but, since his divorce from Miguel, he hadn't quite got out of the habit of issuing commands and always maintained a constant dialogue while painting. Miguel was a dear, but he was twenty-seven years younger, and grew a little tired of being shouted at, even though Ashton liked to think that he had always shouted lovingly. There had been other issues in their relationship and the work was very cathartic. He was throwing paint on a large canvas, which was part of his latest collection.

"More detail!" he shouted.

He picked up a small brush made of fine hairs and dipped it into a jar of light green paint. It was what he called his vein paint. This collection had not been a roaring success. Actually, it had been a storming disaster and, if he didn't shift a few soon, he was going to have a bit of a crisis of a bill-paying nature. He put his glasses on and leant closer to the canvas. His pink glasses matched the pink silk blouse and silk skirt he was wearing. Silk wasn't the most practical of materials for painting, but he was very careful and his clothing, or it might have been his image, were very dear to him. He applied thin lines of paint.

"Nice," he said.

Ashton often appraised his own work and always, without fail, found it to be quite outstanding. He wasn't very objective by nature. But, despite that, he was having a crisis of confidence. He'd been crossdressing for years, way before it had become fashionable, and he'd grown to like the air circulating around his genitals when he wore skirts. But the clothing, and what people thought of him, didn't matter. What did matter was those aerated genitals, which were losing interest. That was another reason why Miguel left, and why his latest collection had become an unmarketable disaster.

"More," he said.

It wasn't that *he'd* lost interest – quite the opposite, as few things filled his mind more than sex. It was just that his body and his mind were running on different rails. Or, put another way, his mind had been making promises that his body couldn't fill. It was writing cheques which couldn't be cashed. He was getting quite obsessed by it. Ashton was painting erections.

"Damn, not like that," he said.

He was very exacting with his vein work and, to his credit, he'd done a considerable amount of research, and seen a great many penises. This attention to detail was not being embraced by the market place. It seemed that erections crossed the line from art to pornography and he couldn't see why. Everyone got them, so what was the harm? Although his motivation for painting them was tied to his increasing difficulty in sustaining one. The harder it became, or more accurately, the less hard, the more obsessed he had become, and the larger the erection on the canvas. His vein-work was outstanding, you could practically see the blood pumping. The problem was that people didn't want to put huge cocks above their mantelpieces. It was irritatingly bourgeois thinking and it wasn't paying bills.

"More, more," he said again and a few brush strokes later the penis was even larger.

He loved having them on his walls. His villa was currently festooned with them, although he'd rather sell them than hang them on his walls. He stood back to look at his latest erection.

"Mag-bloody-nificent," he declared.

This one was about eight feet long. The other problem with spending his day painting penises was that it made him horny. Ashton *really* liked penises especially since Miguel had left and he hadn't had seen any for a while. It made him gloomy. Now that he was getting into the autumn of his life men seemed less inclined to expose themselves to him. He was carrying out all his work from memory.

"More veins," he muttered.

It wasn't as if he liked his penises to be veiny, it was just that it gave them more of a three dimensional quality and a slightly rough look he quite liked. They were like action penises that had been everywhere and done everything. Sort of battle worn. It reminded him of a truck driver he used to know.

"Oh Christmas," Ashton said.

He was worried he was going mad. He looked out of the window into his garden. It was a well tended garden. Ashton had a gardener as well as a housekeeper, and he would have had more servants if he could afford it. Worse, if he didn't shift a cock or two, he was going to have to let someone go, and that would mean he'd have to do something ghastly like his own washing. Ashton liked to change clothes several times a day and generated more washing than a large family. He'd had a promotional idea, and had tee shirts with his latest work splashed across the front and back. They were really quite good value. They hadn't sold well either.

"Okay, what next?" Ashton asked himself.

He might have to go back to painting that faux-religious stuff that had really shifted. It was the moment before his cross dressing, when he'd found God or God had found him. His ego was sufficiently inflated for him to think that God had sought him out personally, ignoring the seven billion other people on the planet, and demonstrating that God had a taste for surrealist art. It was beginning to look as if God wasn't keen on penis art. Ashton had been a believer. He even believed that God was gay and just did that procreation stuff because, well, somebody had to. But the failure of his recent collection to really fly suggested otherwise. Had God gone to the other side? Was God now heterosexual? Ashton felt he needed a sign. And then it happened.

"Oh Christmas puddings," he said.

Ashton had spent his life waiting for divine intervention, and here it was happening before his eyes. There was a naked man in his garden. There were many ways this could be interpreted, although there weren't many theologians who would share Ashton's thinking, and he saw it as a sign. God must have sent him there to let him know that He supported what Ashton was doing.

"Thank you, God," he said.

There were other possibilities. God could have sent him as a plaything. Ashton didn't mind and, although his own penis didn't operate as well as it used to, it was still functioning and had needs that had to be fulfilled. He got up to approach the naked man, taking a professional interest in the penis. He wondered if he could get the young man to stand for him. He didn't mean the penis, but then again, perhaps he did.

"Young man!" he shouted, tapping on his window.

He'd hoped that the young man would have turned his way brandishing a massive, although not quite canvas size, erection and demonstrating that there was nothing wrong with the public display of tumescence. But that's not what happened.

"Hey!" he shouted, banging the glass with the flat of his hand.

A moment later he was forced to reconsider his divine intervention thesis, as the naked man grabbed the clothes off his clothes line and jumped over the wall into the next garden.

Chapter Thirty-Four

"Oh fucking bollocks," Suzy muttered.

Someone had buried an axe in her head. It was an axe flavoured with mojitos and chasers. Who had chasers with mojitos? Suzy tried to piece together the evening. It was hazy but there was one thing that stood out. No strike that, she thought, there were two things that stood out. The first was lying next to her. He was snoring lightly, which she was grateful of as it gave her a moment to relive the moment. She was in Bradley's flat. It was worse than that. She was in Bradley's bed.

"Oh fucking tit-bollocks," she said.

It might have been the headache, or it might have been the moment she really hadn't seen coming. There had been quite a few significant moments before that, and it might have been that, along with the quite prodigious quantities of alcohol that had been forced into her bloodstream, that had prompted it. Bradley tried to kiss her. No, it wasn't that. She'd fended him off and the whole event might have been forgotten and consigned into the bin of bad memories and an unwise ideas, but he'd followed it with a speech. A speech in which he'd professed undying love for her. That was a shock.

"Hey, are you okay?"

It was Bradley. He was awake and also attempting to piece together the events of an eventful evening. The good news was that he was in bed with Suzy. That was very good news, or it would be, if she weren't fully clothed. His big speech thing hadn't gone well.

"Was this a good idea?" Bradley asked.

He could have been talking about being in bed with Suzy, but they both knew it wasn't that. They'd had a discussion, at Sam's flat, and it had resulted in the potentially bad idea. They'd stuffed the cash in a large blue IKEA bag they'd found in Sam's flat and taken it to Bradley's place. They'd taken a bus. Given the wreckage that was left behind with mattress and sofa stuffing everywhere, it was probably a very bad idea. But they'd had more to drink at Bradley's place, and it was at that moment that Bradley hit on an idea.

"I'm not sure," Suzy said.

It was a seduction plan. Suzy had disappeared into the bathroom and Bradley had taken out all the cash, removed all the bands down to the individual notes, and scattered them across the bed. In his defence it would have been the only opportunity in his whole life when he'd make love on a bed of cash. It seemed a neat idea at the time.

"I feel ill," Suzy said.

It looked fantastic, but he hadn't factored in the reason for Suzy's trip to the bathroom. She was throwing up. The subsequent ill-considered kiss was flavoured with many things and none of them were pleasant.

"What are we going to do?" Suzy had asked.

Then he delivered his speech and Suzy had collapsed face first into the bed of bank notes, which was where she now found herself. What were they going to do with the money?

"I guess we better sort it out," Bradley said.

He was reluctant to get up, as he was naked except for his boxer shorts and the notes were covering him. That was another unwise part of the evening. When she'd come out of the bathroom, having only been partially successful removing the vomit from her face, she found him lying in his boxer shorts on the bed of notes. She might have been pissed, very pissed even, but it wasn't too difficult to see where Bradley hoped the evening was going to go. If she'd been any longer he wouldn't have had the boxer shorts either. He gave the on/off boxer short decision considerable debate, but it prompted an up/down decision regarding the state of his penis and even he could see, at that moment, that up would have been at the very least unseemly. It was optimistic too, as he collapsed shortly after her.

"We're going to have to sort it out," Bradley said, and got up, and went to get his clothes.

It was a huge sea of notes and it looked exciting and frightening at the same time and, worse than that, Suzy had seen the men that had come looking for it, and they were pretty frightening.

"Then what?" she asked.

Chapter Thirty-Five

Sam had been running. He was scared, really terrified. He knew when he took the money that he was stepping into something pretty dangerous, but the temptation had been reeling him in like a big fish in a powerboat on the sea. The trappings of a bigger life had engulfed him, starting with the Russian girls, who might have been hookers, and the roulette wheel and the altar of Armani. And all that was before the Contessa had appeared.

"Hello," a man said.

Sam nodded and stepped back into his own world. The Contessa's life was unreal, and it was an unreal he had been enjoying, and had grown used to very rapidly. Of course, if he'd thought about things he would have known that it was just a temporary unreality.

"Nice here, isn't it?" the man next to him said.

What the hell was Sam going to do? He had no money, no passport and no clothes. That wasn't entirely true: he was wearing a particularly lurid skirt, which he was trying to cover with a baggy tee shirt. He'd have to go back to the Contessa's place. But he was fairly certain they'd be waiting for him. He would be walking into a trap.

"Can I sit here?" the man asked.

Sam wasn't sure he could handle another escape like that. Running along the rooftops had been terrifying. But there was no choice. It was the kind of money that people killed for, and it was probably acquired by the kind of people who weren't averse to killing. It tended to focus the mind more effectively than a new range of photocopiers.

"You look nice," the man next to him said and placed his hand next to Sam's thigh, brushing it very slightly.

Sam moved up a little. He'd suffered a lifelong fear of heights, and all it had taken was two violent men with a desire to lynch him to change that. He'd ran for a while until he'd found a bench by a small beach. He just needed to figure out what to do next. He needed some inspiration.

"Do you like cocks?" the man beside him asked.

"I beg your pardon?" Sam said, getting flustered.

The man next to him smiled. It wasn't too difficult to see where he stood on the cock-liking front.

"Your tee shirt," the man pointed.

Sam looked at his tee shirt, or rather the tee shirt he'd stolen off the clothesline. He'd been so concerned about the skirt he hadn't noticed anything else. He pulled the tee shirt away from him and looked more closely.

"Oh shit," Sam muttered.

It was covered in cocks. They were sizeable and very much ready for action. This wasn't the inspiration he was looking for. Sam got up and walked away briskly. The man next to him knew that not everyone was comfortable expressing themselves, and took this as a sign that they were to reconvene to somewhere more suitable. He followed Sam. It wasn't until Sam broke into a sprint that he had to conclude he wasn't being hard to get. Sam spent the next hour on the beach. He would have spent longer, but he didn't have any suncream and he was fairly certain he was turning pink. It was a shade which went well with the skirt.

He would have to go back to the Contessa's villa after dark, a long way after dark. He didn't have a watch, or a phone, to tell him the time, but he knew he had a long wait. There were other issues. He was hungry, and needed to find a toilet. He wasn't sure they'd let him into a bar, or cafe, with a cock-covered tee shirt, even if he had money, which he didn't. He wandered along the beach until he arrived at the harbour. That was where Ernest's boat or, as he called it, his little boaty, was moored. He was fairly sure he would be welcome there but, from his last experience, that would come with a price too. A price he wasn't keen on paying.

He was very nearly at the point of losing the contents of his bowels without being involved in the decision making process, when he found a toilet block. It gave him an unexpected joy, as he thought he might have to find a ditch and, the last time he'd done that, he'd got into all sorts of trouble. It left him with only his hunger to worry about. He walked between the yachts looking for hiding places, until he saw a table on the deck of a large power boat. On the table was the remains of someone's lunch, and Sam didn't waste time pilfering what was left. Five minutes later he found a canvas-covered lifeboat on a yacht which appeared to be locked up. He slid under the canvas, finished the food he'd stolen and fell asleep.

It was a deep sleep in which he was only mildly tormented by the torture that lay ahead of him. The men that had pursued him and, amazingly, found him in the Contessa's villa wouldn't give up until they had their cash back, and that was complicated. They might even kill him, even if he did tell them where it was. Sam swatted his nose. His hand hit something solid. He opened his eyes.

"I know what you're thinking," a voice said.

Sam was looking down the barrel of a gun. The man holding the gun was squinting in the sun.

"You do?" Sam said.

The man squinted a little more.

"Did I shoot five or did I shoot six?" the man said.

As Sam had been asleep he had no idea how many shots had, or had not, been fired. And then he got it. Sam squinted and said, "well, in all the confusion I clean forgot."

"Hey, what are you doing here? It's Sam isn't it?"

Sam focused his eyes. It was one of Ernest's acolytes. The one he'd thought of as the fine boned young man.

"I'm hiding," Sam admitted.

"Hey, we're all hiding," the acolyte laughed.

"I need somewhere to crash out until late," Sam said.

"Crash away," the acolyte said, putting the flare gun away.

Sam relaxed and slept again. He woke when it was dark, feeling sore, and unaware that one half of him was a little pink. He left the safe haven of the boat and, somewhere around the middle of the night, Sam retraced his steps, up a garden wall, onto a higher wall, across a balcony and onto a roof, along the ridge line and dropping onto a balcony. He landed without making a sound. But someone was waiting for him.

"What took you so long?"

It made Sam jump. It was the Contessa.

"You're up late," Sam said.

"I couldn't sleep," the Contessa said.

There were a few things she required for a restful sleep, and her latest muse had not been there to provide one of them. She'd hoped she could keep Sam going all summer. It was most disappointing.

"That's a shame," Sam said.

If it weren't for two violent men, Sam would have liked to have idled the summer away with the Contessa, and leave Derek and the photocopiers behind, but real life had intruded and he had to attend to it.

"I've had a few problems," Sam added.

Sam wasn't sure if he should tell her, or even if she wanted to know. It didn't appear to trouble her. He did need to get his things and go.

"Will I not see you again?" the Contessa asked.

She said it with a dramatic quiver in her voice. The Contessa liked a bit of drama in her life and tomorrow she'd go back out into the social hunting ground of casinos, bars and restaurants to snare herself another young muse. She'd find someone eventually and that wouldn't last forever either. But it was always sad to see one go. Although he hadn't quite gone yet.

"Peralta," she commanded, "shoot anyone who comes through the door."

Sam hadn't noticed Peralta hovering nearby. Peralta's devotion was absolute. He knew that she would always look after him and, in return, he would always protect her. He would have gone further but Peralta's time in the Special Forces had ended with a stray bullet which damaged his ardour.

He nodded and disappeared. Sam didn't doubt he'd do it. The Contessa took his hand and led him to the bedroom. Sam, in a moment of spectacular naivety, grabbed his clothes and started to put them on.

"I don't think so," the Contessa said.

It was clear that she had other plans and had no intention of being diverted from them. She also knew this was to be the last time. It had been a fun interlude, and tomorrow she'd catch up with Ernest and his crowd. But there were problems. The first was that Sam had been on the beach all day without any suncream. He was quite painfully pink. The other was that Sam was discovering that nothing crushes the libido more than the possibility of being lynched by the people from whom you have taken a million quid. He couldn't get it up. The Contessa tried every trick in her book, which was more akin to a library. After forty minutes both of them were sweating, but not from the weight of boisterous sexual activity. The Contessa was ready to admit defeat.

"I'm sorry," Sam said and gathered his thing together.

"I'll just give you a quick massage, to set you on your way," the Contessa said.

The Contessa smiled and lay her hands on him. It had been some time since she'd exercised her massaging skills. It was quite amazing what her hands, with a drop of lubricating oil, could achieve. In her younger days those hands had been legendary and had helped give rise to the most dormant of old men, whose title and wealth she would subsequently inherit. They could have been called viagra hands, but viagra had yet to be invented. And Sam was not an old man.

"That's better," the Contessa said.

Half an hour later, and feeling more relaxed and laid back than a Rastafarian with a big spliff, Sam drifted into a smiling sleep without a care in the world. It was a feeling which stretched to the morning. He had no idea of the time, and the Contessa had no interest in such bourgeois concepts, and it turned out that last night wasn't their last time. She didn't have to deploy her magic hands for long in the morning and, when Sam finally left, he was so laid back he was nearly falling over. It was such a relaxed state, at ease with the world and himself, that he made the mistake of leaving by the front door.

Chapter Thirty-Six

Brandy was enjoying herself by the swimming pool. Of the twenty-three bikinis she'd packed, a number she considered barely adequate, she'd opted for the florescent green one with gold chains for strings, including one which sliced her backside. If her rear view wasn't mesmerising enough, her breasts, and the cups she had attempted to press them into, were involved in a constant battle. She'd gathered a coterie of young men, plus a handful of old men, and she was waiting for Vlad to come striding back and claim her, like the prize she was. But he was involved in 'business,' whatever that was. Worse, he'd brought that shabby man along with him. She hadn't taken to Gary.

She got up and walked around. There was no particular reason for this, but she couldn't help it. It was hard to say precisely how many eyes were trained on her, but it was quite a number and most were hoping that her breasts would defeat the cups, break free and win the battle. Brandy wiggled as she walked and then occasionally, for no particular reason, she would raise her hands and flounce her hair. She put on quite a show. She wondered where Vlad had got to. The combination of the admiring glances and the hotel room was having quite an effect on her and she needed Vlad to sort that out.

She threw a beach dress on. As Brandy had a body which looked like it was constantly attempting to break free from her clothes, the skimpy, minimal cotton dress continued the same battle. She was going to look for Vlad. She slipped her shoes on. They weren't what most women would call shoes, as it wasn't immediately obvious from their style, and general form, that they were designed to operate as an intermediary between her feet and the ground. They made some men unconsciously gulp.

She went looking for Vlad. He wasn't in the room, nor was he in the bar, or the restaurant. Brandy grabbed her bag, which was so small it had been a struggle for the designer to brandish his name across the side, but it held her cards, or rather one of Vlad's, as well as car keys and modest makeup needs.

She walked outside the hotel. She was feeling distinctly unappreciated, and strutted and moved in a pied piper kind of march with which she intended to acquire a coterie of men who would value her. And right now there was no question in her mind that she was scorching, smoking, pavement-singeing hot. She was a risk to global warming. A large van drove by with the words 'Jesus Saves' on the side. Brandy wasn't interested in Jesus. The annoying thing was that the only person she really wanted was Vlad. There was still no sign of him.

Brandy walked past the casino and looked at the sea and thought about her life. She liked their loft-style apartment, and she enjoyed the time she was able to spend in the gym, but she really liked the sea and the sun. They should travel more, she decided. After another ten minutes she realised she was getting herself wound up about nothing, and decided to return to the hotel and the pool, where she could torture the other guests with her bikini battle. It was as she turned that she noticed something. It was Vlad's black four wheel drive car. At least, she was fairly sure it was his. There were plenty of similar cars parked nearby, but this one possessed a drug dealers vulgarity at odds with the rest. She walked up to it.

There were times when she hated the car as much as Vlad loved it. It was the fact that he did love it that irritated her. She had to compete against a machine. She couldn't believe he'd paid over a hundred grand for the bloody thing and here it was. She wondered why it wasn't in the hotel carpark and what it, and very probably Vlad, were doing here. The car had come between them on a number of occasions, the last of which had prompted a big argument. It had got so bad Vlad had given her the spare key. It was more symbolic, as he had not the slightest intention of letting her drive it, as it had over four hundred horse power and had cost him a fortune.

And Brandy knew this. She opened her little bag and, sandwiched between one of Vlad's credit cards and her mascara, was a chunky black key the mere proximity of which had already opened the doors. It made a little 'plip' noise. This was very definitely Vlad's car. She pulled the door handle and the door swung open.

Brandy looked in as a little battle began to stir within her. She wasn't blessed with much of a conscience, but she knew how much Vlad loved the car, and how annoyed he'd be. But she'd spent some time looking for him and she shouldn't have to, and the hotel wasn't that close. Brandy got in the car. Her plan was to wait for Vlad. That would show him. She'd not sat in the driver's seat before. It was high and commanding. She ran her hands round the wheel and waited.

Three minutes later it was obvious that one of the qualities that Brandy was not equipped with was patience. It was for that reason that she'd not had a calling for the caring professions. She liked her life to be a rollercoaster, and the human equivalent of a modern computer game. She looked down and saw a large button marked 'start'. She wondered what Vlad's reaction would be if he found her in the car *and* with the engine running. She pressed the button. The thing whooshed explosively into life. She'd never noticed how much noise it made. She blipped the throttle. The bonnet seemed to buck, as if it was fighting the engine. It was very much like her bikini and her breasts.

Brandy waited another three minutes. It felt like about thirty and, if asked, she'd swear it was all of that. She had been very patient. It was quite warm outside and the air conditioning was cooling her down. A minute later it was no longer cooling her down: it was making her downright cold. Brandy fiddled with the controls. It didn't seem to be having the desired effect, so she fiddled a bit more. While she was there she put on a bit of Beyoncé. She really liked Beyoncé. It was somewhere between adjusting the volume of the music and the air conditioning that she knocked another stick.

"Whoa!" Brandy screamed.

The car was in gear. It lurched forward, but Brandy had this covered. She stamped on the brakes. Except she was sitting slightly to one side, and the pedal she hit was very definitely not the brake pedal. The car vaulted into the air like a leaping springbok.

Chapter Thirty-Seven

Suzy's job was quite well paid, and she was well regarded. She had something she'd always wanted – a career. She'd been lucky with her flat, and had bought herself a nice Mini convertible with a bonus she'd received a year or two ago. While she didn't take the most expensive and lavish Caribbean holidays, she enjoyed some pretty decent trips. She was solvent. She was content with her stuff.

"I think we should put it back," she whispered to Bradley.

They were at work and, now that she'd taken to whispering to him in the office, the rest of the staff had assumed that they'd finally got it together, and had embarked on an affair. Not that either of them had partners, but there was nothing office gossip liked more than a bit of clandestine sexual activity. Suzy had not mentioned Bradley's declaration of undying love. Things were complicated enough.

"Why?" Bradley hissed.

Bradley's considerable collection of designer-tagged suits had come at a price, as had his BMW, and he liked to go out. He went out so much he was rarely sober enough to drive the car and, as his life was so London based, had few places he needed to drive to. But he really loved his BMW. He often referred to it in conversation. It might have been a bit of a seduction crutch. It had upset him when the lease company had taken issue with a matter as trivial as the repayments. They'd taken it away, and it had felt like a child had been removed from him. His apartment was terrific too, way more than he could really afford, which was why he rented it. The battle between assets and liabilities would be a hard fought match that would involve the latter's victory. Bradley really liked stuff.

"Because it's dangerous. You saw what they did to Sam's place," Suzy whispered.

Bradley thought about this, and tried not to think about that Paul Smith suit he'd found himself admiring on the way to work. He'd seen some nice shoes, too. Then there was the car showroom. Gleaming, sparkling with inviting metal and leather. He was conversant with the zero to sixty acceleration times of all the cars he thought were worth being seen in. There had been a really nice Porsche. It was black. The dashboard and the seats were black too, as were the carpets. It was very black. It looked like a big cat, a panther, about to pounce. He wondered what kind of a seduction crutch a Porsche would be.

"How will they know it's us?"

Suzy thought about this. It was true that since she'd seen the cash, she'd even slept in it, there had been a few things that had caught her eye. They weren't crazy things, although there was a rather nice Prada handbag. The only problem was that she wasn't sure what it went with and, when she started thinking about that, it prompted her to look at other expensive labels, which was odd as she wasn't really that interested in designer clothing. It was the lure of the money.

"Someone might have seen us," she said.

"Who?" Bradley said.

Good though his wardrobe was, was it good enough for the kind of man that drives a Porsche? He'd found an old car magazine at the bottom of his desk. He'd taken a quick furtive look, as if it was pornography. It was the picture of a powerboat that had caught his eye, from an advertiser that had gambled that the kind of people who liked fast cars would also like powerboats. It was a good gamble, as was the advertisement for watches. Was he a Rolex or Patek Philippe man?

"There are next door neighbours," Suzy said.

"Are there?"

Bradley had decided that, as he was a Porsche man, he was probably a Rolex man, and if he should make other buying decisions like a Ferrari, then a more discreet watch would be appropriate. He wondered what kind of watch Paul Smith wore. There was probably a Paul Smith watch, which made Bradley wonder if he should commission the Bradley watch. He wasn't sure what it would look like, but it would be big, he was certain of that. It would be designed to say something, and it would need a model name. He gave it a bit of thought and settled on the Bradley Fuckoff.

"Yes, everywhere. Opposite, next door," Suzy said rather more loudly.

Suzy's office door was open, but it had a lock, and it had blinds, and the thought of both had prompted one enterprising colleague to instigate a sweepstake as to whether they'd have sex in the office. Her raised voice had set the whole thing in motion. And then Suzy closed the door. That really got them going.

"Look, I saw those people and they really looked nasty. They ripped Sam's place apart and, if they find him, they will rip him apart, and then they will rip us apart. The money is going back."

Bradley saw the black Porsche fading, the Rolex sliding off and the Paul Smith back on a hanger. There would not be a Bradley watch. This was terrible. He had to do something to repair the situation. He suggested the only thing he could think of.

"Let's have a drink after work and we can talk about it."

Suzy knew the tactic. It would involve mojitos and chasers and, if it hadn't got her into bed, then it probably wouldn't make her yield on this either. But she might need something to sweeten it, and she had a pretty good idea what Bradley wanted.

"A quick drink, just the one, and then we can drive it over and go back to your place," she said putting her hand on his.

It did the trick, not least because it had come out of the blue, like a fighter plane diving out of the cover of the sun, and it made Bradley flush. When he left her office he was surprised to find so many faces pointing his way. Someone even let out a small cheer.

Chapter Thirty-Eight

Sam decided to fight. He had enjoyed the money. He'd grown used to it. He was good at living well and he wasn't going to give it up. His assailants may be big, aggressive and a little bit nasty, but he was made of sterner stuff. He'd give them a run for their money. It was a short lived decision.

"I'll tell you where the money is," Sam pleaded.

Sam was a pretty good photocopier salesman. In fact, he could generally sell most things to most people. He had other skills too, but what he had no facility for was hand to hand combat, or conflict of any kind. This was the end of the road.

"I'll tell you where the money is," Sam repeated, a slight whimpering sound had entered his voice.

"Bloody right you will," the man with the shabby black leather jacket said.

The two of them had grabbed him so tightly that his feet were hardly touching the ground. This was about survival and exploiting opportunities. He needed to separate the nice one from the nasty one.

"You little runt bastard," the other man said.

He had an accent. This was bad. Sam had always imagined that the gatekeeper of hell would have a South African accent with which, slowly, deliberately and sadistically, he would drawl 'welcome to hell'. But Sam was wrong. The gatekeeper would have a Russian accent. It would be rich with subtext and none of it would say things like 'I do charity work' or 'let me look after those kittens'.

"I'm going to break you," the Russian said.

Sam threw fleeting looks up at their faces. They both dwarfed him and neither looked remotely nice. There was no hope that he'd form a bond with his captors. He had to do something soon otherwise he'd end up at the bottom of the sea. Sam tried to think. For reasons that weren't clear his mind suddenly filled with all sorts of thoughts, including the virtues of the Canon XE20 photocopier over the Ricoh P14. Sure, they were both good machines, and it was wise not to forget the HP and the Dell, which were also solid contenders in the marketplace. It depended on whether quality was a greater consideration over speed, or cost per copy. And there were maintenance costs to think about. Sam very nearly asked them about their photocopying requirements when a further, more useful thought, struck him. It might help if he could establish which man was the leader.

"Who's in charge?" Sam asked.

There was no immediate response other than both men tightening their grip on his upper arm, he could no longer think of it as a bicep. It was actually quite painful and Sam was about to point this out when his mind became flooded with other thoughts.

"I am," both the leather jacket and the Russian said.

Had Sam overlooked both the Toshiba and the Sharp? And, of course, there was the daddy, the Xerox.

Then he realised that there was a leadership conflict. Was that exploitable? He had no idea.

"I'll tell you where the money is," Sam said again.

He was fairly sure he'd mentioned this before but, in the circumstances, he thought it could bear some repeating. He looked around. This was broad daylight. There were people milling about. Should he shout something?

"Get in the car first," the Russian said.

Sam hopped along as the Russian strengthen his grip. His hand wrapped comfortably around Sam's bicep. Not that his Russian assailant would recognise the muscle that Sam lifted his arm with as a 'bicep'.

"Did I mention I'll tell you where the money is?"

This was the end of his run. It hadn't been a bad run. There'd been the Russian girls and the Contessa. It had been a great rollercoaster and, if they didn't kill him, or beat him senseless, he'd phone his boss and get back to selling photocopiers. Right at that moment he welcomed the possibility of getting off the rollercoaster. He let mundane thoughts wash over him in an attempt to escape from the unpleasant reality ahead of him.

"Where is it?" the man in the shabby jacket said, ignoring the Russian.

Sam couldn't spill the beans quick enough. If asked he'd have produced a map and drawn a diagram. He would have annotated it in colour too.

"It's in my flat," Sam said.

He wanted to be as cooperative as he could possibly be in the hope that it might lessen the beating, or reduce the risk of death. Or something.

"No it isn't," leather jacket said angrily.

Leather jacket and Russian looked at each other. Gary had been pretty thorough.

"I hid it in the copper cylinder. The water cylinder. It was empty. I mean when I say it was empty, it was empty of water. I wouldn't have put the money in a load of water, that wouldn't have been good," Sam babbled.

The leather jacket and the Russian looked at each other. It made sense. It was possible, resourceful even.

"Over there," the Russian instructed.

Sam could see a demonically black car. It had windows that were tinted as black as the paintwork. Once inside no one would see him. For a second he hoped they had guns. That would be less painful than being beaten to death. Sam prepared himself for the beating, but was distracted by a sudden roar. It came from the demonically black car.

"What?" the Russian said.

They all looked up as the car jumped up over a high kerb and launched itself across a grass verge and towards an ornamental fountain. The Russian looked in horror as his prized, and much polished, black beast bounced over a small stone wall and landed, like a playful hippo, in two feet of water. The Russian ran and wherever the Russian ran, Sam went with him, like a rag doll. When they'd arrived at the fountain the Russian stopped and attempted to take in the enormity of the situation. Sam kept on going and flipped face-first into the fountain. He was under the water. The commotion around him was temporarily silenced and he was only aware of the peaceful bubbling of the water around him. Then he pushed off from the ground, rose into the air and realised that the Russian had released his grip. And Sam ran, but the bottom of the fountain was slippery. There might have been coins. He couldn't tell. He fell and his face slapped the water and he was back in watery silence. It was quite tranquil, but he needed to breathe. He rose out of the water again, slipped again and, on the fourth attempt, made it to the other side of the fountain, and a solid stone wall. With the aid of the wall he vaulted out of the fountain and sprinted. It was surprising how fast he could run with the prospect of death or a beating as an alternative, and it was far faster than the leather jacketed man, who couldn't run at all.

Chapter Thirty-Nine

When Brandy was a little girl her stand out feature was her good looks and, as she grew older, it was accompanied with a body which stood out even further and was almost cartoonish in its unnecessary voluptuousness. Eyes followed her wherever she went and, if anyone didn't know her, they certainly knew of her. It could have presented numerous career opportunities, but she'd never thought that her role on the earth involved a career. She was quite smart, and she diverted that smartness towards a staggering talent for manipulating men. There was almost no end to the things she'd got them to do. Occasionally it was just an academic exercise to see how far they would go. It was power and she liked it. It was a power she frequently deployed with Vlad, completely ignoring his immense size and strength, and that everyone else was shit-scared of him. And that he was a drug dealer.

Not that Brandy would have been attracted to an Anglican vicar or a school teacher, although that might just have been the limitations of her own life. There might be vicars and school teachers out there who would be more than happy to rip off her minimal clothing and ravish her. But most of her previous partners, and it was a sizeable enough number to lie about, had been nightclub owners, bouncers and debt collectors. She was so skilled at bending them to her will that she rarely felt frightened of them. Until now.

"Oh shit," Brandy said, which was very restrained of her.

Vlad was going to kill her. She was sure he was capable of it. It probably wouldn't be the first time. A list of options appeared in her head. She could blame the car. But Vlad loved and trusted the car more than her. She wouldn't get away with it. She could say that she was ill – perhaps she'd had some sort of fit. But Brandy had never suffered a day of illness in her whole life. She was immune to everything, including hangovers. Her robustness was such that she could probably have found a career in repairing nuclear reactors in meltdown. And, if a film was made of that version of her life, there would be numerous gratuitous moments in which she'd get in and out of her protective suit with the most sculpted and minimal underwear.

"Oh shit, shit, shit," she said.

This was bad. She wondered if she could sweet talk Vlad. She'd have to use sex and do that thing that he liked doing, that she wasn't so fond of. But Vlad was going to react like a nuclear reactor in meltdown. In, or out, of her protective suit, she'd be in trouble. Then the solution came to her in a rush. She would have to lie. She got out of the car and fell into the fountain. The ground was slippery with slime and coins and she was wearing very high heels, but she barely faltered. It was worse than she'd thought. Vlad had seen her.

She watched as Vlad lunged at her and she tried to calculate the best lie. She could say that the car had become possessed, or that she'd been kidnapped and the kidnapper had run, or that she'd been abducted by aliens. As Vlad grew closer the expression on his face became clearer, and she sensed the alien abduction plan would not go well. She'd not seen him look as dark and angry as this before.

Brandy ran. Her long legs, made longer by the high heels, set a stride which would have astonished an athlete. Were there a national event for high heel sprinting, she would have been a contender. She ran out of the square and into a side street and then left, and right, into further side streets until she was hopelessly lost.

Chapter Forty

Ashton Hoffman-Lendetta had had a terrible morning. It had started when he'd paid the housekeeper and the gardener. Or rather, he hadn't. The transfer had failed to arrive at its destination, and he'd written some cheques. They'd looked at him dubiously, which was quite an insult. Then they tried to express the cheques which prompted a conversation with the bank in which the bank manager explained, rather impertinently in Ashton's view, that not just was there no money, but he'd climbed the mountain that was his overdraft facility. He'd phoned his agent. That hadn't gone well either.

"No more erections!' his agent had screamed.

There was irony in this, as Ashton had suddenly become quite absurdly priapic. It was a shame Miguel was no longer around, and he could think of little else. He hadn't actually seen a live one in some time, excluding his own, which was less urgent than he would have liked, but absence was making it a good deal firmer. He needed a man. If he could just paint one more final erection from the flesh then, he promised his agent, he'd give them up and move on. His memory was getting pretty hazy, and Ashton was a man who'd seen a good deal of cocks.

"Bugger," he said.

He was in the car. Normally he wouldn't drive, but the staff had walked out. In the good days, the great days, he'd had a chauffeur, but finances had tightened and he'd incorporated it into the gardener's duties.

There were two reasons he'd got in the car. The first was that there was no toilet paper in the house. Either the housekeeper hadn't stocked any, or she'd taken it with her. The other reason was he wanted a man. Worse than that, he *needed* a man. He'd have settled for a boy, but he'd known too many people who'd got into rather nasty trouble. Not that boys were really his thing, although he did have a cut off point at around forty. That was a lot younger than him, and he was getting the feeling he couldn't be choosy. It was why he was in the car.

"Damn," he said, as he drove into a bollard

He'd not driven himself in nearly twenty years and, when he had, he hadn't been very good at it. It involved doing too many things at the same time. Ashton was not a multi-tasker. He couldn't even keep two themes in his head at the same time, which was why he was trapped in his erection collection. He liked the ring of 'The Erection Collection', but his agent had not embraced it. Nor had the public.

"Shit," he said.

There was a hollow dinging sound, which suggested he'd collided with something. He carried on going. He wished there was a man supermarket in which he could push a trolley around and select from a wide range. It didn't seem fair. He was rich and famous, it should be easy.

"Bugger," he said.

He'd bounced over a kerb and remembered that he wasn't actually rich. He was, as his bank manager put it, 'stony broke'. He'd bought the car at his peak. That was quite a long time ago and the car, a big Citroen, was getting a little ragged with age. And that was before he'd got in the driver's seat.

"Hold on," he said and stamped on the brakes.

It had a very sensitive brake pedal, and he smacked his head on the steering wheel. But he'd seen something, or rather someone. It had all the hallmarks of a possibility. At the time of his greatest popularity, men and boys used to hurl themselves at his feet. He tried not to think of what he'd descended to, although he was unaware at this point that he had more descending to do. A young man was running in his direction. He looked familiar. Was he the young man who'd jumped over his garden wall and stolen some of his clothes? He could have painted a fair likeness of the young man's penis, but he wasn't interested in the flaccid. What good was a 'Flaccid Collection?' It didn't even rhyme. He leaned over and threw the passenger door open. It was a long shot, but what did he have to lose?

"Jump in!'

And Ashton was delighted. The young man jumped in. If he'd known it was so easy to pick one up he'd have done so sooner. This was most exciting and, as the young man was so evidently running from trouble,

Ashton stamped on the accelerator pedal. He'd not done that before, but this was like deep sea fishing. He'd caught a live one, and was buggered if he was going to put it back.

His car glanced off a Ferrari, bounced over another kerb, swiped a Range Rover, took the wing mirror off a Bentley, scraped a Maserati, narrowly missed a caravan with the words 'Jesus Saves' on the side, tore off the bumper of a police car, and drove over a scooter before Ashton had it under control. He didn't live far away, but the bumper had become attached to the rear of his car. It took out a blind man and scattered the flowers arranged on the pavement outside a florist.

"Are you okay?"

It was a question that either could have asked of the other, but it was Sam who asked it of Ashton.

"Never better," Ashton said, as the bumper which had attached itself to the rear of his car got caught between the lead of a small dog and its elderly owner.

The old lady was made of stern stuff and held onto the dog, who would have been strangled were it not for the release of the bumper, which shot off the back of the car and through a lingerie shop window and into the crotch of a La Perla clad mannequin. The dog hit the neighbouring jewellery shop window with sufficient force to set the alarm off.

"You're wet," Ashton said.

Ashton knew he should keep his concentration on the business of driving, but he was getting quite excited. He might have been shaking a bit, and that was quite distracting. He turned two more corners without hitting anything and brought the car to a rapid rest.

"Ashton," Ashton introduced himself.

"Sam," Sam said.

Ashton ushered him into the house as quickly as possible and directed him to a basement bathroom. He'd gone through a photographic phase, and this was his darkroom. There was a glass division between the bathroom and the darkroom, as he'd had plans to display, and store, some of his work. It hadn't been used, as his agent had sold his work pretty quickly. That was until he'd embarked on 'The Erection Collection'. They were stacked everywhere.

"Pass me your clothes out and I'll get some dry ones for you," Ashton said.

Sam panicked for a second, but realised he couldn't stay in the wet clothes. It was a compact bathroom with what appeared to be a large window on one side. He pushed the door almost closed and removed his trousers and shirt.

"Grab a towel," Ashton suggested.

Even Sam's underpants were soaking. He took them off too and passed them through the partially closed door, and shut the door. He looked round for a towel.

"Right," Ashton said, but he didn't move.

Something had occurred to Ashton. The key to the bathroom was on the outside. The store and the darkroom were heftily constructed as his work was, at one time, quite valuable. He looked at the key. He wondered if he dared do it. A number of thoughts passed through his head. It was a little crazy. His hands shook as he turned the key, and the lock clicked as the barrels fell in place. His young man wouldn't be able to get out of that. Better still, Ashton would be able to see him through the darkroom window.

"Hello?" Sam said. He shook the door, but it wouldn't open.

Chapter Forty-One

Suzy left the office totally unaware that all eyes were on her. If she'd given it some thought she wouldn't have left with Bradley. That was a dead giveaway. But she was thinking about the money. She was also thinking about the men who had wrecked Sam's flat. Ten minutes later Bradley had them installed in a booth buried in the back of a dark pub. If there was any less light they'd have spilled their drinks. Bradley's plan was twofold, and both folds were obvious.

"This is the only opportunity that we'll ever get to lay our hands on so much dough. We could buy an apartment together, or a villa in Spain together, or a nice cruising boat together," Bradley said.

He was combining the two folds into one strategy and hoped that if he said 'together' enough times, it might do the trick. But Suzy already had her own flat and she liked it that way. She also didn't like Spain and boats made her seasick. There were other issues.

"How will we buy an apartment with the money?" she asked.

"What do you mean how?" Bradley asked.

"You can't just walk into an estate agent with a huge stash of cash," she pointed out.

"Can't you?" Bradley said, although he meant to say 'we.'

"No," Suzy said firmly.

"You mean we have to launder the money?" Bradley asked.

Suzy nodded and took a sip of white wine. She put her elbow on the table and rested her head on her hand, while Bradley, for the first time in his life, thought about how to go about laundering a million quid in cash. Bradley was not a deep thinker and it didn't help that Suzy's blouse had fallen open, and was rewarding him with a direct view of her cleavage. He'd never met a woman who was so unimpressed with him. He was impressed with himself.

"And if we don't get caught because the neighbours have seen us, we will get caught when we try to launder the money."

There was something about Suzy's jiggling breasts that ensured that all Bradley had heard was the word 'we,' which he was fairly sure was said at least four times. It was a good sign as Suzy was all he really wanted. Apart from the money. He wanted that too.

"I saw them," Suzy added. "Two big guys. One had muscles in his arm like your thighs. They looked pretty violent."

Bradley unconsciously stroked his thighs. They weren't *that* spindly. How did she know? Had she been looking at them? The threat of violence was too remote to touch him, but he did see that it would be difficult converting the cash into cars and buildings. An idea came to him.

"Okay, you're right. We can't buy a villa in Spain or a Riva, but we can grab some cash, a small amount, and buy the most expensive and lavish meal of our lives."

The were very few things that Bradley ever said that made sense to Suzy, but there was something in this. They might as well get something out of the experience.

"And then we put the money back?" Suzy asked.

"Yes," Bradley said firmly, although another thought was brewing in his head and he added, "Let's grab a cab."

They finished their drinks and weaved their way put of the pub and into a black cab, which appeared as if it had been bid. They went past Bradley's apartment and Suzy waited in the cab while Bradley went in to fetch the cash. He opened the IKEA bag and took out five hundred pounds. That would be enough for a pretty lavish meal for two. He took another five hundred just in case. And then he thought about the idea that was brewing in his head. It would be late by the time they finished eating. They'd be in the West End of London. What next? A hotel. London hotels weren't cheap and, if they were going to stay in a hotel and cement their relationship or, if not that, have fantastic sex, then it might as well be a lavish hotel. Bradley took another thousand pounds. Of course, they'd want breakfast in bed. That would be nice. And a view would be good. Now that Bradley was giving it more thought it occurred to him that, if it had a view, it might as well have a balcony. They could have breakfast on the balcony. He took another thousand. He'd heard that some hotels had private saunas. They'd want to try that. Bradley had almost made it to the door when he wondered how much a suite would cost.

"What took you?" Suzy asked when he finally made it back to the cab.

Bradley hesitated. He tried to think of a viable reason for why he'd dithered so long. He couldn't. He just shrugged and felt the twenty thousand pounds that was crammed into his pocket. He had great plans for the evening.

Chapter Forty-Two

Vlad couldn't believe it. The car he'd polished to perfection was straddling a stone wall with its nose pressed into a pond of water that was deeper than it looked. There was a nasty mark in the bodywork where it was resting on the wall. He couldn't see the damage to the face of his car.

"How are we going to get it out?" Vlad shouted.

If they dragged it out it would cause even more damage. His mouth had fallen open. He'd worked bloody hard for that car. He'd sold a hell of a lot of drugs. And now look at it. For a second he wanted to cry. Then he looked at Brandy. His face turned black with anger and he lunged at her. Normally when Brandy moved she slunk from one leg to another, rotating her hips and ensuring that her bottom fulfilled the cycle of its fullest movement. Unless a bodybuilding drug dealer was about to kill her. He'd never seen her move so quickly. Vlad tried to get round to the other side of the car, but tripped and landed in the fountain. The bottom was slippery and he fell over twice more. By the time he'd got up Brandy had disappeared.

"Where did she go?" Vlad asked Gary.

"He went that way. He got in a car," Gary said pointing.

Gary hadn't noticed. He'd slipped over too.

"I didn't mean him, I meant her," Vlad said.

Gary shrugged. It took two hours to find a crane and get the car hoisted out of the fountain. The car had some pretty nasty dents in it, but it ran okay.

"Drink?" Gary suggested.

Vlad nodded.

"This is gong to shit," Vlad observed.

Despite the handsome bar, and the glorious view, there was something a little gloomy about them, as they both sat slumped nursing the biggest beers they could buy.

"We've got a choice," Gary said.

Vlad looked up from his beer. He wasn't quite sure what he was mourning. Some part was the cash, a big part; another was the damage to the car, as if it had lost its virginity and would never be the same again. The other part was Brandy, but he wasn't sure if he was mourning her at all. As Vlad hadn't responded, Gary continued.

"Sunday got in an old black Citroen. I think it was a DS. There can't be many like that. We make enquiries and we try and track him down."

Vlad recognised the sense in this. It would be proactive and smart. He just needed another beer. He waggled his beer glass and Gary nodded, as he could see no reason why another beer wouldn't be useful.

"Or, we take his word and head back to London and back to his flat ASAP."

Vlad wasn't sure if he had the energy to jump back in the car again. He needed rest and another beer. His relationship with the car had changed too. Before he'd been dying to give the car some welly but now, with two buckled doors, he felt less inclined. The seals were probably broken and it might make a lot of noise.

"Cheers," Gary said.

The beers arrived with a regularity that didn't trouble Gary, but Vlad was a man who spent a lot of time in the gym. He took supplements that claimed things like 'muscle packing' and 'strength enhancing'. Consequently he didn't drink very much alcohol, but the trauma of events had pushed him into it. Or it might have been Gary, who'd never lifted a weight in his life but, when it came to the consumption of alcohol, was a honed athlete at the very peak of his game. There was no one he couldn't take down. And Vlad, who had now consumed four large beers and some little shot-like things, was moving onto a new phase.

"It doesn't seem fair," he sobbed.

While Gary was very highly qualified when it came to the consumption of alcohol, he was rather less so when it came to dispatching sympathy and advice. But it seemed they were stuck together for a while and he had no choice. Gary very nearly said 'there, there.'

"I mean I worked so hard," Vlad sobbed a little more.

Although Gary had never worked a hard day in his life, he had to point out the flaw in this statement.

"But you sell drugs," Gary said softly, as if he'd suggested Vlad was a librarian.

Vlad lifted his head sharply, which was as much was a surprise to him as it was to Gary.

"I mean, I worked so hard with Brandy."

It was a statement that hung in the air, as it was a further surprise to both of them.

"Did I say Brandy?" Vlad said.

Vlad couldn't believe he'd said Brandy. What was he thinking? He knew he'd have done something violent if she hadn't moved so quickly.

"You did say Brandy," Gary said.

The two men made an uneasy presence in the casually chic bar frequented by stars and millionaires from all round the world, and two large brandies appeared in front of them. Vlad didn't notice and picked his up and began to drink it to take away the pain of his loss. He couldn't believe he was thinking this.

"Are you sure?" Vlad asked.

Vlad needed to check, as his internal thoughts were getting mixed up with his external.

"Oh, yes," Gary said.

It left a silence in which Gary finished his brandy and ordered another with a nod. The bar owner was bracing himself as if a hurricane was approaching.

"I'm sure she'll come back to you," Gary said.

"Are you?" Vlad asked.

Another unpleasant side effect of the alcohol was that Vlad was being introduced to paranoia. He'd never felt that before. Gary could see things spiralling out of control.

"We could do all three things," Gary said and, as Vlad was operating on a delayed service, he laid it out in slightly clearer terms.

"We could find Sunday, and Brandy, and take them back to London, and go straight to his flat."

Put that way it didn't appear as if Vlad had anything to worry about.

"Okay," Vlad said quietly and Gary ordered some coffees.

On the fourth coffee, when Vlad's hands had started to shake, as he also rarely drank coffee, Gary asked the question that had been in his mind for a while.

"Why did you change from Lionel to Vlad?"

Vlad would have pushed his hair back, as he had as Lionel, but his hair had gone with Lionel and, right at that moment, his hands were shaking too much.

"Russians are more frightening than a boy called Lionel from Leytonstone."

Chapter Forty-Three

The bathroom Sam found himself in was spartan. There wasn't a towel, as he'd been promised, and he was beginning to get a little cold. He clutched his crotch. It didn't help much. He was relieved he'd escaped as those men had scared the hell out of him. After a minute or two Sam wondered where the man who'd saved him was. Did he say he was going to get him some more clothes, or dry his own clothes? He couldn't remember.

"Hello?" Sam said.

He shook the door again. It didn't want to open. He assumed it had jammed, as he could see no reason why anyone would want to lock him in a bathroom. He sat on the edge of the bath and waited. It gave him a moment to reflect on the things that had happened to him. For some reason he thought about Derek, or rather what Derek would make of the lurid details, and he smiled. There was the money. If Suzy hadn't dumped him and he hadn't picked up that girl – he struggled to remember her name, and then gave up. But if he hadn't picked up whatever her name was, then he wouldn't be here. Or if he hadn't decided to cook a chicken, which was so far past its eat by date that it was on the verge of decomposition, he wouldn't have had an urgent need to crap, and he wouldn't have stopped where he'd stopped, and he wouldn't have found the money. And if he hadn't blown ten grand at the tables he wouldn't have met the Contessa. The Contessa had been quite a ride. And then there was Ernest and the acolytes. That had been an alarming experience.

"Hello?"

Sam tried the door again. It seemed strange. But then, right at the moment, everything seemed strange. Normality, he reassured himself, wasn't so far away. He'd told them where they could find the money and in a few days he'd be back selling photocopiers. It took another five minutes before Sam began to think something might not be right.

"Hello," he shouted.

His voice bounced back at him. It was a solid prison-like space. He tapped on the wall. It was thick. It was more of a dungeon than a prison. There was a ticking noise next to him. It was the radiator. He put his hand on it. It was getting warmer. It seemed like an unusual time of year to run the heating, but he was grateful for it. He felt a little warmer. Annoyingly he'd dumped his bag outside the bathroom. He tried to peer through the window in the door. He could just see the strap of his bag, but no sign of the man that had rescued him.

"Hey!" he shouted.

Sam was getting a bad feeling. This didn't seem right, because it wasn't right. He got down on his knees and examined the door lock. It wasn't jammed. It was locked. Frying pans and fires were coming to mind, but he couldn't understand what anyone would want from him. He had nothing on him, nothing to give. Or so he thought.

"Are you comfortable?" a voice said.

Chapter Forty-Four

If there was an Olympic event for running in high heels then Brandy would have been a contender. She'd never seen a darker look on Vlad's face. It was worse than when someone had stolen his cash. She was fairly certain he was going to kill her and she had a feeling it wouldn't be the first time for him. She'd run on grass, on tarmac and on cobbled streets, and she was certain she'd lost him. The question was what the hell was she going to do now? Aside from her four inch heels, she had the skimpiest and most minimal of skirts, over a string which contained as much material as the name suggests, and a tee shirt which plunged in every direction. It was clothing that qualified her for few things but, as luck would have it, there was one thing for which she was eminently qualified. She was in a back street.

"Have you come for the audition?" A man asked.

Brandy turned round. The man was in his fifties. He had long grey wavy hair and a vast luxuriant moustache which looked like he was attempting to swallow a small furry animal. He was very proud of it and it projected at right angles to his face. He was flamboyantly dressed and was standing outside a door smoking. He didn't seem that threatening.

"Audition?" Brandy asked.

The man smiled. He had a twinkly-eyed smile and he knew it. He liked working in his industry, as it constantly reminded him that there was life in the old dog yet. He ran his eyes over Brandy, as if they were his hands. He was practically salivating.

"Yes, audition," he said.

He spoke English with an unnecessarily rich French accent. He knew this girl wasn't French. Girls came from everywhere, often from the middle of Europe and English was their second language. That and money.

"Oh," Brandy said, unsure what to say.

He smiled again and cast his eyes lasciviously over Brandy one more time. He couldn't help liking the innocent ones, even when they were dressed to rip a man's genitals off. Actually, he especially liked those.

"Baron's Burlesque Bar," he said and then introduced himself. "Marcel Baron."

Marcel smiled again. His actual name was Jean-Phillipe, but he'd always liked the idea of Marcel and, when he moved from shooting pornographic films into the world of burlesque, it seemed perfect.

"Whose Burlesque Bar?" Brandy asked.

"Baron's," Marcel said, pointing to himself.

He pronounced Baron as Bar-on, and it wasn't his real surname either. He'd toyed with other aristocratic titles such as Lord, Duke and Prince, but Baron had hit the mark and fitted well with Marcel.

"No, I've not come for an audition," Brandy said.

Brandy had only vaguely heard of burlesque, but was fairly sure it involved taking your clothes off. What kind of a girl did he think she was? She was many things, but she wasn't a stripper. It was then that Brandy looked down at her clothing and had a brief and only moment of personal insight. She wasn't *that* far from naked.

"Oh, but you must. You are a very beautiful woman. You are perfection," Marcel said.

He said it in a long slur of Frenchness, with a practiced ease, which would suggest he'd not just said it once, he'd said it a million times. As he spoke his eyes grew tight and almost closed, as if he was on the verge of falling asleep. He was a very laid-back guy.

"Do you think so?" Brandy said.

Despite the continual outpourings throughout Brandy's life regarding her beauty and physical attributes, she never tired of hearing it. She was a beautiful girl, wasn't she?

"I could put together a very beautiful act for you. Very tasteful. Long pink feathers, sequins. Very beautiful," Marcel said.

Marcel liked to pepper most of his sentences with 'very beautiful,' and could see that he was slowly reeling her in. He wondered if he could make her grateful enough. The itching had cleared up, he was ready to go again.

"Do you think so?" Brandy said.

Marcel didn't know that Brandy was a girl with no more clothes than the few square inches she was clad in, no money, no passport and on the run from her violent Russian drug dealer boyfriend. She didn't have that many options.

"Yes, it would be very beautiful," Marcel said and hurled his cigarette down with Gallic disdain.

He turned to the door behind him, which was the stage door to the rear of the club, and he held it enticingly open for Brandy, like a Venus flytrap.

"After you," Marcel said, his eyes twinkling.

Despite her difficult situation, and perhaps to her credit, Brandy hesitated. Marcel had expected this. It was normal. At this point he would bring out Brenda. Brenda was an old pro in every interpretation of the word and she looked after the girls. She ran the show and had been fiddling Marcel out of thousands for years. But, before Brenda, he had one more enticement.

"You are so beautiful you'll make three, maybe four, even five hundred a night."

Brandy had little idea what was required of her, but she was a girl who very much liked the sound of money. She'd had a stab at a few things, but hadn't found much that had focused her mind. Brandy wasn't good at doing things that didn't interest her, such as answering phones. Her work life had never come together, as she'd have liked, and then she'd met Vlad and working seemed less important. But Vlad was no longer in her life.

"Five hundred?" Brandy gulped.

When Brandy wanted to buy something, and it was priced at three hundred and ninety nine, she would only see the three hundred. With possible earnings she was taking the opposite view. She could earn five hundred a night. She looked in through the open door. It didn't look hostile. It felt like theatre, like show business, like Broadway. Brandy couldn't help feeling excited. She stepped in. She had a career ahead of her.

Chapter Forty-Five

Suzy opened her eyes. She couldn't believe it. She closed them again. Bradley opened his eyes and he couldn't believe it either. He'd finally got her. He'd never put so much effort into anything. He'd wined, dined, chatted, been attentive and enraptured by her every word. It had cost a fortune. It wasn't technically his fortune, but he didn't want to bog himself down in details. It was a beautiful suite, huge and overlooking Hyde Park, and the bed was large and luxurious. And he was in it with Suzy. He turned and snuggled up to her. This would be the moment when she declared her undying and fully reciprocated love. He snuggled closer, it was a very big bed, and she turned to him. He smiled. Despite his love for her, he couldn't help noticing that her breath smelled like there had been a death followed by a decomposition. It was normal, he thought, many people had unsavoury morning breath.

"Darling," he said softly.

He'd never said 'darling' before, but they were in bed together and now seemed an appropriate moment to introduce it into their lovers' vocabulary. He'd never said 'darling' to anyone. He'd never wanted to either. This was how great relationships start, he thought. He imagined them, in their eighties, being interviewed and finishing each other's sentences, and brandishing words like 'darling.'

"Darling," he whispered again.

He was getting quite good at using the word. He could see her trying to mouth some words, but nothing came out other than a blast of air which could have stripped wallpaper. Despite the rancid nature of her breath it made him think about the house they'd have together in readiness for the two children he thought they should also have. Probably a Jake and a Chloe, but obviously this would have to be discussed. Then he pictured her heavily pregnant and him hanging wallpaper. He'd not hung wallpaper before, but imagined it wouldn't be too difficult, and he could probably find a YouTube video on the subject.

"Agh," Suzy grumbled.

He pictured for a second a fluttering of Disney-like butterflies singing joyfully in her presence. Her grunt was followed by another rush of air, which might have claimed a few of the imaginary butterflies. Bradley had enjoyed quite a few encounters that were quite varied, including gender, in their makeup, but he'd never come across quite such alarming breath. It made him love her all the more. It was cute, although he thought he might have to get up and open a window. But he didn't want to leave his snuggled position.

"Darling," he muttered once more.

He couldn't think of any other term of endearment other than darling. Should he make one up? He thought for a second and wondered how she'd react to something like Honeysuckles. Maybe it was too soon. One thing he was sure of was that it wasn't too soon to have sex again. Not that he wanted Jake or Chloe right now. He just wanted sex.

"Honeysuck," he whispered.

He panicked. He hadn't quite fully committed to the word honeysuckle and had petered out at the end. He hoped she hadn't just heard the 'suck' part of the word. That wasn't his intention. Not that he'd mind. He began to get quite excited at the thought and redirected his thoughts to the children they'd yet to have. He'd have to buy one of those people carriers. He didn't know much about people carriers and their nought to sixty times, or if they even had one. He imagined that people carriers would be cheaper than the BMW that the lease company had taken away. He hoped so as he'd heard that children were quite expensive.

"Ohhh," Suzy said with apparent agony.

It was another exhalation which would have proved fatal for small furry animals, as well as butterflies, but Bradley didn't dwell on it. The meal had been nigh on a thousand pounds. He'd ordered champagne and the finest wine and brandy. It was rich, and might explain the nature of her breath. There had been very few of Bradley's seductions in which the object of his desire had been entirely sober. Suzy clearly hadn't been. The hotel was inspired. She had literally fallen into his arms.

"Darling," he said, a little louder and with a nudge.

He'd reverted to the safer ground that was 'darling'. But he was getting pretty impatient. He really was ready to go. He wondered if it would be acceptable to ask her to brush her teeth. She might have to floss too. The bathroom had quite a few beautifully packaged products lined up and ready to be stolen. He didn't think they included mouthwash. Was it socially acceptable to say 'darling, could you brush your teeth, floss and use mouthwash?' He doubted it. It might, he thought, be better to take her from behind. He had to think about something else.

"Hey," he said, shaking her.

Of course they'd be the kind of couple who'd have dinner parties for all their mutual fully coupled-up friends. They'd be pretty cosmopolitan about it with a spattering of ethnicity and, obviously, there'd be at least one gay couple. And they would be incredibly liberal if Jake or Chloe announced they were gay. He thought it unlikely he'd share a joint with them, though. There was liberal and there was poor parenting. Although perhaps he might in return for top 'A' level results. Did modern parents do that kind of thing? There was a louder grunt from Suzy that marked consciousness. She turned to him and he was delighted to discover that whatever had been troubling her alimentary canal had been exorcized from her body. Her breath, if not actually sweet, wasn't too bad. He wouldn't have to ask her to brush, floss and gargle. Or take her from behind. He'd be able to see her face writhing in the pleasure and ecstasy. He watched her eyes open slowly, lazily. He could see them focusing on him. It was hard for him to interpret the look that followed. A more objective observer might have called it surprise or even panic.

"What the fuck?" Suzy said with, and this would be the most accurate description, horror.

Chapter Forty-Six

"He can't go anywhere. We've got his passport and about twenty grand in cash," Gary said.

Gary was still holding Sam's bag, and consequently the cash, and Vlad hadn't torn it off him. It was an exercise in trust and it was going quite well. But Vlad was going through a new phase and it was a first for him. He was feeling morose.

"Nothing's going right," Vlad muttered.

They'd spent all morning trying to track down the battered black Citroen but France, and its richer principality, Monaco, was not short of them. Now that they were looking they seemed to be everywhere. Gary's feet were tired and his stomach was rebelling.

"Let's have lunch," Gary said.

Vlad nodded lethargically and Gary steered him to a bistro with tables and chairs sprawled across the pavement, which meant that Gary could light up a fag. He was finding himself in the unlikely role of counsellor and, as Gary's life had not featured one relationship that hadn't failed, it was clearly not his area of expertise. He tried to change the subject back to the matter that had brought them there.

"Sunday can't get back into England, they're pretty hot on passports now, we can go straight back to his flat and grab the money. I'm certain he was telling the truth and it makes sense."

"I mean," Vlad said, suggesting his mind was elsewhere, "when I first met her I knew she was a bit special. I mean not just the looks. I knew she was special. Then there's the body, but it's not just the body. Although it is a hell of a body. Did you notice the body?"

Gary was forced to acknowledge that he had, indeed, noticed Brandy's body and it was quite special, but Vlad hadn't noticed that he'd noticed.

"I just knew she was special," Vlad continued with a hint of a sob.

Gary responded in the only way he knew how. "Beer?"

Vlad seemed to nod, although it may just have been his head floating in a semi-catatonic state. Gary wasn't going to ask again, and ordered two beers. He lit a cigarette, which the old Vlad would have objected to, but the new Vlad didn't notice. Vlad had descended deep into his own thoughts. Brandy had accused him of loving the car more than her and, before she left him, she may have had a point. He *did* love the car and he loved his loft apartment. He liked stuff. Of course he did. He wasn't a college professor lecturing on ethics, he was a drug dealer. But he was a drug dealer who was thinking of getting out of the business. Although it was possible that all drug dealers kidded themselves that that was the case.

"Steak?" Gary said who was finding the morose silence a little uncomfortable.

Vlad's head shook enough, although it might have been from his inner debate, rather than a desire to eat beef, for Gary to take it as a yes and order for both of them. Vlad also liked his muscles, but not so he could pick up heavy objects, or because he could intimidate people, although they were frequently deployed that way, but because, they too, were like a status symbol. A reason to be taken seriously. A man who has got somewhere in life. A brutal no nonsense, no-shit, arse-kicking kind of man. Who was really upset because his girlfriend had left him.

"Pepper sauce?" Gary asked.

The waiter stood nervously. There was tension in the air. He was a professional waiter, not the kind that was just waiting at tables until a great acting job came along, and he'd seen fights flare up. He could recognise a bad sort and this pair were so bad there'd been an argument as to who should serve them. He'd lost.

"I mean Brandy!" Vlad suddenly wailed.

For a second the waiter hesitated and wondered whether he would like it with the more traditional mushroom and brandy, but thought better of it and left to speak to the chef, while Vlad had a huge dawning realisation. Yes, he liked stuff. The car and the apartment, and he'd liked Brandy by his side as a status symbol. People looked. They admired. They lusted and were envious. Vlad had acquired Brandy in the same way he'd acquired his black four wheel drive car. Not from a showroom, but not far off and, unlike the car, he might not be able to return to the showroom and order another, because Brandy was special. He knew that now.

"She doesn't have any money on her and she doesn't have a passport. She can't have got far," Gary said.

Gary had given up trying to redirect Vlad's mind to the matter of the cash, which was what had taken them there, and brought the subject back to Brandy. They were gong to have to find Brandy as well, or they'd be moping around all day.

"We'll find Brandy too. She might have gone back to the hotel room. She might be waiting on the bed, like wearing nothing, not that she wears *that* much. Anyway, waiting for you," Gary said.

Gary was getting a little bogged down in the image of picturing Brandy with even less clothes than she was accustomed to wearing and Vlad was thinking that, while he liked other men to lust after her, he didn't want her to show everything. Her full nakedness was exclusively for him and no one else, even if it appeared that her body, and her clothes, were in constant conflict with each other. He thought about that struggle.

"What have I done?" Vlad said, although it was more Lionel than Vlad.

Gary would have been losing his patience, but he'd ordered a second beer and the steak was really good. He'd never tasted a sauce like it before. Vlad was eating without noticing either the sauce, or the beef, and his shoulders were slumping lower and lower. Gary decided he had to shake him up a bit.

"You're acting like a love-sick teenager!" Gary shouted.

The restaurant went silent, but Vlad didn't notice. He knew it was true.

"You're right," he sobbed, "I do love her."

And neither Vlad nor Lionel had ever loved anyone before.

Chapter Forty-Seven

"Take your hands away!"

Sam's day had entered a surreal phase. Which was no surprise, as he was in the presence of a famous surrealist. Although Ashton was a surrealist who'd drifted back to realism. It had been a conflict between dreams and reality, and he'd grown fed up of dreaming. He wanted a real cock. The good news was he'd bagged one and, although he hadn't intended to, he'd locked it up and, more by luck than planning, he had a very good view of him.

"What do you want?" Sam asked.

Sam wasn't particularly inhibited – he had only recently ran naked across a roof, and a number of gardens – but his natural response was to cup his genitals. Once he'd discovered that the door to the bathroom was locked from the outside, and he was naked and trapped, he tightened his grip. Then the lights went on.

"I want, I want," Ashton said, struggling to articulate exactly what it was he wanted.

And when the lights had gone on Sam discovered that the wall to the bathroom wasn't a wall at all, but a glass panel. A window. That was quite troubling for him, but what was really troubling was what he could see the other side.

"I want these," Ashton said and held his hand out.

Through the glass panel Sam could see paintings. There were a great many of them because, as Ashton's agent had pointed out, they weren't selling. Such was their scale and detail, the vein work was quite exemplary, it took a few moments for Sam to recognise the subject. Sam didn't say a word, then Ashton found his voice.

"Cocks! Dicks! Penises! Wangers! Pricks! Dongs!" Ashton shouted.

This would be Ashton's final picture, he'd decided. It would mark the end of his obsession and the end of this phase of his career. But the subject of that final picture was hidden behind Sam's hands.

"Take your hands away!" Ashton yelled.

Ashton had set up his canvas and had mixed some paint. He could see from the rest of Sam's naked body his general pallor but, as he'd yet to see the penis, he could only guess the colour. They were generally redder and darker, although there was often a colour change from flaccid to erect, and he needed to be prepared for that too. He had his vein brush ready, but he generally found that younger penises were only very lightly veined.

"Will you let me go?" Sam asked.

It wasn't much of a plea in the circumstances, but Sam didn't know what else to say. He wasn't sure if this was worse than the two big men who'd tried to kidnap him. It was certainly weirder.

"The thing is, the thing I want," Ashton began, "what I'm after."

Sam waited to hear what he was after, but Ashton was struggling to express it and then he found the solution. He pointed at the pictures. And Sam got it.

"You want me to get an erection?" Sam said, incredulous.

"Please, if you would," Ashton said, delighted that they were finally making progress.

"But..." Sam said.

If someone had pressed a million quid into his hand, and he knew what that looked like, in return for a first class erection, he wasn't sure he could manage it. If they pointed a gun at his head, and he wasn't far away from knowing what that felt like either, then he doubted he could encourage any blood down there. The blood was already employed elsewhere, mostly terrifying him. He'd have to explain. He had to try and make a connection with his captor.

"I don't think I can. It doesn't work like that," Sam explained.

Ashton understood. It didn't work like that for him either, although he did find that a handful of Viagra often helped. It was this thought that prompted a further thought.

"Do you think a drink will help you relax?" Ashton said.

He said it as if they'd met in a club, and had gone back to his house together with the prospect of having sex with mutual consent. Sam didn't know what to say and Ashton, who was unaware of the bizarre nature of the situation, although he was traditionally a surrealist, took it as affirmation.

"Gin and tonic?" Ashton suggested as he disappeared upstairs.

Sam had a few moments, alone, to think about how he was going to make his escape. He needed a weapon, or something solid, with which he could break the glass. He put his weight against it, but it didn't seem to flex much. He wondered if he could kick it and, if he did, whether he'd damage his foot. He wouldn't get far with a bleeding foot. He might even cut an artery. Things had a habit of going from bad to worse, and that would be worse. If he gave him what he wanted would he let him go? Sam suspected he might, but he didn't think he could give him want he wanted. A second later Ashton returned with the gin and tonics. He'd even figured out how he was going to pass the drink to Sam. He knelt down and removed an air vent.

"Cheers," Ashton said.

Sam looked at the gin and tonic. It was fizzing invitingly, and God knows he needed a drink. He picked it up.

"Cheers," Sam said and took a swig.

Chapter Forty-Eight

Suzy was at work. It was a rare day in which there was nothing urgent to do, and the office was as quiet, and peaceful, as a village cricket match. Normally she really savoured days like this. It was a time to drink coffee and exchange gossip at the water cooler. It was a good day to take a longer lunch and even indulge in a glass or two of wine. But the silence was putting her on edge. She was avoiding Bradley and he was avoiding her.

"What went wrong with you and Bradley?"

It was Fi. Fi liked to keep abreast of all the office politics and, if required, could provide a five minute summary of who was doing what, although it was mostly who was doing who.

"Nothing," Suzy lied.

"You've got to be kidding me," Fi said. "You're crawling around like you're ducking shrapnel and he's practically silent and the other end of the office."

The problem was that Suzy did work with Bradley. It couldn't go on for long. She couldn't believe she'd slept with him. What was she thinking? She'd got caught up in a tidal wave of spending the money, and had gone from an excellent meal to an excellent hotel. A fabulous hotel. She had never stayed in a hotel for work, or for any other practical, prosaic reason. Hotels were for romantic assignations and, as she knew that, she should have seen him coming. She wished she hadn't thought that, as an image of his contorted face came to mind. And his breath. He had terrible breath.

"I'll talk to him," Suzy said hurriedly, and turned to something which she hoped looked very urgent.

Fi took the hint and drifted away in the direction of the photocopier room. She really was a gossip predator. Suzy liked Bradley but, she now knew for certain, she really didn't fancy him. Not one bit. His passion for her was a little disarming. It might have been that that had taken her along. It was very hard not to like someone who so obviously liked you. But there were so many details that made her feel a little queasy. The hairs on his face seemed to jut out in a spiky and unpleasant way. That brought to mind the first kiss. She should have put a stop to it then. It was strangely slobbery, and there was too much saliva involved. There were other things like strange boil-like moles on his chest. And then there were his toenails. She stopped herself thinking about the toenails, and then she remembered his breath. They'd eaten the same things, why was his breath so toxic? What *was* she thinking? Maybe it was the money.

"Money," Suzy suddenly said.

She'd forgotten about the money. How could she have forgotten about a million or so quid? But she had. She'd got out of that hotel room, as if her vagina had been on fire and she was heading for a swimming pool. She'd been so desperate to leave she'd left behind her bra and knickers. The knickers were only cheap, and he could keep them as a trophy for all she cared. The bra, on the other hand, had been specially fitted and was expensive, and one of the few bras she owned that was both comfortable and sort of sexy. She'd have to ask him to give it back to her. Suzy realised she'd forgotten about the money again. She needed to speak to him. She picked up the phone.

"Bradley, can you come to my office, please," she said without waiting for a response.

She could see him moping towards her like a wounded animal. She was going to have to give the it's not you, it's me speech. Then ask him about her bra. That would do it. Then she remembered the money.

"Yes," Bradley said.

His damaged pride was oozing from him in such quantity that it risked staining the carpet.

"We need to talk," Suzy said.

Bradley was an optimist, but even he knew that this wasn't the precursor to the make up speech. She'd made her feelings pretty obvious when she'd left the hotel room, as if she'd just shared a bed with nuclear waste. He knew he should accept it, but he couldn't hide his disappointment.

"We're just not compatible that way," Suzy said.

For a second Bradley's optimism returned. His mistake had been to attempt to seduce her while she was inebriated. If she'd been sober this wouldn't have happened. Then he ran though the words she'd just said and saw that there was nothing he could do. He slumped a little.

"Also," Suzy said slowly, "if you happen to have my bra."

Bradley slumped a little further. He'd hoped there'd be some spoils. Something to remind him of one of the finest evenings of his life up until the point that Suzy had opened her eyes. Or maybe a few moments before that when she let out a few alarming breaths. She had terrible breath.

"Yes," he said, as if his mother had just asked him to tidy his bedroom.

"And we have to work together," Suzy reminded him.

"Yes," he said, as if his father had asked him to cut the grass as well.

"Smile," Suzy said.

Bradley smiled, as if electrodes had been attached to his testicles.

"I'll make it up to you," Suzy said.

Bradley gave her a slightly lascivious grin.

"I'll try and make it up to you," Suzy corrected herself.

Bradley grunted and got up and Suzy had another thought. It was a bolt from the blue. She missed Sam. He didn't have strange jutty beard hair, or weird boils on his chest, or strange toenails, or bad breath. She hadn't realised how lucky she'd been. She wondered where he was, and what he was doing, when something else occurred to Suzy. Bradley had nearly left the room.

"Bradley!" she said sharply.

He turned and faced her, his face showing surprise.

"The money!" she hissed. "Did you put the money back?"

There was a pause. It was a long pause in which there was enough space to back a security van. Any more space and it could have accommodated a brace of police cars too.

"Not yet," Bradley said, and disappeared into the office.

Chapter Forty-Nine

"I just need to see it in the flesh, and then I'll paint it, and that will be that."

Sam would have struggled to explain his current position to Suzy, or anyone else. Some men had looked intent on killing him. This man just wanted him to get an erection. He'd been very persistent, and Sam was trying. He was really trying. He had his back to Ashton. He needed *some* privacy. But, despite the fact he woke up most mornings with an erection, it was proving rather elusive.

"I might need some help," Sam said.

"I can..." Ashton said, offering his hand.

"That's not what I meant," Sam said quickly.

Ashton sighed. It was just his luck. How had he managed to bag the only young man incapable of getting it up? He wouldn't even let him see it, which was annoying, as it would help him to get an idea of colour and form. It was also annoying, as he'd crushed three viagra pills into the gin and tonic. The boy should be positively priapic.

"Okay," Ashton muttered, and went upstairs.

He could sort of understand that the young man may not be into other men – he'd heard there were people like that – and he wondered how he could find something suitably stimulating. He'd heard that the Internet was rich with pornography, but the most technological Ashton became was putting batteries into a massage device Michael had insisted they buy. It was more commonly thought of as a sex toy and he was pretty certain Michael had taken it with him. But he did have a computer and, for occasional emails, wifi. His agent had given him a portable machine with a piece of fruit on the back. It was in his desk. Ashton found it and looked around for a button marked 'on.' Then he gave up and stabbed buttons at random. It did the trick as the thing lit up. He found a page which invited him to search for things. His mind went blank again.

Ashton's memory of pornography, particularly heterosexual pornography, was rooted in the seventies. He'd shared a flat with a young actor whose appetite for women and sex was voracious. The actor, now on his fifth marriage, had a stack of video tapes, which he watched when he wasn't actually having sex. Ashton tried to recall the titles. He remembered they favoured alliteration. One sprung to mind and he tapped it in. Astonishingly he found it. Ashton hurried down into the basement with the laptop.

"Here, watch!" He commanded.

Sam looked at the slightly fuzzy image. The men wore their hair long and possessed large, droopy moustaches. They might have worn flared trousers were they not naked. There was an awful lot of activity before the title appeared, 'Hot, Horny and Hellbent on Humping.'

They watched it together in what would have been silence were it not for the series of grunts and moans which accompanied the action and then, as the final credit lifted, the action stopped and the story began. The men *were* wearing flared trousers. The title gave no clue to the possibility of a narrative, but what followed was an insight into the aspirations of the director. He'd convinced himself that art and pornography weren't mutually exclusive and, by peppering the film with unusual camera angles and dappled lighting, it might disguise the horrendous dialogue which the appalling acting only made more painful. In this way he would eventually be recognised as the true artist he was, but the director did not know what the future held. As it turned out he had prison and rehab to look forward to, followed by rehab and prison. This was his finest work. Ten minutes later, after being subjected to dialogue so leaden that even Ashton had lost his erection, Sam made a suggestion.

"You can fast forward it," he said.

"You can?" Ashton asked.

Sam pointed to a bar at the top of the screen, but Ashton struggled with hands shaking with irritation, and frustration, to muster the required hand eye coordination to put one on the other. Fortunately another title came to mind. He opened another page and tapped it in.

"This will be better," Ashton declared.

Sam looked with interest. He knew he had to make a decision. It felt like he was defusing a bomb. He was going to have to do this, if not for queen and country, for himself. He gripped his penis and prepared himself for the opening scenes. Although the story that was to follow was quite different, the film began in much the same way showcasing the highlights. Sam concentrated and the words, *Glorious Geisha Girls Give Oily Massages,* appeared. For a couple of minutes it was quite encouraging, with a substantial number of naked, entangled people and then it launched into a plot that was more convoluted than the writhing mass of people. After a while Ashton tried fast forwarding it, but he kept landing on moments after the action had finished and more bad dialogue had begun. Finally he found a scene in which there was distinctly more action than talk.

"Excellent," Ashton said.

They watched with different levels of interest. For Ashton it was anthropology, and for Sam it was desperation. He could see the images of beautiful women writhing helplessly over each other, and the oil was a nice touch, it really brought the breasts alive and gleaming beautifully. He just couldn't connect with it. It was accompanied by a lot of unnecessary grunting and moaning, which seemed disproportionate to the amount of stimulation being provided, and tended to suggest simulation rather than the real thing. Sam never knew he could be so picky and he tried to encourage his blood to circulate in his genitals, but it seemed reluctant.

"Too slow?" Ashton said, who'd grown bored. "Let me try another."

Another title had appeared in his head. He was amazed he hadn't thought of it earlier. It was entitled *Big Boys Bashing Big Boobs*.

"Oh," Sam said.

The boobs were indeed big, quite massive, and they too were oiled. He thought if he got out of this he might do more to explore oil in his sex life. It made him think about Suzy, which was unexpected. He'd certainly massaged her, but had he used oil? He couldn't remember. But something was happening. There was growth. Then he checked out the film and found the other part of the alliteration. The big boys were entirely as billed. Do penises grow that big? He wanted to say he doubted it when one of the big boys responded enthusiastically to the big boobs and made quite a mess on them. If it wasn't real, it was certainly very realistic, and whatever had begun to happen had stopped happening.

"Another gin and tonic?" Ashton said, who was going quite red in the face.

Sam watched Ashton leave. There was no question *he* was enjoying it. Sam sat down on the toilet. What the hell was happening with his life? He rested his head in his hands and looked down at his extraordinarily flaccid penis. It was receding faster than the Italian army, and it had work to do to get him out of this place. Then Sam noticed something glint in the corner. It was near the door and it looked like a key. He got up. It *was* a key. He picked it up and tried it in the door. It clicked. The door was unlocked. He heard Ashton coming down the stairs. He wouldn't have long.

"A nice fresh gin and tonic," Ashton declared and leant down in the corner of the neighbouring room and passed it through the vent.

Sam didn't waste any time. He opened the door, ran through and closed the neighbouring door, and ran.

"What?" Ashton screamed, "No, no," he whimpered.

Five minutes later Sam was out of the house and running towards more trouble.

Chapter Fifty

"She's not in the room, or by the pool, or the lobby, or at the beach, or in the shopping centre, or the casino," Vlad said.

Gary tried not to sigh. He was certainly getting irritated by the situation. They'd spent the day looking for Sunday and Brandy, although he was getting the distinct impression he was looking for Sunday, while Vlad was looking for Brandy. He needed to get back to London and rip Sunday's flat apart. He'd been thinking about leaving Vlad to it, but there would be issues with that.

"It's getting late, let's get something to eat," Gary suggested.

One part of Gary didn't want to cross Vlad. Although Vlad didn't *sound* like he could do the business, what with all the whining about Brandy, he looked like he could, and that was a little worrying.

"Yeah, good idea mate," Vlad said.

Vlad hadn't quite dropped the Russian accent, but it had become quite slight, as if he could be his true self with Gary. Vlad's emotions had been oscillating all day and they were both getting tired of it. But despite that, and despite all the hassle, Gary was growing to actually quite like Vlad, which was strange for both of them.

"How about here," Gary said.

It was quite a chic place with dappled lighting and, as it had been warm, Gary had left his leather jacket in the hotel. Vlad had lent him a shirt, as Gary had ripped his in the tussle with Sam. Vlad had found it a little odd that he hadn't packed more than one shirt, as he'd packed several. It was a smart shirt and, without the jacket, Gary looked, if not actually good, somewhere close to the border of respectable. The dappled lighting helped.

"Can we sit here?" a woman asked.

"Sure," Vlad said.

Vlad hadn't noticed the two women. But he was wearing a tight, short-sleeved linen shirt, and there was some rippling going on, which had caught their attention. Although the ambience was being kind to them too, as a harsher light might describe them as middle age, possibly even on the ripe side of middle age. But they were handsome, buxom good-time girls and Gary was delighted at this unexpected turn of events. They introduced themselves.

"This is Trish and I'm Sal," Sal said.

They offered their hands for shaking and Vlad went first.

"You have big hands," Trish observed.

Vlad was more practised at knowing where an evening like this might lead and, after the agonies of searching for Brandy, he was up for it. It wasn't as if he hadn't tried.

"We could hear you speaking English," Sal said.

"What brings you to Monte Carlo?" Trish countered leaning on the table slightly.

The bad light worked both ways and, now that they were close, there were slight reservations regarding Gary, but they were the kind of predatory pair who wouldn't let too much light get in the way of a good time.

"We're here on business," Vlad said.

Gary liked the sound of that, as he'd never been anywhere on business, let alone somewhere as exotic as Monte Carlo.

"What business are you in?" Trish asked.

She wasn't really concerned what business they were in, although a large yacht in the harbour would be a welcome bonus. Not that they required the aphrodisiac of wealth.

"Money," Vlad said and, for the first time in a while, he smiled.

It occurred to Vlad that Brandy had been very high maintenance and that might have been taking its toll on him. He needed to chill, and tonight would be a good opportunity.

"And what brings you here?" Gary asked.

Trish and Sal looked at each other. They worked on the cosmetics counter in a large London department store and, during the day, they were the picture of respectability. Come nightfall they were something else. They'd been conducting a tour of France's swinger clubs and had decided to dip a toe in Monaco. So far it had been a little too tame for them.

"A holiday," Sal said.

They'd decided that their activities may appear too sordid for the average man, although Gary, who was riding on Vlad's coattails, wouldn't have cared. He'd not had an encounter with a member of the opposite sex for such a long time he'd given up trying. Hope had disappeared long before that. This was more like the drug dealer's life he'd hankered for.

"Excellent, let's make it a great one then," Vlad said, regaining his stature.

The meal romped along nicely accompanied by a few, but not too many, bottles of wine. Vlad paid with a wad of cash, but Trish and Sal weren't interested in the money.

"I know a place we can go," Trish suggested, and they tripped out of the restaurant and into a bar arm in arm, and as if they'd known each other forever.

The bar was a large open space with wood floors and a curved polished bar with brass jewellery, and an array of illuminated optics containing spirits. It, too, was restrained with the lighting, although there were other reasons for that. They took a table and Vlad ordered cocktails. Gary smiled at the girls. He smiled at Vlad, and he smiled at the waitress, who had appeared with the drinks. Gary was not known in the police station as the 'old smiler,' or 'smiley Gary' or any other smiling variation, and his face rarely cracked into anything quite so joyful as a smile. This was because he rarely found himself having a good time. But today was different. And then the lighting dropped a little more and spot lights were trained on a curtain in the corner of the room. There was a small stage he hadn't noticed. A leg appeared from the curtain. It was long, smooth and naked. A small band struck up, and even more of the leg came into view until it was accompanied by the rest of the body. A mostly naked body of, as a compère had drawled, a very beautiful girl. If this was sordid, then Gary was all for it. A minute later girls were writhing against each other.

"Nice, eh?" Sal said.

There were moments, when men weren't available, when Trish and Sal might enjoy a little cross-gender sex. They had few limits, and they were more than capable of recognising an attractive girl.

"Yes," Gary said, trying to keep his eyes from disappearing onto stalks.

The girls were quite athletic and admirably supple and Vlad was also having a good time. It was just what he needed to forget about Brandy and move on. There were times when he had to remind himself he was a tough-talking drug dealer, as his internal conversations were becoming increasingly sensitive. Watching naked girls was helping him get back to more normal territory.

"Isn't this great," Gary said, beaming.

As is the way with all these places their alarmingly expensive cocktails were replaced with more alarmingly expensive cocktails but, as Vlad had cash in his pocket, and they were both having a good time, it didn't seem to matter. It was an act, a little later on, that prompted nostalgic thoughts in Vlad. She was a tall girl who'd wrapped herself in two pink feathers, which just allowed a discreet glimpse of occasional nakedness. By the standards of the previous acts it was quite tasteful. She had legs that were very much like Brandy's. She moved around until she found a low table on which she lay back, straightened her legs and very slowly opened them. It would have been very tasteful, but she dropped a feather. Vlad couldn't help noticing that her pubic area was trimmed in a very particular way, which further reminded him of Brandy. He'd assumed that it was a cut that Brandy had arrived at on her own, and not a fashionable way in which many young girls like to wear their pubic hair. If the girl hadn't dropped the other feather, she might have been new to this, Vlad wouldn't have had a clear view of her breasts. They too were exceptional and remarkably like, but Vlad didn't finish the thought, as he could now see her face. He jumped up.

"Brandy!"

It took everyone by surprise, particularly Brandy who was now scrabbling around on the floor trying to pick up her pink feathers, and Marcel, who could smell trouble. But there was a further distraction.

"Stop!"

They all looked up as a naked man in an excited state ran across the stage chasing another naked man. Gary recognised him immediately.

"Sunday," he said to Vlad, and got up and ran onto the stage.

Chapter Fifty-One

Sam ran. Barefooted and bare everything, he ran. The side door of the mad artist's house led to a small alleyway. It was dark, and cobbled, and he ran just ahead of the frenzied man, looking for cover. As he ran there was a slapping on his stomach. The strange thing, although it might have been a consequence of that slapping, was he could feel himself growing. There was nothing remotely stimulating about the experience. He couldn't understand it, but blood was definitely redirecting itself. He saw an open door and ran through it.

"Stop," the artist shouted.

But Sam kept on going. He could have stopped and fought. He was younger and fitter and could easily have overpowered him. But he thought something might get in the way if he fought a man with an erection, and he didn't fancy that. He carried on running. Then he got caught under what seemed like a spotlight.

"Sunday!"

It was a stage. Someone was calling his name. He looked to one side and saw an audience. Someone rose from the audience. Sam carried on running until he was out of the glare of the lights and in the wings, at the end of which was a door. It was a fire exit with a push bar. There was a noise behind him and a scream of pain. The mad artist had tripped and fallen on, Sam guessed judging by the sound, his sword. Sam pushed the bar and the door flew open.

He was in a car park. He hesitated and then he saw a van. It was large, like a Winnebago, and it had letters painted across the side. The door was open. He put his head in, and the van appeared empty. He looked back at the slogan on the side of the van. It said, 'JESUS SAVES!' At this point Sam didn't care who was saving him, so got in.

He walked through the van and then noticed some men outside. He ducked down. Two of them were policemen. He could hear them arguing. He crawled on the floor until he arrived at a further door. It was slightly ajar. He looked in and saw a bedroom. Sam crawled in. There was a mobile phone lying on the bed. He heard a door slam, panicked and looked around. He grabbed the phone and looked for somewhere better to hide. There was a wardrobe behind him. He could hear footsteps approaching. Sam got in the wardrobe.

Chapter Fifty-Two

Despite vowing not to avoid each other, Suzy and Bradley had spent the rest of the day avoiding each other. It wasn't until Suzy got home that she realised she was going to have to do something about it. Not about them, about the money. That was a heap of trouble she didn't want to get involved in. Except she was involved. She drove to Bradley's flat.

"Suzy!' Bradley said with some surprise.

Suzy nodded, being business-like, and pushed past into the flat. She wasn't going to take any shit, and she absolutely wasn't going to have a drink. They had to grab the money, and put it back where they found it, and that would be that.

"Where's the money?" she asked.

"What money?" Bradley said.

Suzy glared at him. He slumped a little. He'd felt this way before. When he was twelve he'd been given a Scalextric set for his birthday. It was wonderful, but his mother took it away when he'd hit his younger brother. He'd really cried about that, more than his younger brother had. He often thought he should have hit him harder.

"They will track you down and they will kill you," Suzy said.

She might have borrowed the line from that Liam Neeson film, although what she really meant was 'they will track me down and kill me'. It was much more frightening put that way.

"I counted it," Bradley said.

"Did you?"

"I did."

She knew he was prompting her to ask how much, but she didn't want to know. It was bad money and it had to go back.

"How much do you think there is?"

"I don't know."

"I do," Bradley said.

There was a pause. Bradley was moving towards a plan. The good news, for Suzy, was it didn't involve having sex with her, the bad news was that it involved the money.

"You think Sam either took or found that money," Bradley said.

"Yes," Suzy said slowly.

"And the bad guys are after him. Money like that, cash like that, probably came from drugs or, if not drugs, a heist of some sort. Remember that big robbery a couple of years ago?"

"Er, no," Suzy said.

"The thing is it's dirty money. It's stolen, or illegal, and Sam found it, or stole it, from some nasty people," Bradley continued.

It concerned Suzy that he'd given it so much thought. Bradley never gave anything *that* much thought. It was making her nervous.

"And do you know how much there is there?"

Suzy shrugged.

"I'll give you a multiple choice. Is it one million four hundred and seventy-six thousand, one million five hundred and twenty-three thousand, or one million two hundred and twelve thousand pounds?"

"I don't know," Suzy admitted.

"The thing is," Bradley began and Suzy sighed.

"What?" Bradley asked.

"Why do you always start your sentences 'the thing is?'"

"Do I?"

"Yes."

"No I don't."

"Yes you do."

Bradley thought of another way to express himself, but nothing was coming readily to mind. He had a good point he wished to make.

"The things is if the bad guys find it where Sam left it and find one million two hundred and twelve pounds, will they think who's stolen the rest? Will they be relieved the majority is there? They'll assume Sam's taken it and he's already in the shit. They won't, because of the way they think, think 'oh someone's popped in and has taken a bit and left the rest'. They wouldn't think that."

"So what are you saying?"

"The thing is, if we take a hundred grand each, and put the rest back, no one will ever know."

And Suzy didn't say anything. She left a pause which was long enough for Bradley to recognise that they should seize the moment. She was having doubts. He'd already packaged it up nicely.

"Here," he said and thrust a package in her hand.

It was a plastic Sainsbury's shopping bag. It was orange and it was the size of a couple of house bricks but slightly lighter. It was a hundred grand. It was a Caribbean holiday and a new kitchen for her flat. It was handbags and shoes. It was designer clothing, or a new car. His argument did make some sense.

"Let's go," Bradley said suddenly. "You drive."

Suzy felt a little numb. In the cold light of total sobriety she couldn't figure out whether it was exciting or crazy. Half an hour later they were in Sam's flat and, with a bit of fiddling, the money was back concealed in the disused hot water cylinder. Once it was done they both fell onto the sofa. They were on a strange high. The adrenaline had been rushing. And then, with a disproportionately loud ringtone, her phone shook and jangled.

"Shit," Bradley said, clutching his heart.

Suzy looked at the number. She didn't recognise it. She had to answer it.

"Hello," she said tentatively.

"Suzy? It's me. It's Sam."

Chapter Fifty-Three

Brandy had struggled with the pink feathers all day. The other girls had been really helpful, and there were moments when she could swish them in perfect time, and others when they crashed like faulty windscreen wipers. There was a real camaraderie. She felt like a team, and she fitted in. No one seemed to envy her, quite the opposite, they were pleased to have her there. She'd rehearsed as Marcel had suggested, but she found it hard to concentrate on the music, the business of opening her legs, *and* the feathers. It didn't seem to matter now.

"Brandy!"

It was Vlad. She couldn't believe it. He'd found her. She'd hoped that he would be pining for her but, as she tried to remember the dance steps, and when to open her legs, she'd thought a little less about him. She wasn't sure if he was angry, or happy to see her, and the lighting wasn't good enough for her to tell. What she could see was that he appeared to be with that dreadful bloke, Gary and, more importantly, two women. Brandy hovered for a moment, unsure what to do. She hadn't been working long, but she'd enjoyed it. It had a kind of power. And Vlad, she thought, didn't really appreciate her.

"Brandy!' Vlad shouted.

Everyone thought Brandy was stupid, but she knew what kind of a man Vlad was, and how he'd acquired his money. The danger might have been a small part of the appeal, but she liked the car, and the apartment, and all the other stuff. But it wasn't a life that was allowing her to grow as a person. Although Brandy had only entered the world of the burlesque club the previous day, and the business of removing her clothes for a living, she'd thought a lot about growing as a person. There might have been flaws in her thinking.

"Brandy!" Vlad shouted again.

Marcel knew how to sort out rowdy punters and the big ones didn't scare him. He strode purposefully up to Vlad. He found that Vlad was bigger close up than he appeared to be at a distance. It didn't matter. He knew how to deploy some bravado. He was big on bravado, more so than actual fighting skills, but then with bravado that big he hadn't need to fight.

"Don't shout at the girls," he yelled at Vlad.

Although Marcel was a big man himself, and was wrapped in his considerable armour of swaggering boldness, Vlad didn't notice. He didn't even hear him. He got up and moved towards Brandy. And Marcel put his hand on Vlad.

"Vlad!" Brandy shouted.

There was a pause in which no one said a word, the band had stopped playing, and the air was filled with tension. Then Vlad punched Marcel. Marcel had been threatened a lot, but no one had ever punched him. He flew through the air in what felt like slow motion. It gave him enough time to think about many things. He thought about his ex wife, and the daughter he only occasionally saw, and he couldn't help thinking that, despite the evident momentum of the punch, it hadn't hurt that much. He landed on a table, and that did hurt. The table broke in two and propelled the drinks, which had been resting on the edge, across the room. There were two men on a neighbouring table, who hadn't seen the commotion begin, and assumed that the drinks had been lobbed at them. They pitched in. Women began to scream. The screams were quite primal in nature and seemed to prompt further aggression from the men.

"Vlad," Brandy said quietly.

Two men were on top of Vlad. They had established, or assumed, that Vlad was the alpha male in the pack and their own status would be enhanced if they took him on. It wasn't wise. Vlad threw his arms out and the two men landed on two further tables. Marcel had only just made it back onto his feet. There was no messing this time. He phoned the police.

"Vlad," Brandy said forlornly.

Vlad looked up. Their eyes locked. There was much that needed to be said. Vlad would have got down on his knees and begged forgiveness, and Brandy would have explained how she wished to grow as a person. It would have been likely that she would have had to repeat it a number of times, as even Vlad would have found it hard to equate stripping, even classy stripping, with personal growth. But there was no opportunity for such an exchange of thoughts as Marcel punched him. It was a fabulous punch, beautifully timed and elegant, and it broke two of Marcel's fingers and fractured the others. But Vlad didn't see it coming and he staggered first to one side and then the other. There were few remaining tables that hadn't already been smashed in half but, on the final stagger, Vlad managed to find one. He crashed through it and went out like a light.

"Vlad!" Brandy shouted.

She wanted to run to him, but she feared that if she did she'd be blamed and lose her job, and she didn't want that. Instead she picked up her pink feathers and ran off stage and into the welcoming arms of her fellow burlesque dancers. A second later half a dozen gendarmes burst into the room waving firearms and shouting. Trish and Sal were still seated and had managed to grab their drinks before they were propelled off the table.

"Well, I didn't expect that," Trish said to Sal.

Chapter Fifty-Four

"Can you come and get me?" Sam asked.

It was a big ask but, right at that moment, he was getting fed up, and he hadn't quite given the logistics of being picked up much thought. He was ready to return to the mothership, although he wasn't sure what that was either. A quiet evening perhaps, an occasional takeaway. Some kind of normalcy.

"Where are you?" Suzy asked.

Sam hesitated. Should he say he's in a wardrobe? Probably not. Should he say he's stark naked? Probably not. Should he mention that he's being pursued? Best not.

"Er, Monte Carlo," Sam admitted and, to preempt her response, and for no particular reason, he said, "where are you?"

Suzy hesitated. Should she say that she's sitting in his flat? Probably not. Should she mention that she'd taken the money? Maybe not. Or that she's put it back? Probably not. Should she admit she's taken a hundred grand? Best not.

"Me? What do you mean? Nowhere, I mean at home," Suzy said, as guiltily as was possible in just a handful of words.

Worse, she was with another man. Worse still, she'd slept with him, although her memories of the event were pretty hazy. She'd certainly woken up and neither of them were wearing clothes. Hold on, she thought, didn't he say Monte Carlo?

"Did you say Monte Carlo?"

"It's a bit of a story," Sam said.

Suzy left a barren pause in the hope that it would shift focus from her. She needn't have worried. Sam had problems of his own.

"I sort of got kidnapped," Sam explained.

"Oh," Suzy said with concern.

It was concern born from many things, including the theft of the money. It was more self interest than concern. She knew the money spelled danger.

"Is this related to the thing you said you had hidden in your flat?" she asked.

"Sort of," Sam explained.

"Sort of?" Suzy asked.

And then Sam added, "Did I say I had something hidden in my flat?"

"Sort of," Suzy said.

If it was only sort of related to the money perhaps the money wasn't so dangerous. Suzy had not been in possession of the hundred grand for long, yet somehow spending plans had appeared in her head. Not overly lavish ones like Bradley, whose spending plans were ambitious enough to put him in the red before he'd peeled off the first note.

"It was an artist who wanted to paint me naked," Sam said, without giving the admission much thought.

"What?" Suzy said.

"But before that," Sam explained quickly, "it was to do with the money."

"Oh, dear," Suzy said, mentally restraining her spending plans.

"The two men," Sam said.

"The men that ripped your flat apart?" Suzy asked.

"Yes," Sam said.

"The two big guys?"

"Yes," Sam said.

He could feel his chances of being rescued were disappearing fast. It was a long shot, but he was running out of options.

"Sounds like you're in big trouble,' Suzy said.

"Yes," Sam admitted.

It was then that he felt the caravan move. A door had been slammed and the engine started. Someone was walking towards the bedroom.

"I'll call you later," Sam whispered.

He could hear the bed being patted and some irritated tutting. After a few minutes whoever it was left, and Sam was on his own, and wondering what to do next. Then it came to him. He didn't have any clothes on and he was in a wardrobe. He opened the door a slither to shed some light. Everything seemed very brown and rather rough to the touch. He looked closer.

There was good news. One size tended to fit all. The bad news was that they appeared to be monks' habits. The wardrobe was hot and airless, and he decided to wait until he had to make his escape. Besides which the material was very rough, chafingly so and, as he crawled about, the chafing seemed to have an unexpected effect on him. He looked down at his nakedness and sighed. There was no question he'd arrived at a state that the artist would have approved of. While he was pondering why that might be the case, unaware of the prodigious quantities of viagra that had been dissolved into the gin and tonic he'd drunk, something else occurred to him.

"Shit!"

The person looking for something in the bedroom was probably looking for the mobile phone that was in his hand. The phone began to ring and vibrate.

Chapter Fifty-Five

The Hump was sitting in his car. He was fretting. Vlad had called him and given him an address and told him to keep an eye on the place. He didn't know what that meant, but there was a tone in Vlad's voice that made him take it seriously. It wasn't as if he was any good at this sort of thing. He'd left the skip hire business with his hapless nephew. It was a bit high risk, as the boy had failed every exam he'd ever taken, and had shown no aptitude for anything. But that wasn't why he was fretting.

"What's all this about?" he asked the Lobster.

The Hump did not like the Lobster, and the feeling was palpably mutual. But Vlad didn't know who to trust. He'd called the Hump first because he thought, on balance, he could probably trust him more. Then he'd phoned the Lobster, as he knew that neither of them trusted each other. He hoped that the mutual suspicion would keep them from doing anything silly.

"Didn't Vlad tell you?" the Lobster asked.

The truth was that Vlad didn't trust either the Lobster or the Hump, but he thought he could trust the Lobster *and* the Hump. Vlad hadn't told the Hump much, but the Hump didn't want to admit that to the Lobster.

"Of course," the Hump said.

Surveillance was a very lengthy and boring business and they'd got this far in near total silence. It was mostly because the Hump was agonising over a small gambling debt he'd acquired, after a sure thing had proved not to be so sure, and the debt wasn't so small either. He had financial problems.

"So why do you ask?" the Lobster said.

The Lobster was contorted with anxiety and his complexion was a more severe shade of red than normal. But he had issues of his own, including a tax bill of over twenty grand he didn't have a hope in hell of covering. He was a terrible accountant, who'd mistaken losses and profits, and got himself in a twist that the Inland Revenue were not sympathetic to.

"I'm just checking. I mean if someone appears, what are we supposed to do?"

This was a concern to the Lobster too, as he was barely capable of carrying his own weight let alone getting involved in a chase. Hadn't Vlad's instructions been clear? He thought so.

"Vlad said we follow anyone who turns up," the Lobster confirmed.

They fell into a silence, which was relatively comfortable as neither wished to talk. For the next hour both of them obsessed about their respective financial crises. It didn't put either of them in a good mood. An hour later the silence had become tiring and the Hump broke it.

"Is this about the missing cash?" the Hump asked.

"How did you know about that?" the Lobster asked.

"Vlad mentioned it," the Hump said.

Before Vlad had tortured him about it he'd heard it from one of the runners, who'd heard it from one of the street dealers, who'd heard it from one of the buyers, who'd heard it from a girl who worked at the gym, who'd overheard Vlad. This sort of thing got around fast.

"I guess so," the Lobster finally said.

The Lobster knew that, very probably, the solution to all his financial problems lay in that small one bedroom apartment on the first floor. He knew that Vlad had significant quantities of cash and he guessed this was where it was hidden.

"Is that why he went to France?" the Hump asked.

"I guess so," the Lobster said.

They fell into a further silence, but their thoughts were running on similar lines. They both knew that Vlad was big and scary, but he was in another country. If ever there was an opportunity, this might be it. The only problem was that the Hump didn't want to mention it to the Lobster, and the Lobster sure as hell wasn't going to mention it to the Hump. The silence continued for a further hour until the Hump made a suggestion.

"Do you think we should check everything is okay inside?"

Going inside was not part of the remit, but Vlad's instructions hadn't been a masterpiece of clarity. There might be, they both thought, some room for interpretation.

"I think Vlad asked us to keep an eye out, didn't he?" the Lobster said.

"He did," the Hump confirmed.

"And that's what we're doing," the Lobster said. "But..."

The 'but' hung in the air while one of them decided what to do with it. It might have been a football suspended in the air waiting for it to be tapped into goal, but neither of them were big on sporting metaphors. But they were both desperate for cash.

"But," the Hump continued, "it might be useful, useful for Vlad, if we at least check out everything is okay inside."

"For Vlad," the Lobster confirmed.

Neither of them moved for a moment and, for a second, the Lobster thought of what he might say to Vlad were he suspended upside down, and having his toenails forcibly removed with rusty pliers. It was a useful image as, unpleasant as they were, the Inland Revenue didn't do that kind of thing. But Vlad did. He wondered how many toenails would be removed before the Lobster convinced Vlad that it wasn't his fault.

"Just for Vlad," the Hump said.

The Hump had only rarely seen the very unpleasant side of Vlad, but had heard enough to take him seriously. He just had to make it clear to Vlad that he was the innocent party, just operating on his behalf.

"Okay," the Lobster said.

But both were waiting for the other to take the first move. It was a game of musical chairs, and the music hadn't stopped. For a second there was a possibility that they were both going to move at precisely the same time, but neither had the coordination for that. Instead a car appeared.

"Who's that?" the Lobster asked.

"I don't know."

They watched as a man and a woman got out of the car and walked to the front door. They pushed open the front door.

"Maybe they're going to another flat," the Hump said.

They watched the house carefully until a light went on.

"No," the Lobster said. "That's the flat."

Chapter Fifty-Six

"Where the hell are we going?" Myrtle asked.

"Now don't say that word," Josiah said. "I didn't know we couldn't park a caravan in Monaco."

Myrtle was irritated. This was their big adventure, although Josiah liked to say that everything was part of God's big adventure. God was certainly funding it, or rather the Charismatic and Episcopal Church were funding it, although technically it was Christ's United National Truth. At least that was what it was called until it was closed down when the website was produced and issues had arisen to do with acronyms. There had been money left in the account and Josiah had never left Arkansas, and knew that God's word needed to be spread.

"We can head up into England and continue the pilgrimage."

Myrtle didn't say anything, as she had now seen as many churches as she ever cared to see. She wanted a bit of glamour and had talked Josiah into taking her, and very probably God's word, into Monaco. It looked great and everyone was so chic but Josiah had insisted that they wear the church's ceremonial uniform, which was like a monk's habit, and rougher than a badger's ass. Myrtle had taken to swearing in her head.

"Can we have a day off?" Myrtle suddenly suggested.

"A day off?" Josiah said.

He didn't understand the question. How could you take a day off from being in God's bright glow? He was finding Myrtle's increasingly rebellious attitude a little troubling. He'd hoped that she would embrace her time with him and maybe, if God was willing, look towards marriage. Of course the church didn't condone sex before marriage and they were in separate bedrooms. She was in the large one with the wardrobe, and he was in a smaller bedroom surrounded by leaflets, which were piled high. In fact the church wasn't that committed to sex *during* marriage, which suited Josiah fine, as he had not the slightest desire to procreate.

"A day off from churches and spreading the word and stuff," Myrtle pouted.

In her head she hadn't said 'stuff' but 'shit'. Josiah's swearing vocabulary wasn't very extensive, which was why the obvious acronym was missed. But she knew that saying shit would get him riling. She said 'shit, shit, shit, shit,' in her head.

"What do you mean?" Josiah said.

She wondered why she had to spell it out. She'd heard from her mother that Josiah was interested in marriage, although it was more about God being willing than her. Right at the moment she would be very willing to bare her breasts, drink cocktails, and take drugs. Not that she'd ever done any of those things.

"I mean wear normal clothes and have lunch in a nice restaurant," she said.

Josiah tried to digest this. He'd been cooking wholesome God-fearing food in the Winnebago, although it had featured a lot of beans, and that was proving to be an issue for him. He didn't approve of the decadent ways, particularly of the French, although he hadn't known that when he'd left Arkansas. His geography was terrible and he couldn't really tell France from Italy, or Spain. Who would have known that there was a nightclub called the Vatican? It was quite shocking.

"Oh..."

Myrtle very nearly said 'shit'. The problem was that when Josiah didn't know what to say he just went silent on her, which she found very irritating. She was going to suggest the beach, and she'd heard that Europeans took a far more relaxed attitude to clothing. She looked outside. It was very different from Arkansas. The people looked different. They looked happy and carefree. Myrtle used to be carefree but, as she'd got older, there was a marriage imperative, and she found it very difficult to be carefree about that. She'd hoped for a sign. A message. Perhaps not a miracle, like the wine-turning walking on water thing, but an indication. It had never occurred to her that God didn't exist until she'd spent so much time with Josiah, who went on about Him all the time. Now she really had her doubts.

"Can we go to the beach?" Myrtle suddenly said.

She hadn't meant to, it had just come out. Josiah didn't say anything, but he gripped the wheel a little harder. He'd never been to the beach, but it reeked of the kind of decadence he loathed. Myrtle pouted a bit more. God, she thought, could have given her a sign then. He could have got Josiah to say, 'that's a great idea!' But neither God, nor Josiah, said anything.

"Humph," she said.

She'd liked to have said something a bit coarser, but couldn't bring herself to. She'd found a romantic novel under her bed. It must have been left there by a previous owner. There was a man on the front cover. A real man. He had a muscled torso and long black curly gypsy-type hair. She'd begun to read it, she couldn't stop herself. Then something occurred to her.

"Do you ever get any signs from God?"

It was a question that Josiah was far more comfortable with than a suggested trip to the beach. Not that he would answer honestly, instead he slipped into his preachy tone.

"Of course, there are signs everywhere," he boomed.

Myrtle tried not to sigh. She was wondering whether the romantic novel *was* a sign. It was God's way of showing her the rest of the world. The things she was missing. She wasn't that far into the book yet, but could sense that there would be some serious ravishing on its way, and that was a whole lot more interesting than seeing more churches.

"Like what?" she said flatly.

Josiah didn't care for her tone and responded with a belligerent silence, and an even greater determination to see more churches to help cleanse her soul. Myrtle got up and went to her bedroom. She sat on her bed and let out an enormous fart. The bean diet was driving her crazy. She slid her hand under the pillow and grabbed the paperback. When she pulled it out she noticed something she'd not noticed before. There appeared to be some pages which were more creased than others. Why would that be? She turned to them and began to read.

"Oh my, oh my," she said.

The generously-locked gypsy prince was doing some ravishing. For the briefest of seconds she wondered whether a gypsy could be a prince. Surely, she thought, he would be one, or the other. Then she realised she was missing the point. She read on. The point was travelling her way quite quickly.

"Oh my, oh my," she said again.

It was quite shockingly graphic. But there were a few words she didn't understand. What was 'tumescent?' She reread the sentence a few more times and each time it seemed to her that the sense of it all turned on this one word. She had to look it up. She looked around for a dictionary, but couldn't find one. Then she looked for her phone, but couldn't find that either.

"Shit," she said.

She felt a little pleasure in saying the word. She farted again and then made a further rebellious decision. There hadn't been enough room for all the cans of beans in the kitchen and Josiah had stacked them in Myrtle's room. She opened the window. She was feeling so angry with Josiah, or it could have been God, or it might have been the gypsy prince. Or it might just have been the beans. She picked up a can and threw it out of the opened window. It felt good. They were out of the city and on a small motorway. It seemed safe enough. She threw out a few more. Then she chucked out the rest. She threw them two at a time. She didn't care whether it was God's will.

But it might have been. A man had stopped on the motorway to have a piss. He knew he shouldn't, but he just had to and, while he was taking that piss, he stumbled on two men who were well known in the community and great supporters of the family. Despite that, one had inserted his penis in the backside of the other, and they didn't want any witnesses to the act. They disconnected and turned on him. It would have been very unpleasant for him, but God's will intervened, and the two men were taken out by two flying cans of beans.

"Tumescent," Myrtle said, as she knew nothing about the path of the cans of beans, and God's will.

She had to find out what it meant. She went back up to the cab.

"Have you seen my phone?" she asked Josiah.

There was the one area which Myrtle had said was non-negotiable. If she came on the trip so did her phone. She'd have gone mad without the company of Facebook.

"No," Josiah said.

Myrtle looked around until she found Josiah's phone. It was small and old and plastic, and the kind of phone that was just a phone. She tapped her number in until it connected. She could hear it ringing in her bedroom. She ran in and searched around the bed. It wasn't there. Strangely, it seemed to come from the wardrobe. She opened the door. She wasn't sure what she'd expected to find, but she certainly hadn't expected a naked man to hand her the phone. Hold on, she thought, what's just happened? And then she knew. It was clear. It was obvious and if it wasn't a miracle it was pretty close. It wasn't the first naked man she'd seen, although she'd seen very few but, taking a detailed look, she knew exactly what tumescent meant.

"It's a sign," she said to the naked man, "it's God's will."

Then she slammed the door and locked it.

Chapter Fifty-Seven

"We're being followed," Suzy said.

She felt more nervous now than she had before, and before there had been over a million in cash in the car. But before they were taking the money back, now they were taking it away. A hundred grand each. They were stealing it. That made her nervous.

"Are you sure?" Bradley said casually.

He didn't feel casual. Something had exploded in his stomach, and it was a cocktail of adrenaline and fear. He leaned over and looked in the wing mirror. There was a car there, but then this was London. There was always a car behind.

"Turn here," he said.

Suzy turned, and she watched in the rear view mirror, while Bradley watched in the wing mirror. They were holding their breath.

"He's turned," Suzy said.

Bradley slunk down in his seat. He was half inclined to make a run for it if they had to stop at the lights. That wouldn't do much for their relationship, but then Suzy had made it abundantly clear that they didn't have a relationship. If that's the case it's each to his own, Bradley thought.

"Turn again here," Bradley said.

They turned into a small anonymous road, which led nowhere but to a ladder of other anonymous roads. It was the sort of road which someone only enters if they happened to live there. Or if you were being followed.

"He's still there," Bradley said.

"Don't look round," Suzy said.

They carried on slowly until they got to the end of the road. There was a tee junction leading to the main road. It was clear, and Suzy turned directly without stopping for long. The car followed them.

"Shit," Suzy said.

"We're going to have to try and lose them," Bradley said.

"Of course we're going to have to lose them. What the hell else are we going to do?" Suzy said.

Bradley didn't say anything, a little wounded by her tone. She had more to say.

"Are you going to get out and fight them?" Suzy asked.

Bradley didn't answer, but slunk a little further down in his seat.

"I thought not," she said.

Right at that moment, as well as not fancying Bradley, she didn't much like him either. She was happy with her flat and her car, and the stuff she had in her wardrobe. He'd talked her into taking the money. He'd talked her into more than just that, but she didn't want to think about it, as it gave her an unpleasant taste in her mouth.

"Traffic lights," Bradley said.

As Suzy was driving the car in a pretty attentive manner she was more than aware of the traffic lights they were approaching. What would have been more useful would be a suggestion as to what they should do when they arrive at the lights. They were red.

"We don't want to stop," Bradley observed unhelpfully.

Suzy knew that too. She could just about make out the shadow of two men. Two large men. One seemed to have a red face, which was strange. Her Mini was the 'S' version, which meant it was quite quick. Not that she'd ever driven it that quickly, and wouldn't have bought it had she realised how expensive the insurance was going to be, but right now she was grateful for it.

"They're changing," Bradley said.

Suzy slipped through the lights and the car followed her. She was going to have to ignore Bradley and choose her time. There were more traffic lights up ahead and Suzy thought that if Bradley pointed them out, she might just stab him.

"Traffic lights," Bradley said.

Suzy turned and glared at him, but he didn't seem to notice. As they grew closer the lights began to change. When they arrived at the lights they were unquestionably glowing red and she dropped a gear. And Suzy floored it.

"Shit," Bradley shouted and his head flew back.

For a few seconds the world stopped still for Suzy, as it did for a pedestrian who thought he could make it, a cyclist who didn't care, and an ambulance driver who was reaching for his siren. The pedestrian jumped back and caught the cyclist who flew into the side of the ambulance. And Suzy got through.

"Shit," Bradley said again, which was a fair appraisal of his bowels' response.

Suzy was hunkered down at the steering wheel and racing through the gears. The car was roaring with the pleasure of finally being let loose, and Bradley was still shitting himself.

"That was exciting," Suzy said.

"You can slow down now," Bradley shouted.

"I've lost them," Suzy said, making it very clear as to who had done the losing.

She turned into a side road and made a further turn, and then another turn. They were taking a different road in the opposite direction. Twenty minutes later she was back at her flat. Bradley, as far she was concerned, could take the bus back to his place. She wondered if she should change the car. Maybe a small upgrade, just five or ten grand, she thought. She'd do it tomorrow. She had the cash, after all.

The problem was that she was too excited to finish the evening so soon. The adrenaline was pumping. So, without giving it much thought, she invited Bradley in for a drink.

"What?" Bradley said.

Despite the uncomfortable fact that Bradley had very nearly crapped himself, and would have happily hidden in a corner for an hour or two until his heart rate returned, and the feeling he was going to die had disappeared, he knew an opportunity he didn't want to miss.

"Sure," he said as casually as he imagined a man who wasn't shitting himself might say.

Chapter Fifty-Eight

"Go," the gendarme said.

Vlad had nearly made it to the hospital, but he'd come to in time to be taken to the police station. The police had began by taking statements but, while many of them could speak English, they weren't very keen on writing it down. They also didn't really care who had started it. They weren't very keen on Marcel either. The last mayor had wanted to close him down, and had very nearly succeeded forcing Marcel to tone it down from pornographic to burlesque. Marcel was surprised to find that trade had increased, which irritated the new mayor.

"Go," the gendarme said.

If they could have said the same thing to Marcel they would have, but he was a resident and there were other members of the council, and the gendarmerie, who were very frequent patrons of Barons. Vlad and Gary were being escorted to the border.

"Go," the gendarme repeated.

Vlad and Gary drove in silence. Half of Vlad's face was swollen and turning dark, like his mood. In a short period he'd lost his money and his girlfriend, and his car had taken a battering. It wasn't going well.

"We don't have either Sunday or Brandy," Vlad pointed out.

Gary had an idea about how they should proceed, but he feared it wouldn't align with Vlad's. He knew his best bet would be to persuade him. He'd just have to do it with subtlety, and that wasn't in his character.

"What was the name of that club?" Gary asked.

"I don't know. I can't remember. Why?"

Gary paused. He reminded himself that he needed to go gently.

"I think it was called Barons," Gary said.

"Was it?" Vlad said.

Vlad wasn't sure in which direction he was driving. He needed to clear his head. What he really needed, he knew, was to think about the money. He'd lost sight of it with the Brandy business. That had reminded him of Brandy.

"I've got their telephone number," Gary said.

It hung in the air. He'd fiddled with his phone and a number had appeared. Gary realised he'd have to spoon feed him.

"We've got Sunday's and Brandy's passports. We don't know where Sunday is, but we do know where Brandy is. We also know where the money is. If you call Brandy and tell her you'll be back for her, then we can go to Sunday's flat and pick up the money."

This sounded like a good idea to Vlad. He just had to decide which he wanted to do first. Should he call Brandy first? He knew he should, but he feared the answer wouldn't be too positive. What the hell had got into him?

"Right," Vlad said, and pulled the car into a small petrol station.

He checked the fuel gauge. The car needed fuel, but then it always needed fuel. It was a car that *really* liked petrol. In some ways the car was as needy as Brandy. He got out of the car and filled it. After he paid for it, he parked the car on the forecourt.

"What's the number?" he asked Gary.

Gary told him and Vlad entered it into his phone. He looked up at Gary and said, "Excuse me."

Vlad got out of the car and he walked along a grass verge and then, on a whim, over a fence. He was in a field. It was quiet. He pressed the button and waited for the line to connect.

"Hello, I'd like to speak to Brandy," he said.

There was a pause at the end of the phone. It was Marcel and Marcel didn't want to lose Brandy, who was a new asset to his business. She was a glowing asset. He'd never seen a body like hers, and Marcel had made it his life's work to see a lot of naked female bodies. Brandy's body didn't conform with its unnatural disregard for gravity. Word had spread and he'd seen a few locals, and a few of the old crowd who used to come when the performances were more pornographic, return.

"She's not here," Marcel lied. "Can I leave a message?"

Vlad would have got angry but, as his most recent attempts at reconciliation had been less than successful, he hoped he could express it more clearly in a message. He decided to leave a message and call her later.

"Can you tell her that I miss her. I've got to go back to London, but I'll be back for her in a few days."

"Sure," Marcel said.

Marcel has said 'sure' when people ask him if he wants a coffee, and 'sure' if they offer a cigarette. Normally it meant he wanted a coffee or cigarette, but not always. Sometimes he just said it to get someone off the phone.

"Thank you," Vlad said and hung up.

He walked back to the car, feeling a little better. He got in.

"Everything okay?" Gary asked.

"I think so," Vlad said and he set the sat nav, pulled the car onto the motorway, and accelerated into the fast lane. They were going home.

Chapter Fifty-Nine

"Oh shit and bollocks" Suzy muttered.

She'd found a new dimension to herself and it was a bit shocking. How come she never knew she was an adrenaline junky? There was something indefinably thrilling about being in a car chase. And winning. She'd whupped their asses and now she had to dump the motor. The thrill of it had changed her internal vocabulary. She'd become Bonnie.

"Hey babes."

It was Bradley which meant, by a process of elimination, that he was Clyde. Not the Clyde she would have chosen for herself, but the Clyde that was lying naked next to her in her bed. Although she had to admit that, while this time she had been drunk on adrenaline, she was sober in all other regards. Consequently she remembered most of the evening. And she'd gone and done it again.

"Oh, hi," she said in a slightly dismissive tone.

It sounded more like she'd bumped into the postman in the street, and not like she'd just spent a night of passion and intimacy. Although the passion had mostly been Bradley's, who had worked very hard. He'd pulled all the stops out and had been spectacularly attentive.

"Shall I get some coffee?" Bradley suggested.

"Through there," Suzy pointed.

Bradley got out of the bed and walked to the kitchen. It was the first time Suzy had taken a look at his naked body, as it had been either clothed, or too close for her to see anything. It wasn't too bad and, she reluctantly admitted to herself, the sex hadn't been too bad either. Still, she was going to have to dump him and buy a new motor. There were still vestiges of the adrenaline in her bloodstream, or her memory of it was conjuring it up. She'd never called a car a 'motor' in her life. Bradley returned with two coffees. For a second she was irritated that he'd made assumptions about how she liked to take her coffee, but then she remembered that he made her coffee almost every day at work. Bradley knew precisely how she liked her coffee.

"It's Saturday," Bradley pointed out.

To Bradley it was a line that suggested infinite possibilities, including walking along the banks of the Thames arm in arm, eating alfresco under an umbrella and the light patter of rain, or taking in an art gallery, or a boat trip. To Suzy it raised further complications about how she was going to dump him.

"Oh," Suzy said.

What Bradley would have liked, prior to the alfresco-art-gallery-arm-in-arm thing, was more sex. It was just the small matter of how to initiate it. Given that they were both lying naked in bed together, this was a strange problem, but he was finding Suzy hopelessly unpredictable, and there was no way of knowing what she'd do if he slipped his hand between her legs, or on her breasts, or even her stomach. After giving it some further thought he downgraded his ambitions to her hand.

"I think I ought to change the car," Suzy said.

She was wondering what to do with Bradley's slightly sweaty hand, which was resting on hers. She knew it was just the first stop in a journey, unless she diverted it immediately. The worse thing was she wasn't entirely sure what she wanted any more. She certainly wasn't going to drive to the south of France, or wherever to pick up Sam. Strangely, since she'd spoken to Sam, she'd lost interest in him.

"Suzy," Bradley said.

He hadn't moved his hand. Instead he'd moved his head. It was close to Suzy's and he was coming in for a kiss. Fortunately his morning breath was a little more palatable this time, but she wasn't quite ready for a kiss. She had a choice to make and she had to make it soon. She placed her hands either side of his face, which Bradley found intimate and exciting and then, rather than pulling it towards her for the anticipated kiss, she directed it to between her legs. She was, she reminded herself, a Bonnie kind of woman, and Clyde wasn't complaining.

Chapter Sixty

Myrtle had moved up to the passenger seat, and was watching the scenery pass by at as much speed as a religious fanatic driving a caravan could muster. But her thoughts were elsewhere. She was excited, but confused too. Had she imagined it? Was it all an hallucination? Was it a sign? Was it God's work? Did God send down naked men to women who felt in need of one? If He did, it was a bloody good service and one she wished she'd known about earlier. She was still trying to absorb it and decide what she was going to do.

"What signs has God given you?" Myrtle suddenly asked Josiah.

Josiah, like many religious fanatics, didn't do much questioning. There seemed little point, as it was all about faith, and if you're questioning, you don't have faith. It had never occurred to Josiah how neatly circular this was, and his normal response was to answer a question with another question.

"Isn't the sun evidence of God's mighty hand?" he said.

"Well, it's evidence of something," Myrtle said thoughtfully.

When they'd left the States Myrtle had felt quite fond of Josiah, as she might a faithful Labrador. But that had changed, and the list of things she absolutely hated about him had grown quite long, and the thing she *really* hated was the preachy tone. He adopted it whenever God was involved and unfortunately he tried to involve Him in everything they did, which was why she'd rather be struck down by a lightning bolt than enter into marriage with Josiah. And that was before she thought of having sex with him. He would want to procreate, she was certain of that, but that would be all he'd want to do. He wouldn't do that gypsy-prince thing.

"Is that enough?" she asked.

She meant it with reference to God's signs and not a potential life with Josiah, which was how he took it. He frowned. He was here to spread the word, and the person he'd chosen to spread the word with seemed like she was having doubts. He had to think of a sign and fast. If he lost Myrtle what hope would the rest of the world have?

"The daisies in spring, the dew on the ground, fresh spring water, the blossom on the trees, the wind in your face, the green of grass, the blue of the sky," he said.

It was easily the most he'd ever said to her and it didn't have that preachy tone. It was quite romantic, and she could see some sense in it. Why were we so keen on tricks like walking on water when nature said so much? It still didn't explain why there was a naked man in her wardrobe. She decided not to ask Josiah if he thought it possible that God had given her a naked man. She changed the subject.

"How long until we get to England?" she asked.

Josiah seemed constantly confused by the geography of Europe, because at times it seemed so small, and other times rather bigger than he'd thought. This was one of those times.

"A good few hours yet," he said.

After his brief foray into romantic territory he was back to the prosaic. This was another thing on her irritation list, as Josiah was incapable of answering *any* question with some degree of fact. She would have liked a precise number of hours, or miles, or something specific. That was the problem with God and his signs, nice though they were, was that they weren't very precise. She stretched and looked at the sat nav, although she had suspicions that he had no idea how to operate it, but it had a time of arrival.

"About ten hours?" she said.

"If it is God's will," Josiah said.

As far as Myrtle could tell, Josiah was unfamiliar with the words 'yes' or 'no' or he was incapable of saying them. Ten hours was quite a long time for her God-given naked man to be scrunched up in the back of the wardrobe. For a second she remembered a book she'd read as a child in which the back of a wardrobe led to a fantasy land of witches and lions. Although, given that her wardrobe contained a naked man, it might lead to a different kind of fantasy. That was another thing. Since she'd started reading the romantic novel her dreams had become a little more lurid.

Rather alarmingly so. It was probably *that* that had summoned the naked man.

"Okay," she finally said.

Myrtle had ten hours to speak to the man, because if they stopped there was no way of knowing where Josiah would be, but when they were driving she knew *exactly* where Josiah was. This was her moment.

"I'm just going to lie down for a while," she said.

Myrtle got up and walked back to her bedroom. She opened the door and then closed it behind her. Then she locked it, she wasn't sure why. She looked at the wardrobe. She pictured it bursting open and streams of people pouring out. In this fantasy there was no question that most of them would be naked. It was quite exciting. She moved forward and pulled over the bar that prevented the wardrobe from opening when they were on the road. Then she stepped back, as if it was likely to snap at her. Nothing happened. She lent forward and opened the door. The good news was that she hadn't been hallucinating. The bad news was that the naked man was no longer naked. He was wearing one of their monk-like habits. It made him look religious, which wasn't the fantasy she had in mind. They looked at each other.

"What are you doing in my wardrobe?" Myrtle finally asked.

"I'm glad you asked," Sam said, as if he were taking tea with a country vicar, "I was hiding from someone."

Myrtle jolted. A thought had hit her. It was a lightning bolt of realisation. She'd assumed all along that the naked man in the wardrobe was a sign from God, but there was a possibility that she was only half right. Yes, he'd been sent, but not by God. On the other hand, he didn't seem very demonic.

Chapter Sixty-One

"Are you sure?" Suzy said.

The other thing that Bradley liked, almost as much as sex, was buying cars. He *really* liked looking at cars, and today they were armed with a pretty healthy budget. He'd directed her beyond the modest, through to the middle ranking and, right now, they were looking at something pretty damn sexy.

"It does zero to sixty in five seconds," the salesman said.

Suzy didn't really know what that meant other than it went like stink, which would be handy should she find herself in another car chase. Bradley had a further suggestion, which he was holding back. He knew the timing of that suggestion was critical.

"And a maximum speed of over one hundred and seventy miles an hour," the salesman continued.

It was hard to say who this excited more. It certainly excited Bradley, and it gave the salesman a little frisson every time he said it. To Suzy it seemed a little dangerous. Unfortunately dangerous was good for the new adrenaline junky Suzy. Dangerous was exciting.

"Very nice," Bradley said.

So far, this had been one of the best mornings of his life. The unrequited love which had seemed like a dagger in his heart – Bradley could be quite dramatic – was now requited. Perhaps not fully requited but, as they'd spent some time actually having sex, that was a very welcome step in the right direction. She was quite demanding and for a moment he had nearly been asphyxiated, but there were worse ways to go. And now they were in a car showroom.

"Would you like to talk about it together?" the salesman asked reverentially.

The salesman knew that Bradley was sold. It was a Porsche Boxter. He was more than sold. He was salivating. It was a dream come true and now that they'd been left together, like a committed couple, a married couple even. Now was the time to deploy his suggestion.

"I think it would be nice to buy it together," he said.

There were two parts to this plan. The first was he'd be able to drive a Porsche Boxter, and how cool was that? Even cooler since his BMW had been taken back by the lease company. They had been very specific about their payments. Also, if they owned it together, jointly, then that would bind them together. There was a further part to his plan.

"Do you think?" Suzy said.

She really didn't know what to think. It was certainly bloody expensive, although she had the cash on her, and they'd given her a good price on the Mini. All that talk of high speed danger had got her in a fluster. It was like a moment of weakness. Bradley sensed it and went in for the kill.

"Because we've been forced to ditch your car, we can go back and grab the cash for this one and then that's it. We don't touch it again."

It would mean going back to Sam's flat and that might prompt a high speed chase. But she'd be driving a Porsche Boxter, and that did zero to sixty in five seconds, apparently. Grabbing the cash for the car was an appealing idea and, in a moment of weakness, Suzy went for it.

"Okay," she said.

An hour later, after a discussion with the salesman, his manager and the owner of the business regarding taking significant sums in cash, Suzy drove their new car out of the showroom. The sun had come out and they'd opened the roof and Bradley rested his hand on her inner thigh and, right at that moment, Suzy didn't mind too much. Later that evening they were going to collect the cash. There was no way of knowing what the excitement, and resultant adrenaline, would do to Suzy.

Chapter Sixty-Two

"We can't do this all day and all night without eating, sleeping and taking a shit," the Lobster pointed out.

It had also occurred to the Hump. The obvious solution was for them to operate in shifts. One of them could be watching while the other was eating, or sleeping, or taking a shit. It was the only way forward. The problem was that the Lobster didn't trust the Hump, and the Hump didn't trust the Lobster. It was why the Hump was pleased that the Lobster had made the suggestion. He'd point *that* out to Vlad if it all went wrong.

"Do you think so?" the Hump asked.

"Yes," the Lobster said, mostly because he wasn't far from crapping himself.

"Okay," the Hump said.

"You go first," the Lobster said and added, "I'll be back in six hours."

They both knew he'd be back in less than six hours to catch the other out.

"Okay," the Hump said, and the Lobster got out of the car.

Although they hadn't spoken much, it felt suddenly quite silent. The Lobster had spent the last four hours desperate for a crap and, once he got home and onto the toilet, whatever was in there had appeared to solidify, and was reluctant to make an exit. It made the

Lobster even redder. He would have been redder still if he knew what the Hump was up to.

The Hump had waited a decent time for the Lobster to leave. He hadn't ruled out the possibility that the Lobster was lurking behind a tree somewhere waiting to catch him out. He guessed he'd be back much sooner than six hours. The Hump got out of the car. Getting into the house wasn't difficult and, once in the house, getting into Sam's flat was easy. He searched the flat. He checked under the bed, in the mattress and the various holes in the floor and walls. Nothing. He couldn't find a thing. The whole thing was a wild goose chase. The Hump sat down and sighed. He wondered how he was going to pay his gambling debts. Obviously they were vicious, nasty and unpleasant people and they'd applied interest on the debt. He'd thought about getting a loan but, while the people were vicious and nasty, their interest rates were reasonable compared to a pay day loan company. These were strange times, the Hump often thought.

"Quiet!'

The Hump jumped. Someone was coming up the stairs. He had to hide. He only had a split second to make a decision and he wasn't the kind of man who did anything in a split second. But they were almost at the top of the stairs. He slid under the bed. He feared for a second that the Lobster had returned with Vlad. Vlad when he was angry was even nastier than those pay day loan people.

"Quickly," one of them said.

The Hump could make out two pairs of feet and, unless Vlad had taken to wearing high heels, it was a man and a woman. He didn't think it was Brandy, as the heels weren't high or pointy enough. The Hump often had fantasies about Brandy. He couldn't stop himself. He tried to redirect his thoughts. They were doing something. He crawled a little further forward to get a better view. He could see more of their legs. It definitely wasn't Brandy. He was more familiar with every contour of her legs than he was of his own. It was the couple they'd followed and lost.

"Where's the spanner?" a voice said.

"There," an irritated female voice said, as if she meant to say 'right in front of your face.'

It was a tone that the Hump was familiar with from his ex wife. He'd never quite placed the same importance on fulfilling domestic tasks as she had. He leaned a little further forward. They were doing something. He thought it unlikely they'd broken in to repair some plumbing, which tended to suggest that the spanner was in some way relevant. He crawled to the opposite end of the bed, which gave him a greater view into the sitting room. They'd opened a cupboard. It looked like an airing cupboard.

"Just take a little," the woman said.

The Hump didn't know but there was now something of an issue as what a 'little' actually meant. It certainly wasn't the price of a coffee, or a sandwich, or a pair of shoes. Or a fancy car. But, when held in the hand, it didn't look *that* much.

"Is that enough?" the female voice said.

"I'll take a bit more," the male voice said.

Ten minutes later the Hump was alone in the flat. It took him a while to crawl out from under the bed. He wasn't the most supple of men. It took him even longer to find the spanner which was, incredibly, right in front of him. He wasn't great at plumbing, but then there had never been a pot of gold at the end of a plumbing task. Eventually he reached into the underside of the copper hot water tank and pulled out a wad of cash.

"Bloody hell," he muttered.

He had no idea how much a 'wad' equated to, although he was fairly certain it would settle his gambling debts. He took a couple more for good measure. Ten minutes later the copper tank was back in place and he was back in his car. He'd hidden the money in the boot under the spare tyre. He was sweating a little. He'd exerted himself a fair bit, but it was mostly the fear and excitement. His timing was perfect and he very nearly hit the roof when the Lobster got into his car.

"Everything alright?" the Lobster asked.

"Fine," the Hump managed to say.

Chapter Sixty-Three

Suzy was driving like a Formula One driver with her hair on fire. She'd run through the gears and occasionally through the lights, and she'd managed to get the car to rocket from standstill to sixty miles an hour in what seemed like about five seconds. There were a couple of moments when people got in her way and she just found the gap, and pressed the pedal. She didn't let the size of the gap, or the extent of the on-coming traffic, deter her.

"You'd better slow down," Bradley said.

Bradley normally enjoyed going fast, but sixty in a thirty zone was not a good idea with a pile of stolen cash in the car. He was feeling a bit car sick, too. He was going to suggest it was his turn to drive, but she'd got straight into the driver's seat and made it clear she wasn't prepared to negotiate. She hadn't quite grasped the concept of shared ownership.

"I suppose," Suzy said.

She was Bonnie and she was wondering if they could 'knock off' a petrol station or two on the way back. How difficult could it be? She wasn't sure what 'knocking off' really meant, or what it entailed, but she did know they'd be up the road and in another post code in seconds.

"Get out of my way," she yelled to a road user with whom she did not wish to share the road.

Despite the hugging nature of the seats, Bradley was holding onto the sides with what was beginning to seem like dear life. The woman was a bloody maniac. It was his fault. If he hadn't encouraged her to take more money she wouldn't be possessed, as she appeared to be. It had brought out the crazy woman in her. For a second he pictured himself giving evidence in court when a near collision with a fire engine took his mind away from the image. It was too frightening to give him moments for reflective thought.

"Bloody idiot," Suzy said of the fireman.

She really liked the Porsche Boxter. She liked it so much she wondered whether they should share it. It would be far more convenient if they had one each. She'd mention it to him later, although she suspected he'd say they'd already taken enough money. She had a plan to get round that.

"I like this car," Suzy said.

Bradley smiled. He reminded himself that they were coupled up and there appeared to be a future ahead of them. If they didn't die in a horrific high speed car crash. Despite that, it was great. It was what he had wanted. He snuggled his hand further up her inner thigh and didn't find any resistance. It gave him a little spark of excitement.

"It's great, isn't it?" he said.

It was a glimpse of the future. They'd be one of those cool couples who would have a cool house, a cool kid and a cool car. Bradley's glimpse into the future was a romantic one with blue skies and happy times. He'd protect her from the harsher elements of life and, as a couple, they would be more than the sum of their parts. They'd have great dinner parties and they'd be very liberal when their child announced he was gay.

"Fucking great," Suzy said.

Bradley thought it a little coarse, but decided not to mention it. Suzy's mind was elsewhere. She was wondering when she was going to take the beast out next and what she was going to get out of him. She hadn't given it much thought as to whether Bradley would be there too. She'd formed a lasting bond with the car and a second later she was outside her flat. She switched off the engine and turned to Bradley.

"Bradley," she said.

Bradley wasn't sure what was coming next. With Suzy he had no idea what was coming next. He'd like to say that it was part of her charm, but she had a habit of saying unpleasant things to him and kicking him out of bed. It was hard to find that charming. He'd like her to say something romantic. Deep down Bradley craved the romantic. It was why he had images of walking hand in hand along the banks of the Thames and alfresco meals in light rain. And that was before the cool house, the cool kid and the cool car. Although he knew her mind did not operate the same way as his.

"Let's fuck," Suzy said, and got out of the car.

Chapter Sixty-Four

"I'll just be a minute," Myrtle told Sam.

She'd formed a plan. She needed to address her appearance. She grabbed some clothing which, while not actually sexy, was approximately feminine. Most of her bras were grey and shapeless apart from one, which was grey and a little bolder in its aspirations. She had a jumper which was too small for her, which is to say it was tight. Used in conjunction with the bra it prompted a curve which men's eyes followed. She had a small amount of makeup, which she'd hidden from Josiah who, she suspected, would consider it to be the work of the devil.

"Better," she said to herself.

There was a full length mirror in which she attempted to admire herself. She looked quite nice, but had difficulty in seeing herself that way. She wondered if her breasts were too obvious, and then thought that if ever there was a moment for them to be too obvious, this was it. She applied a little eyeliner and mascara. The caravan was shaking a bit, and she wasn't very skilled at applying makeup, but the result wasn't too bad. She was ready to open the door. She grasped the handle. It wasn't just the van that was shaking. She was nervous.

"Hello," she said.

"Hello," Sam said.

He could see that she'd made an effort, but wasn't sure, given recent events, whether this was a good thing or not. He feared he might have drifted, once again, from the frying pan. The woman smiled at him.

"My name's Myrtle," Myrtle said.

"Hi, I'm Sam," Sam said and offered his hand.

She leaned forward and shook it. Sam smiled back. Unlike the mad surrealist artist with the obsession with penises, he hadn't been kidnapped. He'd got into the van on his own accord. Although he'd also entered the bathroom of the artist of his own accord. He just hadn't known he was going to get locked in.

"Where are we going?" Sam asked.

Myrtle was a little mesmerised. Was she being tested? Was this about temptation? Where *was* she going?

"I try to be good and treat my neighbour well. And follow God's word. I mean, I'm not like Josiah. He *really* follows God's word. I'm just trying to hang on in there and do my best."

Myrtle hoped that she'd made a sufficient case for her piety, although she doubted it. But if a naked man in her wardrobe was a sign from God, she really did believe.

"No, I mean where is the caravan going?"

"Oh, I see," Myrtle said, but her thoughts had petered out, as she battled with God and temptation.

"Where are you from?" Sam asked.

Myrtle was about to explain about the Church of United National Truth, but sensed that the question was more general than that.

"Arkansas. It's in America," she explained.

"Is it nice there?" Sam asked.

Myrtle had never questioned whether Arkansas was nice or not. It was where she came from, and where her family were from.

"Folks are nice there," Myrtle said.

"What does it look like?"

Myrtle thought about the question. She'd looked out of the window of the caravan and seen Europe go past. She'd seen Italy, and Spain, and France, and it had looked different.

"It's big and flat and there aren't many people," she said.

"And the buildings?" Sam asked.

"They're old," she said, and then she thought about it a little more. "Maybe not so old. Mostly wood."

That was the most she'd ever thought about her homeland, and it had relaxed her. If this was temptation then it was, she thought for a second, very tempting.

"Where are you from? You've got a cute accent," Myrtle said.

"I'm from London," he said and then added for accuracy, "London, England."

"Oh, that's were we're going, England," she said brightly.

This, Sam thought, was good news. Very good news. He didn't have a passport, or any money, but this would give him a passage back. He smiled at Myrtle. She'd pronounced 'England' with three syllables, as if it were an alien place. This was Sam's moment to secure his passage.

"Do you mind if I come along for the ride?"

Myrtle wondered if this was the moment of temptation. It didn't seem like it. What harm would it do?

"Can I just get out of the wardrobe?" Sam asked.

"Of course," Myrtle said.

Sam pulled himself up. He stepped out of the wardrobe and into the little bedroom in which there was little else but a double bed. It seemed a bit intimate.

"Shall I sit there?" he pointed at the bed.

"Sure," Myrtle said.

She sat down next to him. She wasn't too close, but she hadn't chosen the far end of the bed either. She'd never sat on a bed with a man before. Her peer group back home were all a little unfamiliar with men too, as they were all related to the church. It probably explained why there were so few people in her town, she thought. The streets of Europe seemed full of people who were procreating all the time. Procreating was in her mind, and stories of gypsy princes, and temptation. But, if Sam wasn't a message from God, what was he doing there? She decided to ask.

"Why were you in my closet?" Myrtle asked.

Sam thought for a second. Should he tell the truth? If he told her that he'd been hiding from a man who wished to paint his erection, she wouldn't believe him. Or he might have to explain to her what an erection was. That brought him to another thought. While he wasn't widely in touch with his body, he knew it well enough to know that it didn't normally react the way it was reacting. The coarseness of the material of the cloak he was wearing was rubbing against him, but it was more than that. The artist must have put something in the gin and tonic.

"It's a long story," Sam explained, playing for time.

If he told her that he was running away from some violent people, probably drug dealers, she wouldn't think too highly of him. That just left telling a lie and he wasn't very good at that.

"I was trying to help someone," he began.

He hadn't thought very far ahead and was going to have to weave a story together one sentence at a time.

"She got involved with some bad people," he continued.

"She?" Myrtle said with obvious disappointment.

"It was my sister," Sam said.

"Oh," Myrtle said, a little happier.

Right at that moment Myrtle would have accepted almost any story, however flimsily it was fabricated. She wanted him to be a good man. She wanted him to stay. She wanted him. She was about to move closer when a thought occurred to her.

"Would you like a drink?"

"I would," Sam said, smiling.

Josiah had views about profanities and alcohol and almost everything else with which pleasure could be associated, but there was a little red wine, which represented the blood of Christ. Myrtle didn't give it much thought. She sneaked into the kitchen on her hands and knees so that Josiah couldn't see her. She grabbed the bottle, and two glasses, and returned to Sam.

"Great," he said, looking at the bottle.

The wine was cheap, and in a plastic bottle, but it was a large bottle with a plastic top. She passed it to Sam, who opened it and poured it into the two glasses. He raised his glass.

"Cheers," he said.

It was slightly sharp, and on the knife edge of undrinkable, but Myrtle, who was rarely allowed to drink alcohol, whopped it down like pop. Sam filled it up.

"So, why are you touring Europe?" Sam asked.

Myrtle burped and tried to remember why they were touring Europe and then it came to her.

"Josiah says we need to spread the word of the Lord," she finally answered and presented her empty cup for refilling.

"And you?" Sam asked, "do you want to spread the word of the Lord?"

There were colliding thoughts in Myrtle's head. Some had come from the romantic novel which she'd been reading, and some were from the alcohol which was going to her head. The one thing that was absolutely clear was that the word of the Lord was not amongst them.

"Not really," Myrtle managed to say.

She wasn't sure if she should mention the suggested marriage and then, without her being able to stop it, stuff just came out.

"No, I don't. And I don't want to marry Josiah either. I came along with him because I wanted to live a little more. I wanted to see the world."

Then, after this revelation, Myrtle moved closer to Sam. When it came to seeing the world she had quite a lot in mind. She moved even closer and with a boldness she'd never experienced before, she had no idea where it had come from, although the plastic bottle of red wine might have been to blame, she put her hand on his leg. Or rather she'd intended to put her hand on his leg, but the van had jerked, as if it had hit a pothole, and her hand landed on his lap.

"Oh my," Myrtle said.

She couldn't believe she'd said 'oh my'. It was something a wanton woman might have said, and she couldn't think where it had come from. Then she remembered something else from the romantic novel and, now that her hand was in his lap, she noticed something else, which also answered one of her earlier questions. This was tumescence. She grabbed it rather roughly, not helped by the sandpaper characteristics of the Jesuit-style material of the cloak. And then things went a little crazy.

"Oh Lord Mother of God," Myrtle said.

The earth was moving exactly as it had been described in her romantic novel. Everything was jumping up and down. The strange thing was that she didn't feel any different. Was this what an orgasm felt like? She was still gripping Sam's tumescence, but his face did not look like he was finding it pleasurable. Why was there so much that she didn't know? Then she noticed that the countryside was moving slower outside. They were slowing down.

"I think there's a problem with the van," Sam said.

They'd almost come to a halt. Was this divine intervention? Had God stopped them before they had a chance to get going? She went up to the cab to see what the problem was.

Chapter Sixty-Five

The Lobster and the Hump sat in the car in an uneasy silence. The Hump was feeling a good deal more content as he now had the financial wherewithal to pay his gambling debts and a little more. He was thinking about taking a holiday. The Hump had never really been on holiday before so this thought was as close to decadence as he ever managed. The Lobster was feeling pretty smug.

"Anything happen?" He asked the Hump.

"Happen?" The Hump replied with a guilty tone.

"Yes, happen," the Lobster said.

"No, nothing happened," the Hump said compounding his guilt.

The Lobster smiled to himself. When he'd got back to the car he'd found it empty. The Hump was nowhere to be found. Except the Lobster found him in Sam's flat. He'd moved pretty quietly, which was quite a feat for the Lobster. And the Hump hadn't heard him. He'd seen the Hump take some money. This meant that, should Vlad ask, he could confirm that he was witness to the theft. He'd seen the Hump take the money. The genius part was ensuring that the Hump didn't see him.

The Lobster sat and waited for the Hump to leave. He was a man prone to perspiration at the best of times but today, with the prospect of what he intended to do ahead of him, it was pouring off him. The atmosphere had become quite fetid in the car. The silent war of attrition between them and his body odour was his primary weapon. Eventually the Hump had to admit defeat.

"I'll be back in six hours," he said.

They both knew it wouldn't be six hours, but it no longer mattered. The Lobster waited a further thirty minutes to make certain that the Hump wasn't watching him, left the safe haven of the car, and entered the flat. It was quite a mess inside, but that didn't matter.

"Bingo," he said, touching the copper hot water tank.

He examined the pipes it was connected to, and looked around for an appropriate tool. The Lobster was not a man who ever wielded tools of any kind. His hand skills in this area, and many others according to his ex wife, were minimal. He tried turning the nuts with his hand, but they wouldn't turn. He'd seen the Hump extract money from the cylinder, but he hadn't seen how he'd achieved it. He rocked the copper tank back and forward. There was movement. A corner of a bank note appeared. He leaned down and tugged at it. It slid out. It was a twenty.

"Ker-ching," he said.

It was like a one-armed bandit which always paid out, he thought. He was getting quite excited. As well as the twenty grand he owed the Inland Revenue, he could resolve a few of his other financial problems. He'd seen cash pass through the business, and he knew what the angry side of Vlad looked like but, right at that moment, he was blind to it. This vessel contained the answer to all his problems. He tried the joints again. They wouldn't budge. He looked for a spanner, but the Lobster's eyesight and his powers of observation were such that he was unable to see the adjustable spanner that was in front of him. His ex wife would not have been surprised by this, as he'd had the same blindness with dirty washing and dishes which were destined for the dishwasher. He just couldn't see them. And he couldn't see the spanner either. He applied all his weight onto the cylinder and it rocked back. Another note appeared. This time it was a fifty.

"Ker-ching, ker-ching," he said.

He literally had his hands in the corporate till, but then so had the Hump. And he knew that the Hump had had his hand in the till but, crucially, the Hump had no idea that he'd had his hand in too. It might cost him a toenail but, as he rarely saw them, it wasn't a problem. He'd blame it all on the Hump. The only problem was how to extract the money. Then an idea came to him. He searched the flat until he found the solution. It was a broomstick.

"Perfect," he said to himself.

The Lobster pushed the cylinder as far back as it would go and wedged the broomstick against it. He released the cylinder. It didn't move. The Lobster got on his hands and knees and slid his hand between the floor and the base of the cylinder. He could feel the notes, but it wasn't quite enough. He lay down on the floor. That was much better. He slid his hand, and then his forearm, into the cylinder.

"Oh yes, yes, yes," he said.

He pulled out a bundle of cash. It was quite the most excited he'd been in many years. He looked at the bundle and tried to estimate the value. Then he decided he didn't care. It wasn't enough. He put his forearm back up the open base of the cylinder. It was then that the broom, which had been under some pressure, sprang across the room. There was a millisecond when the Lobster wondered what was going to happen next. Then the cylinder sprang back and dug itself into his arm. The Lobster was trapped.

The only thing that had ever been astronomical in the Lobster's life was his blood pressure, and it had just lifted higher, as if it was breaking free of the Earth's gravity. His eyesight grew faint, as if someone had turned the lights out, and his face managed to find another redder shade, as if it were glowing like the sun. The Lobster's life, in all its appalling frustrations, shot by like an ancient black and white film shown on a clattery projector, as if it had no significance, and as if he was dying. But his face was no longer red, as if his blood were no longer pumping. But it wasn't as if. His life *had* been insignificant, and his blood was no longer pumping. Three minutes later he wasn't dying any more. He was momentarily grateful that he wouldn't have to suffer the Hump any longer, but he couldn't be certain of that.

Chapter Sixty-Six

The sweat was pouring off Bradley. He lay back on the bed still breathing heavily. He realised, at that point, that he'd never lived. He'd never *really* had sex. He'd had sex certainly, but not like this. He felt light headed. His brain felt fuzzy. Is that what was meant by fucking your brains out? Or was this having your brains fucked out? He felt more like the object than the subject. He had no idea what had got into Suzy. She was like a wild cat. Of course *he'd* got into her. Many times. But it wasn't like that. She'd hurled him about like a sex toy.

"Not bad," Suzy said.

If Bradley hadn't been breathing so heavily he might have taken issue with that. Not bad? It was pretty fucking good. And, while Bradley wasn't the most insightful of men, he had a feeling that this wildness came from the money and the car. The danger had sent her a little feral and it was something he was really enjoying. He felt emboldened by the aftermath of fine sex, as if he could do anything. It was like Dutch courage but with sex.

"Two Boxters?" he said.

Suzy knew what that meant. It meant another raid and another get-away drive. She was up for that. The advertising business was beginning to seem very tame. She was thinking about a full time career in crime. She'd never known adrenaline like it and the adrenaline agreed with her.

"We'll need some more money," she said.

Just the thought sent a frisson through her and she grabbed Bradley, threw him on his back, and mounted him like it was the Wild West. She would have ridden him like the Wild West too, but Bradley was more likely to have a hernia, or a heart attack, than an erection.

"Give me a minute," Bradley said.

Suzy knew enough about men to know that a minute wouldn't do it. Nowhere near. If there had been more men available, fresh ones, then it was very likely that she would have mounted them too, but that wasn't the case and she threw herself back on the bed with a slight huff. They had a few minutes in silence in which Suzy let the adrenaline subside.

"I'll make a coffee," Suzy said and got out of bed.

She padded naked to the kitchen. It was the first time that Bradley had seen her nakedness at less than close quarters and it was strangely more intimate than their buccaneering sex.

"You don't take milk, do you?" Suzy shouted from the kitchen.

"I do take milk," Bradley shouted back.

Suzy watched the kettle boil. It wasn't in a hurry. It gave her a further moment to come down from wherever she'd gone. She'd never stood naked in her kitchen before. She couldn't think why. And then she remembered. She lived on the ground floor and there was a window overlooking the street. She no longer felt a slave to convention. She'd broken speed limits and taken cash, large sums of it. This was the new her.

"You don't take sugar do you?" she shouted to Bradley.

"I do," he shouted back, "two spoons."

Suzy realised she had no idea how Bradley took his coffee, or anything else. Bradley had become a tool like the Porsche Boxter. That said, she was fairly certain she wasn't going to tire of the car. The kettle had boiled and she threw hot water in the cups and walked back into the bedroom. She passed a cup to Bradley. He took a sip.

"Thank you," he said.

It was instant coffee. The granulated shit, he thought, to which water was applied to create an approximation to the coffee bean derived drink, coffee. It occurred to Bradley than when he made the coffee, which was not most of the time, but all of the time, she was pretty exacting about how it should be achieved. She didn't hold herself up to the same standards. It would have, if he'd thought deeply about it, prompted irritation in him, but the second sight of her unabashed nakedness had stirred something else in him.

"We need to go to work," Suzy said.

She could feel that reason and sense were coming her way. She knew that there was madness in what they'd been doing, but each time she took a hit from the thrill of the madness of it, she ignored everything else. She diverted her thoughts towards what she was going to wear for work when Bradley's hand landed on her. It wasn't on her arm or even her stomach. It was rather more intimately located. Hell, why not, she thought.

Chapter Sixty-Seven

"I'll make some tea," Josiah said.

He'd said it in a clipped tone, which Myrtle hadn't heard before. It was a little unsettling. He'd laid eyes on her tight top and makeup, and he'd clammed up. She'd expected a rant about God and he hadn't delivered it. Instead they were sitting at the table about to have tea. She had no idea what was going through his head.

"Tea," Josiah said.

His mind was in a turmoil. One part of him was outraged. He did not expect a potential wife of his to dress quite so provocatively. He'd seen the women in the squares of Madrid, and Verona, and Monte Carlo and many other places. He knew it wasn't *that* provocative. But it was at close quarters and she looked different. Very different. It wasn't that he hadn't looked at her before. He had. He just might not have seen her.

"Assam, okay?" he said.

Josiah was playing for time. He knew he had to say something. He just didn't know what. He hadn't decided how he felt, or perhaps he had. He was just in denial. He'd also had a brief glance when they were in Paris - he'd asked for God's forgiveness as it was entirely accidental - of a street prostitute. He'd only glimpsed her for a fraction of a second. Maybe less, but he'd seen her stockings and suspenders, and overflowing breasts. He'd never seen anything like it in Arkansas. And Myrtle looked nothing like that.

"Or lapsang souchong?"

Someone had left a collection of teas in the van and, right at that moment, they were proving useful to Josiah. He wondered if he'd been honest with himself, or with God, about his intentions on the trip. He certainly wanted to spread the word of the Lord, and he'd wanted to see more of the world. And the world he'd seen was very different to the world he was used to. He'd seen churches that were a thousand years old in cultures which hadn't changed for even longer. At times he'd felt closer to God. But he'd also wanted to know whether he could become a married man.

"Camomile?"

Myrtle did not know what to make of it. There was something going on in his head and she didn't know whether he was going to explode or cry. She'd nearly cried too. She'd seen temptation and she'd liked it. But there had been a problem with the wheel, or axle, or it might have been a bearing, no one seemed to know, and the van had jumped up and down. The earth had moved just like it had in the romantic novel she had secreted under her bed, but not in the way the novelist had intended. It can't have been a coincidence that it had happened just as her hand had touched his tumescence. God had intervened and stopped her sinning.

"English breakfast?"

It wasn't the outraged part of Josiah that was bothering him. It was the other part. The part he didn't know he had. It was the part that was buried under years of devotion to the Lord and God's word and an acre of piety. It came hand in hand with marriage and the bible referred to it as procreation. Everyone else thought of it as, Josiah's thoughts paused. He'd nearly said the word 'sex' in his head. It wasn't a word he'd ever used, even when it was applied to determining gender.

"Chai tea?"

Josiah had come to the end of the tea collection. He was going to have to make a choice soon. He looked out of the window. The countryside was rushing by quicker than it had been when he was driving. They were on a transporter. It had taken a while to establish who could repair the van and the nearest place was in England, which was where they were heading anyway. The driver had taken one look at Josiah and told him he could stay in the caravan.

"Maybe English breakfast tea," Josiah said.

Myrtle nodded. She felt a little self conscious in her tight top. She tried tugging it down to make it less obvious, or her breasts less obvious, but the bra seemed to bite back. She had a suspicion that one of breasts had popped out. She didn't know whether she should fish about and pop it back in, or just leave it there. She glanced down quickly. She was surprised how big her nipple looked.

"Milk?" Josiah choked.

He reddened. He hoped it was clear that the milk referred to the tea and not her breast which, like their trip to the Louvre and Mona Lisa's eyes, seemed to be following him around the room. He poured the hot water onto the tea bags, and followed it with the milk, and wondered what he was going to say next. He turned to Myrtle, and what he said next was a surprise to them both.

"You look nice," he said.

Myrtle couldn't believe it. Sam was back in the wardrobe. He'd rearranged a few things and he'd managed to fall asleep. And now she was about to have tea with the man who had shown an interest in marrying her and had just delivered his first and only compliment. What was God trying to say to her?

Chapter Sixty-Eight

The jolt, as they drove over a ramp onto the ferry, woke up Gary. He'd been snoring loudly for the last four hours. For a while it had irritated Vlad, who'd tried to combat it with the prodigious hifi the car was equipped with but, loud as it was, it hadn't stirred Gary. In the final hour he'd begun to find the snoring reassuring. Although he hadn't quite forgotten about Brandy, the distance had lessened his yearning, and redirected his thoughts to business. The money.

"Morning," Gary said, not fully aware of the time of day.

They hadn't formulated a plan, but neither had any intention of wasting any time.

"You've got the address?" Gary asked.

"No, what is it?" Vlad said.

Gary gave it to him and Vlad fed it into the sat nav. It was another three or four hours and, should they be successful, was the end of the journey for the two of them.

"Shall we eat?" Gary said.

The boat had a number of restaurants and they gravitated to the most expensive with waiter service without a discussion. Gary was surprised to find it was lunchtime, and processed that discovery quickly enough to decide a steak and a glass of wine would be appropriate.

"We go straight there," Vlad said.

His accent had become more Russian as he thought about grabbing the money, and ripping the testicles off anyone who stood in the way.

Chapter Sixty-Nine

Sam was aware that there were three of them in the room. Myrtle and Josiah were on the bed. Something had gone on between the two of them but, thankfully, it hadn't included sex. He could just make them out through a louvre in the wardrobe door. He'd been crammed in the wardrobe all night. They were asleep.

Sam nudged the door. It was locked from the outside. The caravan shook. He needed to get out of there. He looked around for a suitable tool, but there was nothing obvious. Then he remembered he was in a wardrobe, and wardrobes had hangers. He raised his hand until he could feel a coat hanger. It was wooden. The next was plastic. It took a while to locate a wire coat hanger and a few seconds to unravel it. It didn't take long to release the catch. Sam tumbled out of the wardrobe rather more noisily that he would have wished. A head appeared. It was Myrtle. She smiled at him silently and gave him a thumbs up. Sam didn't know what that meant, but took it as a cue for him to make his exit. He crawled out of the bedroom.

The caravan shook a bit more, as they if were boarding something. It was followed by some recorded announcements. Sam recognised them: this was the channel tunnel. He opened the door. They were already in the tunnel and the caravan sat precariously on the transporter.

Sam jumped down and moved into the next carriage. Released from the captivity of the wardrobe he was confronted with a new problem. Eventually, he found a toilet. When he left the toilet, he continued to make his way through to the other end of the train where there were coaches.

"Have you gone to the dark side?" a voice asked.

Sam jumped. He looked around. The door of a coach was open, and the voice had come from within. He peered in.

"I'm sorry?" Sam said.

Sam had forgotten that he was wearing a hooded monk-like habit. He'd grown used to the coarseness of the material, and whatever had been in the gin and tonic that the artist had given him had now made it out of his system.

"You have a commitment to the Jedi order, a commitment not easily broken," the voice said.

And then Sam got it. A face appeared from the coach. Sam recognised him instantly. It was a tall man.

"Where's your light sabre?" the tall man asked.

It wasn't the height of the man that was his most intriguing feature. He was dressed in a shaggy furry costume. He started to make animal-like grunts and groans to authenticate his character.

"Chewbacca," Sam greeted him.

It was hard to see, but below the furry costume the man was grinning from ear to ear. A girl appeared. She seemed to have buns on her ears.

"Princess Leia?"

They smiled. More faces appeared. All of them in costume and character. Star Wars. The coach was filled with them. It felt like home from and home and, better still, a possible passage to London.

"Where have you been?" Sam asked.

"Comicon Paris," a stormtrooper replied.

"And," Chewbacca said, "we're off to Comicon London."

"Brilliant," Sam said, genuinely excited (although, had Suzy been there, she might have said tragically excited).

Another figure stepped out of the coach. He was immensely tall, and breathing wheezingly. A darkness seemed to surround him. Two stormtroopers appeared either side of him. They had small, but powerful, Bluetooth speakers that were playing a march-like tune.

"You are part of the rebel alliance?" a deep, deep voice said.

For a second Sam froze. The voice made the ground rumble, although it might have been the train, which had begun its journey. He could feel it in his chest. He had never been in the presence of true evil. The temperature seemed to drop, as if the sun had gone in. The force was strong in this one.

"Isn't he great?" Chewbacca said enthusiastically slapping the dark figure on the back, "we're very proud of our Darth Vader."

It was hard to see but, under the mask, Darth Vader was smiling too.

"Nice to meet you," Darth Vader said, and they shook hands.

"What happened to your light sabre?" Chewbacca asked.

"Someone nicked it," Sam said.

"The bastard," Darth Vader spat out with some venom.

The darkness returned. In their world there were many moral outrages, like kicking away a disabled person's walking stick, or putting obstacles in the path of the blind, but few eclipsed the theft of a light sabre. They were all incensed.

"Don't you worry about that," Chewbacca said, and then followed it with a series of wails, and plaintiff cries.

Chewbacca went into the coach, leaving Sam with the dark side.

"We're short of an Obi-Wan Kenobi," Darth Vader said cheerfully.

Sam knew that this was his moment. He hadn't shaved for the best part of the week, as there had been little chance between evading the drug dealers, being kidnapped by the artist, and trapped in the Jesus bus. He had a light dusting of beard, which was brown and somewhere between Ewan McGregor and Alec Guinness. He was quite a passable Obi-Wan Kenobi, as good as their Princess Leia, if not as good as

Chewbacca, or as committed as Darth Vader. He needed to summon the full Alec Guinness.

"You have gone to the dark side, Luke," Sam said.

He'd deepened his voice, tightened up his diction, and added a soupçon of the Shakespearean actor. It wasn't bad and it raised a cheer. Sam had to access his inner geek and try and summon up further Obi-Wan sayings. It turned out his inner geek was closer to the surface than he'd thought. A young lad appeared, and Sam addressed him.

"Luke, may the force be with you," Sam said.

"I am your father," Darth Vader boomed.

"I have a bad feeling about this," Sam, or rather Obi-Wan Kenobi, countered.

Darth Vader turned to him. He was a big man made bigger by the cloak and the helmet and the six inch heels that Sam couldn't see.

"You can't win, Darth. If you strike me down I shall become more powerful than you can possibly imagine," Obi-Wan Kenobi said.

Chewbacca suddenly reappeared with a light Sabre. It was throbbing and flashing.

"A Jedi needs his light sabre," he said, passing the sabre to Sam.

Sam examined it. He whooshed it through the air. It would have been impossible for him not to. It had good balance.

"Come in," Darth Vader said, entirely out of character.

Sam stepped up into the coach. He was surrounded by jostling stormtroopers. He would have to access the force to stay strong, Sam thought, but then wondered if he was getting a little *too* into character.

"Beer?" One of the stormtroopers said.

It seemed a little early in the day for a beer, but he didn't want to break his cover. Sam took a can and made his way deeper into the the coach. At the rear there was a table around which sat a collection of aliens. It was like a recreation of the Mos Eisley Cantina bar scene from the original, and unquestionably finest, Star Wars movie. There were bizarre octopus-like suckers sprouting from their heads. It was very convincing. They were talking in a foreign language. It was foreign to English, foreign to Earth, and foreign to each other. They were smoking.

"Ooh-gaga-goga," one of them said.

Sam didn't know the language, no one knew the language, but he knew when he was being offered a joint. Sam very nearly mentioned the early hour, but then he remembered he was on his way to a Star Wars convention. Sobriety wasn't going to help. He took a very deep drag.

Chapter Seventy

Sex, Suzy thought, was better with adrenaline. It was a new revelation for her, and explained why Tory MPs were in the habit of half asphyxiating themselves in the limited confines of a cupboard, in pursuit of thrills. Not that she'd want to do that. But she understood thrills and adrenaline. She was multitasking this thought while manoeuvring the Boxter through a width restriction at only twenty miles an hour above the legal limit.

"Jesus," Bradley said.

There were many things that were an aphrodisiac for Bradley. Chief among them were naked and willing women. They really turned him on. What didn't turn him on was being scared shitless. They were on their way to Sam's flat to collect some more cash so that he too could have a Porsche Boxter. Right at that moment he thought it most likely he was going to die a horrible death. It wasn't much compensation that his death would be in the passenger seat of a car he'd always lusted after.

"Can you slow down a bit please?" he asked Suzy.

He knew it would fall on very uninterested ears. If his relationship with Suzy could be described as a relationship, there was no question who wore the trousers. Right at the moment she could probably piss standing up.

"This is how Boxter drivers drive," Suzy said.

She was beaming like a mad zealot, and she wasn't sharing this car with anyone. It was hers and all they had to do was return to the bank of Sam. After that, she assured herself, life would go back to normal. She'd look for a new boyfriend, as she didn't think it likely she'd get back with Sam.

"Stop!" Bradley screamed, whacking his hand on the dashboard.

Suzy slammed the anchors on, at which point Bradley's head hit the dashboard. She dropped a gear, tugged the wheel hard to the left, and then the right, and floored it. The car roared and she looked over and smiled at Bradley. His face had turned a sort of grey colour, like the colour of her grandmother's ashes. It was then that it occurred to Suzy that perhaps Bradley thought *he* was her boyfriend. Why would he think that?

"Please," Bradley said, pleadingly.

Suzy wondered if she'd been leading him on. They had had sex. Quite a few times in truth, but he must understand that this was just a transient time. After this caper, she'd never used the word caper before, they would go back to their old lives. She'd mention it later. Perhaps after they'd had sex. She was feeling a little fruity at the moment. She pushed the accelerator pedal a little harder.

"Here we are," Suzy said.

They had made it to Sam's flat in record time. There was no form of travel, including a helicopter, which could have achieved it quicker. It was a miracle, Bradley thought, that there was no loss of life. There were at least three cyclists whose bowel movements would be freer for a week. Bradley's trousers certainly felt damp. They got out of the car.

"Look Suzy," Bradley said, "I don't think I can go through with this."

They walked slowly towards Sam's front door without the caution of previous visits, as if they were about to insert a card into a cash machine.

"I know, I can't go threw with this either," Suzy replied, "it's just a transient period and then we'll return to our old lives."

Bradley stopped. Suzy sensed he was about to turn round, and she put her hand out to stop him. But Bradley had other thoughts in his head.

"Hold on, what do *you* mean 'you can't go through with this?" Bradley asked.

"What did I mean?" Suzy asked.

"Yes, what did you mean?" Bradley asked.

"What did you mean?" Suzy asked.

"I meant I can't carry on stealing the money," Bradley said.

"Oh," Suzy said.

"What do you mean 'oh?'" Bradley asked.

"Well, I thought we should just take the money, as we agreed," Suzy said.

They carried on walking. Bradley was looking at the ground, following the contours of the pavement.

"So what did you mean by 'you can't go through with it?'" Bradley asked again.

"I didn't say that, you did," Suzy pointed out.

"Yes," Bradley said, "but you said, 'I know' as if you agree."

"Did I?" Suzy asked.

"You did."

"Don't you need your own Porsche Boxter?" Suzy asked, changing tack.

"Do I?"

"Don't you?"

Bradley shrugged and they carried on walking. His mind was in a turmoil. First he'd wanted the money and then he hadn't. Then he'd wanted the car and then he hadn't. He'd always wanted Suzy. He even wanted the nutcase Suzy who was only six inches away from mowing down a lollipop lady. He stopped again.

"You didn't mean the money or the car. You meant us," Bradley said, almost fighting back tears.

"Bloody hell," Suzy muttered.

The Bonnie version of Suzy was not much impressed by sensitivity, and whimpering and tears were not going to do it for her. She was just itching to grab the money, jump back in the car, and race home. If she still had any kind of itching after that, he could scratch it if he liked, but she'd smack him if he started whining.

"Let's just grab our money and fuck off," Suzy said decisively.

"It's not your money," a voice said.

They stopped walking. Bradley looked at Suzy. Suzy looked at Bradley. The voice was deep and the English accented. It sounded Russian. They turned round.

Chapter Seventy-One

"We're here," someone said, and shook Sam.

The aliens had inhaled industrial quantities of dope and it had prompted an argument which was incomprehensible to everyone else, and had progressed into a fight, most of which Sam had missed, as the dope and fatigue had sent him into a deep sleep. He hadn't noticed their arrival in England and, if there had been passport control, either side of the border, it had passed him by. He needed to get to his flat and get some clothes, although he didn't think it likely he could stay there. He wondered if he could stay at Suzy's. He doubted it.

"Hungry?" Chewbacca said.

Sam was. They stopped at a motorway service station and had a fry up, which Chewbacca paid for. Sam had moved away from the aliens, who were chain smoking dope, and away from the Storm Troopers, who were drinking an unending supply of cans of beer. They were quite a rowdy lot and he passed by unnoticed except for Chewbacca.

"You don't have any money on you?" Chewbacca asked.

"I'm afraid not," Sam said.

"And I'm guessing you don't have anything under that cloak."

"That's true too," Sam admitted.

"No passport either?" Chewbacca asked.

Chewbacca, when he wasn't Chewbacca, was a criminal lawyer and he was sensing something wasn't quite right. It didn't matter. He quite liked the not right. He was a man with multiple lives of his own, in addition to Chewbacca.

"Looking forward to Comicon?" Chewbacca asked.

"Yeah, it will be great fun," Sam said.

"You weren't intending to go there, were you?" Chewbacca said.

He'd said it in a friendly way and, despite his intimidating size, he had an easy going demeanour.

"No, not exactly," Sam admitted.

"But you do do a good Obi-Wan," Chewbacca said.

"One must feel the force," Sam said.

"What were you running from?" Chewbacca suddenly asked.

"I got a message from a missing droid," Sam said.

"Don't you hate it when that happens?" Chewbacca said.

Chewbacca didn't press any further, although Sam guessed he might, and they made their way back to the coach and on to Comicon. When they got there Sam feared that he might not get in, as he didn't have a ticket, and it was patrolled more assiduously than UK border control. But there was something about the Storm Troopers and Darth Vader that would ensure access to anywhere. The music helped and they'd marched in without a hitch. There was a sizeable corner devoted to Star Wars fanatics and there were quite a few Darth Vaders, but none that compared with their own, and a few Chewbaccas, but nothing to challenge their Chewbacca. He was becoming quite proprietorial about his gang.

"You're easily the best Obi-Wan," Chewbacca said.

"The force is strong," Sam said.

Sam spent most of the morning floating between stands and talking to people whose likemindedness was a little alarming. He'd even got used to his role as Obi-Wan Kenobi and the coarseness of the cloak. It was after midday when he bumped into Chewbacca.

"How about lunch?" Chewbacca suggested.

"I'm up for it," Sam said.

Chewbacca led him out of Comicon and up to a smart restaurant at which he'd reserved a table. They sat down and, for the first time, Chewbacca removed his furry head. The man below had sandy hair and a smiling face, which was difficult to put an age to. Sam pushed the hood back on his cloak revealing his full face.

"My name is.." Sam began to say, but Chewbacca put his hand up.

"Obi-Wan and I'm Chewbacca," Chewbacca said.

Sam wondered whether Chewbacca was also running from something. He seemed to have money, and was clearly at home in restaurants, as he'd ordered a bottle of Fleurie with alacrity. He poured it and Sam swirled the wine in the glass. He'd smoked a bit with the aliens, and shared a few cans with the Storm Troopers, but couldn't quite quantify his sobriety. He decided it didn't matter and took a sip. The wine was good.

"This looks good," Chewbacca said surveying the menu.

It didn't seem that long since they'd had a fry up, but Sam was hungry again. The biggest issue in making his escape had been eating and taking a dump, and Sam now knew that it was best to do either when the opportunity arose.

"It does," Sam said, drinking a little more wine.

"What was the message contained in the droid?" Chewbacca asked.

It was another way of asking what, or who, Sam was running from but, as the message allegedly came from a droid, and Sam's only known identity was as Obi-Wan Kenobi, it seemed harmless.

"It started," Sam told Chewbacca, "with an IKEA bag filled with cash. The droid did not say where the cash had come from, but it had shit, I mean DNA on it. My DNA. It was probably drugs money."

Chewbacca smiled. He liked the sound of this.

"What happened next?"

"There was a casino and high class prostitutes," Sam admitted.

Chewbacca loved the salacious. He could have forged a career as a tabloid reporter.

"And then there was a Contessa," Sam said.

He wondered if he should reference her breasts in the description. It *was* a very significant feature in her appearance.

"With enormous tits," he added.

It was the kind of detail Chewbacca enjoyed. There was more.

"Then two large men came looking for the cash. They ransacked the..."

Sam searched for another word for his flat and Chewbacca provided it.

"The Millennium Falcon?"

"Yes. But I escaped into the clutches of..."

Sam wasn't sure if it would be better to miss out the surrealist artist with a pension for erect penises. He wasn't sure he had the stamina to go through that again.

"There was a van with 'Jesus Saves' on the side," Sam said.

He said it as if the vision from the droid had grown blurry but, if Chewbacca had noticed, he didn't say anything.

"I hid, I mean he hid, and the only clothing he could find was a monk's habit."

"And that's when you found us?" Chewbacca said.

"Yes," Sam said.

They both ate a little more food and drank a mouthful more of wine and looked at their surroundings. It was a strange combination of a smart restaurant populated with Star Wars and comic characters. Some of the female characters had quite dramatic cleavages.

"So what happens next?" Chewbacca asked.

"Good question," Sam said.

Chapter Seventy-Two

The Hump was getting pretty irritated. One half of him was tempted to go and grab some more cash, the other was too worried about getting caught. And he was feeling knackered. Where the hell was the Lobster? If he took a bit more cash, and there seemed to be plenty of it, he might get caught by the Lobster. God, that man stank. His thoughts didn't change much over the following hour until it occurred to him that perhaps the Lobster wasn't coming back for several hours. When they'd said six hours on and six hours off neither, he thought, had meant it. But perhaps the Lobster had. If that was the case he had to get a move on. The Hump got out of the car.

He looked around him. The coast seemed clear. He walked slowly to the house. The front door had been broken open so many times there was very little holding it together. He gave it a small push. It fell open. It was very inviting. He'd just take a little bit of cash, not too much, he thought, and then he'd get back in the car. He was half way up the stairs when he heard a noise. It was a car. It had a distinct engine note, brought about by many cylinders operating in a large capacity, and developing significant power. It could only be one engine and one person.

"Vlad," the Hump said.

It prompted an instant sweat. What the hell was he going to do? He shuffled down the stairs. He could hear voices. He couldn't make them out, and he couldn't discern Vlad's Russian accent. But there were people there and therefore no possibility of escape. He went back up the stairs. If he got caught in the flat it would be even worse. He'd heard toenail-removing tales about Vlad. The muscles in Vlad's arms were larger than Hump's thighs. The Hump was a dead man.

"Shit, shit, shit," the Hump said.

It didn't hold back the tidal wave of sweat. He knew that even if he could come up with a perfectly reasonable explanation as to why he was in the building, when expressly told he shouldn't enter, he would still look guilty. It was worse than that. He *was* guilty. He'd taken some cash. Not a huge amount, but he had taken some. The talking outside had stopped. Somehow he guessed this was not a good sign. Then he saw the answer. It was a window on the landing. There was a bit of a drop the other side, but nothing compared to the distance that Vlad would drop him. He tried to open it.

"Come on," he pleaded with the window.

The window hadn't been opened since 1998 when it had been painted over, and no one had opened it when it was painted over again in 2004, and then again in 2010. It was ready to be painted over once more. He yanked at it. The Hump was not a physically strong man nor, he was discovering, was he emotionally that hardy. Someone was coming through the door. He was going to die. It seemed to be of sufficient motivation for him to find a strength he didn't know he had.

"Please, please, please," he said to the window.

He would, if he could, have promised the window anything it wanted. He would have taken it for a long weekend in Venice, or bought it fresh flowers every day. If it would just cooperate this one time. The Hump was desperate. He was so desperate he stopped promising the window weekends away and went for a higher power.

"Please God, if you open it for me, I shall be good," the Hump said.

He'd never thought about being good before, but this was a desperate time. He also knew he should offer more, as he had plenty of past sins to atone for, but there wasn't much time. If God was going to reach out to him he had to do it sometime soon, or he'd be meeting him in person.

"Please God, it's Darren here, if you would just open this window for me I will be good the rest of my life. I will do charity work. I will help others," he said.

The Hump was quite pleased with himself. It was pretty good. He tugged at the window. The window seemed as solid as the wall. There wasn't even a creak. It didn't appear as if the all-powerful one had heard him. While he'd never asked for God's services in the past, he had hoped for a little more. Then he realised why.

"Er, God, it's the Hump here. I'm in a bit of a bind. I just need a bit of help."

No one had called him Darren in some years. Even his mother called him the Hump, which made it unlikely that God, given the seven billion plus people on the planet, would know that his birth name was Darren. Now was not the time to be coy about it. He'd not conversed with God before, and was finding it wasn't as reassuring as he'd hoped. He could hear the creaking noise of footsteps ascending the stairs. This was it. He should have spoken to God sooner, or been a better person. He gave the window another yank. And it slid opened. It took him a few seconds to realise that God had heard him. Then Hump crawled through and jumped.

The Hump didn't know whether God was familiar with the layout of the house. He certainly wasn't and the construction of a deep basement meant that the fall was a considerable one. As he fell the Hump considered his commitment to good works. Would it be better to attend church regularly, or should he think about manning soup kitchens and helping the poor? Of course, now that the window had opened he no longer needed God's help, and his commitment, even when he was falling, was lessening. Then it occurred to him that if the fall was taking that long he was probably going to die.

"Please God," he said again.

His mind made a series of commitments which, at that moment, he felt quite committed to. Then he looked down. There was to be no soft landing. There was concrete. Worse, there were garden ornaments scattered haphazardly. He couldn't make them out. The elderly owner of the flat was very fond of those garden ornaments and would take exception to the notion that they were haphazardly arranged. She would have pointed out that it was very clearly a reenactment of the birth of baby Jesus, if a slightly unconventional one. Her husband had objected, as he could see flaws in the reenactment. For a start, he was fairly certain there were no pitchforks involved, nor wheelbarrows, windmills, or fishing rods. There was another objection that her husband had argued quite vociferously about, and it was also the last thing the Hump's eyes focused on, and the last word he uttered.

"Gnome," the Hump said.

He would have said 'with a pitchfork' but it was the pitchfork that ensured that it was the last gnome that the Hump ever saw, although there were plenty of pitchforks ahead of him.

Chapter Seventy-Three

"It's not your money," Vlad said.

Vlad was tired from the journey, but he was equally tired of being messed around. He wanted his money, and he wanted it now.

"It's my money and I want it now," Vlad said.

Had the training and the education come Vlad's way he might have made a passable bass opera singer and, right at that moment, his voice rumbled through Bradley's guts which were, after the journey with Suzy, a little fragile.

"We don't have your money," Suzy said.

She amazed herself, and Bradley, with her cool, unruffled demeanour. It was either because she saw her future in crime, or because there was no way she was giving her car back.

"Why are you here?" Gary asked.

"I'm going to see my boyfriend," Suzy said.

"Your boyfriend!" Bradley shouted.

Bradley couldn't believe it. What did he have to do? He'd nearly asphyxiated himself ensuring that she'd had an orgasm. He'd practically crapped himself in the car and he was crapping himself with this bodybuilding drug dealer. Besides which, wasn't *he* her boyfriend? Wasn't he the one with whom she had most recently been enjoying athletic sex? It wasn't fair. Gary picked up on it.

"You're going to see your boyfriend with someone who thinks he's your boyfriend?" Gary said.

It left an uneasy silence. Suzy hadn't quite dumped Sam in her mind, and hadn't quite accepted Bradley. It was a detail that didn't matter to Gary. Someone wasn't telling the truth. Gary was about to point this out when he was interrupted by a bloodcurdling scream.

"What the.." he said.

Vlad pushed past them and entered the house. He climbed the stairs and nearly missed the opened window on the landing. He looked out. It was a bit of a mess.

"Shit," Vlad said.

Gary arrived a few seconds later.

"What's the problem?" Gary asked.

Vlad pointed out of the window and down into the basement.

"Who's that?" Gary asked.

"The Hump," Vlad replied.

Gary looked at the unmoving body that lay prone below them.

"The who?" Gary asked.

"The Hump," Vlad confirmed.

"How do you know?"

Vlad pointed. Although the Hump was face down, and there was a lot of blood, it was no question it was the Hump. The evidence was on his back.

"Isn't that a bit.." Gary was about to say politically incorrect, but stopped himself.

He looked down at the collapsed form of the late Hump. It looked like he'd been attacked by gnomes with pitchforks. It seemed, at the very least, a little prophetic.

"Quick," Vlad said.

Vlad knew they didn't have much time. There would be police all over the place in seconds. With a dead man, and drug related cash, it was hard to see how it could get worse, but Vlad had yet to enter Sam's flat.

"We've got a problem here," he said to Gary. "Look after them."

Vlad pointed at the couple outside and vaulted the stairs three at a time. He entered Sam's flat. It was a bit of a mess.

"What the fuck," he said.

Then Vlad saw the Lobster. The Lobster's complexion was the most human and normal he'd ever seen. He even looked – Vlad paused to try and figure out how the Lobster looked – peaceful. He'd never seen the Lobster as peaceful. That didn't seem right.

"Lobster," Vlad called.

The Lobster remained peaceful and untroubled, although he had hoped he'd never see the Hump again. Vlad moved across the room and shook him. He really was, Vlad thought, a very irritating man. He shook him again.

"Lobster!" he shouted.

Vlad was a big bad man who'd never seen a dead body, and it was dawning on him that he'd just seen two in as many minutes.

"Fuck it," Vlad said.

He then looked a little closer and realised that the Lobster was guilty of something which would have, had the Lobster been capable of feeling pain, warranted toenail extraction. The Lobster had his hand in the till, although it looked more like Mr Herriot extracting a baby calf. Vlad pushed back the hot water cylinder with one hand, grabbed the Lobster with the other, and tossed him across the room. He very nearly said 'bastard', but restrained himself in light of the Lobster's very recent passing. Some respect was due. It would be short lived. Vlad undid the bolts holding the cylinder in place and pulled it out. He turned it upside down and tipped it into the IKEA bag.

"Fuck!" Vlad shouted.

He had a very clear idea of how well filled the bag had been, and it was a good deal more than the small corner of the bag that the notes were now occupying.

"Who's taken all my money?" Vlad growled.

"Bastards!" Vlad shouted.

Vlad stood up slowly. His shadow filled the room. He grabbed the bag and, for good measure and no particular reason, he grabbed the Lobster. He threw the Lobster across the room. Irritating bastard that he was, he didn't make a sound. Vlad picked him up and threw him again. Vlad felt better, and it really hadn't made any difference to the Lobster.

"Bastard," he muttered again, and went downstairs.

He found Gary and said, "Some fucker has stolen most of it."

None of them noticed the arrival of a coach. It might have ended there but Suzy, who was still doing the cucumber-cool thing, recognised someone. It hadn't occurred to her that she probably shouldn't mention it.

"Sam?" she said.

Vlad was feeling a burning fury and he needed someone to direct it at. The name Sam rang a bell. More than a bell.

"Sam?" he said.

Gary turned and saw Sam. This was the man that they'd been looking for. The one that they'd nearly caught. That was, until Vlad's car had bucked like a rabbit.

"Sam," Gary said.

"I want my money back," Vlad said.

It took a moment for Vlad to determine precisely what happened next, but it began with two very tall men, both taller than Vlad, although that wouldn't have worried Vlad. Beyond that there was music, like a march. Vlad heard it, but didn't take much notice. It was the small army behind the two men that did concern him.

"He does not have your money," a deep commanding voice said punctuating it with a slight, but clearly discernible, 'pah'.

It was Darth Vader. Next to him was Chewbacca. Chewbacca was actually one step behind Darth Vader, as Lord Vader was also a mixed martial arts fighter who Chewbacca, in his capacity as a criminal lawyer, had defended on more than one occasion. Darth liked to fight, and this seemed like a worthwhile cause.

"Go," Darth Vader said. "Do not come back."

It was a sentence followed by another customary 'pah,' although Darth's evident breathing difficulties didn't seem to lessen the impact. The Stormtroopers were jostling behind them. It appeared to Vlad as if they were jostling for a fight, but they were all struggling, after a ten hour drinking binge, to stay upright. It was the noise of the sirens rising above the music of the march that focused Gary's attention. The neighbours had been twitching curtains, which wasn't enough to get the attention of the police, until someone spotted a dead body skewered by gnomes with pitchforks.

"We need to get out of here," Gary said.

Vlad nodded and they jumped in the car. The police arrived two minutes after they'd left.

Chapter Seventy-Four

Suzy snicked the car in gear, balanced the clutch and brushed the throttle. There was no question that she had an affinity for that vehicle, although she was questioning her affinity for others around her. It seemed as if this little caper had come to an end, although both her and Bradley were a hundred grand up – plus, in her case, a Porsche Boxter. But, this time, she drove back to her flat gently without troubling the speed limits. Consequently there wasn't much adrenaline flowing in her, whereas Bradley was feeling almost relaxed. And he'd never felt like that in a car that was piloted by Suzy.

"Why do you think Sam was wearing that monk's habit?" she asked.

Bradley was hoping that the appearance of Sam wouldn't scupper his plans, and he was fairly certain she'd viewed him with some distaste.

"He was Obi-Wan Kenobi," Bradley explained.

"Who?" Suzy asked.

"From Star Wars," Bradley said.

Suzy sighed. She'd suspected as such from the thing that was hanging from his belt. What the hell was that called? She couldn't remember and wasn't going to ask. Then she remembered it was a light sabre and, worse than that, she recalled Sam whirring his dick around in the style of Luke Skywalker, or someone. She'd almost felt a flutter when she'd first seen Sam, then the Star

Wars guys turned up. That was just weird. She didn't want a boyfriend who dressed up as a science fiction action hero. Were she to fill out a form for a dating agency that would be number one on the list. She looked across at Bradley.

"That was close," Bradley said.

She'd also thought that Sam wasn't committed enough, but Bradley was too committed. He moved his hand onto her thigh. She wasn't sure what to do with it.

"Oh, what the hell," she said.

She hadn't meant to say it, it just came out. But she left the hand resting on an inner part of her thigh. She had no idea that it would stay there for the next thirty or so years, and that she'd have quite so many children. But then who knows what the future will bring?

"Sorry?" Bradley said.

"Nothing," Suzy said.

Chapter Seventy-Five

Vlad had made a few decisions. He was in the yard directing skips in the absence of the Hump, whose passing had gone unmourned, and he'd been looking at the books. He was concluding that it was a more lucrative business than he'd thought, and either the Hump had been running it badly, or stealing from him or, very probably, both. He hadn't missed the Lobster either. If he hadn't died, he'd have dumped him. In the old days this might have meant that he'd dumped him in a convenient hole, or in the sea with a solid pair of boots which did not act as flotation devices. But now it meant he'd dispensed with his services. The Lobster had been a bloody awful accountant. So Vlad had cleaned up his life a little, but he was, at heart, a drug dealer. He'd taken on a partner.

"Alright, Lionel?" Gary said.

In the course of all the things that happened there was not one moment when anyone thought it might be Gary. His life as a policeman was so innocuous, and so inconsequential, that no one suspected him of anything other than idleness and incompetence. It was a perfect cover. They had reduced the operation and downgraded the class of narcotics and were seeking to buy a neighbouring business through which they could launder the cash with an eventual plan to phase out the dealing. The only limit was the extent of their greed.

"Yeah, I'm ready to go," Vlad, who was now Lionel, said.

They'd agreed that reverting back to Lionel would help distance him from his previous activities, and he was growing used to it with only occasional moments when he'd slip into his not very native Russian. It was an old habit.

"Good luck," Gary said.

Gary had even dumped his leather jacket and, while not quite a paragon of sartorial elegance, had tidied his wardrobe up a little.

"I hope I won't need it," Lionel said.

Lionel was driving to Monte Carlo, where he hoped to introduce himself to Brandy as Lionel and, if that went well, bring her back with him. He wasn't hopeful.

Chapter Seventy-Six

"Did you have a good holiday?" Derek asked.

Sam looked at the boxes, which were packed with photocopiers that had to be delivered that afternoon. He was back to his old life. He knew what was coming.

"Did you get any action?" Derek asked.

It was the question Derek always asked, and it was accompanied with a strange movement of the hips. Derek talked frequently about getting action because he had never, in his whole life, got much. He'd resigned himself to the fact that getting action was a vicarious occupation for himself. He was married, although his wife hadn't married him because she anticipated lively between-the-sheets action, but because he seemed stable and responsible, which neither of her previous boyfriends had been.

"Yes, loads," Sam said.

There was a small silence, as the generally accepted protocol was that Sam would demur at the question, and Derek would spend the rest of the morning pressing him. It was over too soon for Derek, which was one of his wife's complaints.

"You did?" Derek said.

Although Derek had accepted the status quo regarding his own sex life, and enjoyed taking a prurient interest in others, he didn't want to be reminded too forcefully of the barrenness of his own existence.

"It started with two Russian girls," Sam said.

"Two?" Derek asked.

"Yes," Sam confirmed.

"At the same time?" Derek said, his eyes dilating like dinner plates.

"Yes," Sam said, not mentioning that he may have paid for the evening.

"What was it like?" Derek asked.

Derek should have been very accustomed to wearing glasses, as they'd perched on his nose since he was twelve, but despite the familiarity, they began to steam up. They were clearer at the top of the lenses, so he tilted his head.

"It was great," Sam said, adding, "they even did each other."

It had, Sam remembered, been very good, although a narcotic might have been involved. He didn't think that Derek would respond well to that admission, or that the money he'd spent that night wasn't his.

"Girl on girl action?" Derek said.

Derek had to tilt his head a little further as the condensation on his glasses rose a little higher. There were times when he should have been grappling with the relative merits of the Canon C7000 over the Rocoh 960 or the Zerox P21, but his mind was filled with fantasies of girl on girl action. More specifically, girl on girl action in which he also featured. He knew that technically that would make it something else, but it was a detail that didn't matter.

"And did they," Derek paused, as he had to admit defeat and remove his glasses altogether and clean them, "did they, like, blow you?"

"Together," Sam said.

Although Sam had no knowledge of the services and skills of high class prostitutes, he guessed that he'd got precisely what one might expect for the money he may, or may not, have paid. The evening was very hazy. What was less hazy was his position with Suzy. He knew that her respect for either him, Chewbacca or Lord Vader was not vast, but appearing as Obi-Wan Kenobi had been the last straw. Apparently his light sabre was hanging at his side. Only he thought that was cool.

"Wow," Derek said.

Derek wanted to ask the specific logistics of a two handed blowjob, but even he found it a little too much to ask. He tried to imagine it, but it wasn't possible to achieve that and wear his glasses, and he had some lists to check off.

"It was great," Sam said wistfully.

Suzy had looked at him as if he were a little crazy and disappeared with the gay bloke from her office. They'd driven away in a very fancy looking car. Then the police had arrived.

"Will you be back for a repeat?" Derek asked.

Sam smiled. After the police there had been an ambulance and an undertaker. Sam might have been in huge trouble had Chewbacca not reappeared in a business suit. He was questioned for hours but his alibi, at least for the previous twenty-four hours, was solid. Chewbacca was an able defence lawyer.

"No," Sam said, "I think that was a one off."

Sam had concluded that his whole holiday was a one off. Although he suspected that the Contessa wouldn't kick him out if he passed by her apartment. It had taken a while to get his flat into some order and he'd been forced to make temporary repairs to his sofa and mattress with gaffer tape. He didn't seem to mind, which suggested it had been worth it.

"Then," Sam said, "a Contessa with enormous tits flew me to Monte Carlo in her private jet."

Derek smiled. His glasses cleared up. It was all a joke and Sam's sex life was as barren, and without hope, as his own.

"You're taking the piss aren't you?"

"Maybe," Sam said, and began loading the photocopiers into the back of the van.

The End

The Encore

Suzy was surprised that such a simple, menial task could give her so much pleasure. She moved in repetitive circular movements. It was a lubricated massaging motion. It was as if she were kneading and nurturing, gently over the surface. She was washing the car. Suzy ran her hands along its feline form with an obvious delight, which would have given a psychiatrist much to think about. Although Suzy wouldn't describe it as fetishistic. It was just the pride of ownership. It was her's and she intended to cherish and preserve it until she, and it, reach an old age. At some stage she'd probably get married and have kids and neither would stand in the way.

It had been an exciting week. She'd been promoted into a new, glamorous and significantly higher paid job. She'd recommended Bradley for her old job, but they had other plans for him, and he was heading up a new digital advertising department. He was at the same level as her and their combined salary was pretty impressive. Bradley wanted them to buy a house together and he had suggested, just the once, that she sell the car to help fund the deposit. That, Suzy had explained, was so not going to happen. She was waiting for him. Bradley had booked a spa hotel in Bath for them and she had only agreed because she'd planned a country route which would favour rapid, roof-down motoring, which would probably scare the crap out of him. He was late. A moment later a car appeared. It was one of those Toyota hybrids which Suzy now despised, ensconced as she was, in Porsche ownership. Bradley got out.

"Are you okay?" he asked.

He had, she noticed, that scared-rabbit look he had when she'd driven him somewhere. She'd begun to find it quite cute. She had no idea what was happening to her, as all the traits that had previously irritated her, were now really quite charming. She imagined that there must be a word for this process of male-female bonding, but she had no idea what it was. She polished out a small mark she'd just noticed.

"What happened to your car?" She asked, casually.

Bradley looked around, as if he were being tracked down and hunted.

"They came," he said, "they came."

She didn't quite take it in as there was a more pressing concern. A bird had crapped on her car. She'd heard it could be very corrosive. She had to get on top of that immediately.

"Sorry, you were saying?" Suzy asked, still smiling.

She'd bought the most advanced cleaning equipment for the car and a second later the bird poop was a distant memory. The black sheen had returned. On the one hand it was a shame to fire this vehicle rapidly through the air and risk contact with flies and bugs, but on the other hand she was raring to go. She intended to bring the cleaning equipment with her. She'd learned more about the car too.

"Did you know it has three hundred and twenty-five horsepower?" She said.

"What?" Bradley said, sweating.

"The car," Suzy said and continued with the polishing.

She had every intention of unleashing the entire stable.

"The cash. The car. They came," Bradley repeated a little maniacally.

It was so maniacal that neither of them noticed a car rumble up to the kerb. Loud though the car was, it wasn't quite as piercing as the slightly squeaky voice that punctuated the air a second later.

"Oh Vlad, I mean Lionel. It's beautiful."

They turned and saw a tall, blonde, pneumatic woman, made taller still by the highest heels either of them had ever seen. She was giggling with excitement. But she wasn't alone. The tall, muscular bald-headed man, Suzy had seen in the car outside Sam's fiat, walked up to her and put his hand out. They both knew what this meant, but Suzy couldn't help emit a strangled and desperate plea. It was worse than when that footballer had knocked the ball over the goal in that international penalty shoot out. Or when she'd discovered that George Michael was gay. It was worse, Sam might have observed, than the moment when

Luke Skywalker discovered that Darth Vader was, indeed, his father.

"Noooooooooooo."

Suzy handed the keys to the car over to Vlad, who was now Lionel, and he gave Brandy one of the gifts he'd promised. And now she was very happy.

Really, the end

If you enjoyed this book you can find more Giles Curtis comedies on Amazon -

'Newton's Balls'

Martin is dying and he has one wish. He asks his daughter, Megan, to find a man. But not a normal man, he is the product of Martin's quest, and obsession, for higher intelligence. A man made from the finest genetic material, a cocktail of stolen DNA, including the forefathers of science. A super human who will solve the world's problems. At least that's what Martin hopes.

But Kevin is a man with a rampant hedonistic thirst, a talent for deception, and the centre of the ensuing chaos that brings a city to a standstill. He is a man who knows how to throw a hell of a party.

'The Hedonist's Apprentice'

Travis's life is perfection. He has the looks, the car, the apartment and the women. Lots of women. Debbie says the sex is revelatory, which doesn't help Sheryl. And then there's Colin.

Colin's life is bleak and without hope, and his sex life is so inconsequential that it is hard to assign it a proclivity in any direction. All Colin's dreams come true when, thinking he's working for MI6, he shadows Travis's life and goes on a journey of orgiastic debauchery. But things aren't quite as they seem as the noose tightens on Travis's perfect world.

'The Calamitous Kidnap of Oodle the Poodle'

Bryan Brizzard, a notorious bastard, and owner of short haul airline company Bryanair, hates everyone. He hates his suppliers, his employees, his passengers and his wife and children. But, Dom Hazel discovers, he really loves his poodle, Oodle. And Hazel is an animal assassin. But this time it's a kidnap and Brizzard's mansion is set in the Essex Woods where Hazel, who's trying to be faithful to Julie, finds temptation and confusion. And dogging. The plan threatens to fall apart as Hazel leaves behind more of his DNA than he intends.

'The Badger and Blondie's Beaver'

Madeleine misses her old life in Paris. Her work as a forensic scientist is going great, but now she's marooned in the country and her social life, or more accurately her sex life, is a disaster. When she's called upon to extract a severed head from a weir, she meets Sam. Sam is her perfect man, but murder, mannequins, cocaine, the drug squad, Customs and Excise, multiple arrests and the Mafia get in the way.
Sam, Oliver and William are three young graduates desperate to make a fast buck. The plan seems so simple, it just involves the not entirely legal business of transporting silver which, by way of a cunning disguise, has been fashioned into dildos. But the journey refuses to go to plan.

'A Very UnChristian Retreat'

Hugo has only himself to blame. The bookings in their holiday complex in France are few and Jan, his wife, is forced to organise a yoga week. She remains in Godalming, which leaves Hugo alone with the irresistible Suzanna, who gives off signals he has difficulty interpreting. Jan is talked into hiring a private detective to lure Hugo, but his problems have only just begun. Hugo meets Lenny and Doris who claim to run art parties, which turn out to be more of the swinging sort. Hugo's friend, Gary, books in his gay friends, who have a penchant for the feral. But wild is how Lenny and Doris like it. Hugo doesn't tell Jan, and an unpaid telephone bill means she can't tell him about the Christian Retreat group who are on their way.

And then the chaos really begins.

'It's All About Danny'

"How does he manage to go away for a few weeks and come back a Nobel fucking Prize winner?"

Kathy can't believe it. Nor can Danny, who has tripped through life gliding past responsibility, commitment and anything that involved hard work. But when he is rejected by all the women in his life: his girlfriend, landlord and his boss at 'Bedding Bimonthly,' he has no choice. His better looking high-achieving brother, whose earnest phase has taken him away from the big money in the city, invites him to build a school in Africa with him.

Danny discovers that all the flatpack battles he has fought have given him a talent for it, and it lends his life new purpose. But his life changes when, during a fierce storm, he saves the only child of an African chief, who claims to have mystical powers. The chief invites him to make a wish. Danny can't decide whether he should wish for world peace, a cure for cancer or to be irresistible to women. Shallowness prevails.....

Does the Chief have strange powers or has Danny changed? He misses Kathy his girlfriend, who realises she's made a mistake. And then the wish turns into a nightmare...

'Looking Bloody Good Old Boy'

Arthur Cholmondely-Godstone is in the business of pensions. He offers a unique pension, from a nonreturnable sum, and he introduces his clients to a new way of living. He encourages them to explore radical views, try extreme sports and to eat, drink and smoke as much as they can. Or put another way, Arthur does his best to kill them.

Born from an old family and gifted with the family gene, which ensures him an unbreakable constitution, he is also the last in line and the family need an heir. But the family gene is cursed with a minimal sperm count, and his dissolute ways don't help. He is certain there is a child in his past, all he has to do is search his back catalogue of women, while keeping his clients in bad habits.

Brayman is proving to be irritatingly indestructible and Eddie B, the rock star who used to be a rock god, is trying to kill himself, which would be great, but he needs to finish his gigs before Arthur can collect all the money.

And someone is trying to kill Arthur.

'The Wildest Week of Daisy Wyler'

Daisy had lived her life as if on a merry-go-round, and she'd never stepped on a roller-coaster. There had been a husband, children and even grandchildren, but things had changed. A change dictated by her fickle ex-husband, and which prompts a new life in London.

But Daisy wants more. A bigger life, a wilder life. An exciting life. She finds an unlikely friend in Sophie, her neighbour, and there is an imminent party planned for Sophie's 'sort of' boyfriend, the dissolute Lord Crispin. Crispin's parties are legendary and favour the excessive. And so begins the wildest week of Daisy Wyler.

Find out more on gilescurtis.com